WHAT IS COUNSELLING
Y?

Books are to be returned on or before the last date below

Other books in this series

Reflective Practice in Counselling and
Psychotherapy by Sofie Bager-Charleson   ISBN 978 1 84445 360 3

Creating the Therapeutic Relationship in
Counselling and Psychotherapy by Judith Green   ISBN 978 1 84445 463 1

Counselling and Psychotherapy in Organisational
Settings by Ruth Roberts and Judy Moore   ISBN 978 1 84445 614 7

To order, please contact our distributor: BEBC Distribution, Albion Close,
Parkstone, Poole, BH12 3LL. Telephone 0845 230 9000,
email: **learningmatters@bebc.co.uk**. You can also find more
information on each of these titles and our other learning resources at
www.learningmatters.co.uk

WHAT IS COUNSELLING & PSYCHOTHERAPY?

NORMAN CLARINGBULL

Series editor: Norman Claringbull

LearningMatters

First published in 2010 by Learning Matters Ltd

British Library Cataloguing in Publication Data
A CIP record for this book is available from the British Library.

ISBN: 978 1 84445 361 0

Cover design by Code 5 Design Associates
Project management by Diana Chambers
Typeset by Kelly Winter
Printed and bound in Great Britain by TJ International Ltd, Padstow, Cornwall

Learning Matters Ltd
33 Southernhay East
Exeter EX1 1NX
Tel: 01392 215560
info@learningmatters.co.uk
www.learningmatters .co.uk

FSC
Mixed Sources
Product group from well-managed
forests and other controlled sources
Cert no. SGS-COC-2482
www.fsc.org
© 1996 Forest Stewardship Council

Contents

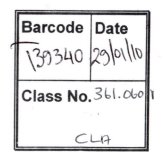

Preface and Acknowledgements

It is an exciting time to be a counsellor. It is a great time to be a psycho-therapist. Times they are a-changing and never more so than in the talking therapies. Counselling and psychotherapy in the UK are at a crossroads in terms of their professional and academic development. Nowhere is this more evident than in the intense debate that is taking place about the possible futures of all the 'talking therapies'. No one attending counselling or psychotherapy seminars or conferences, reading professional journals, or simply talking to therapist colleagues, can fail to be aware of the passion-ately advanced arguments and counter-arguments. Much of the debate is centred on therapist regulation and its likely ongoing impact on practitioner education and professional practice. It feels like the end of an era. Counselling and psychotherapy's 'greats' are being ruthlessly reappraised and its long-accepted orthodoxies are being irreverently challenged. The old certainties of the therapeutic craft are fading and radical changes in therapist training and practice seem inevitable. All of us who are in any way involved in the talking therapies are now being compelled to take a fresh look at our calling and at ourselves. In 1966, Robert Kennedy famously (and erroneously) claimed that a Chinese curse condemns enemies to 'live in interesting times'. It seems more likely that, for all psychological therapists, from trainees to advanced practitioners, our own 'interesting times' could prove to be a blessing rather than a curse if we use them to properly shape our professional tomorrow.

So, anyone concerned with the talking therapies, at any level, will inevitably be affected by these developments and might even want to contribute towards them. This is especially so in the case of the rapidly emerging, new genre of graduate and postgraduate trainees and practi-tioners who will be at the forefront as personal therapy practice increasingly evolves into being a mainly university-educated profession. It will help the therapy profession's 'new thinkers' to better consider their future if they first critically and reflectively examine their ideas about counselling and psychotherapy's past (its *history*). They will then be better placed to examine what counselling and psychotherapy is currently about (its *present*), and then they can productively explore how counselling and psychotherapy might evolve (its *future*). Put simply, the overall question is: Therapy – what's the story there then?

The story of the personal therapies is, of course, just that. It is a story; it is at best an approximation; it is not a matter of absolute fact. All tales are inevitably dependent on the partialities of their tellers and the preferences of their listeners. Similarly, therapy's tales are also based on an ever-varying selection of interpreted personal, social and academic histories. Like the process of personal therapy itself, counselling and psychotherapy's various stories depend on who is doing the telling. Just as therapists try to interpret their clients' stories and make guesses about their future needs, so too must therapists interpret their own stories about the therapeutic profession and make some guesses about its future directions. Sensible practitioners will evaluate the tales told in this book in the same way, it is hoped, that they evaluate the tales told to them by their trainers, their teachers and their clients. That is to say, to value these stories as essentially being attempts to be truthful but always open to critical questioning. At the end of the day, the best tales that therapists can tell are their own and it might be that some of their stories are more credible than others. The trick is to find out which is which. That is what this book is all about.

FOUR CORE QUESTIONS TO THINK ABOUT

1. Where have counselling and psychotherapy come from?
2. What do therapists do?
3. Where do therapists work?
4. Where are counselling and psychotherapy going?

ACKNOWLEDGEMENTS

With thanks to Di Page, Luke Block, Lauren Simpson and all their colleagues at Learning Matters for all their help, advice and encouragement.

Thanks also to Paula Biles-Garvey, Tina Graham, Barbara Allen and Alex Bossman for all their contributions to Practitioner Reflections.

PART 1

WHERE HAS COUNSELLING & PSYCHOTHERAPY COME FROM?

The story of the talking therapies – how they evolved

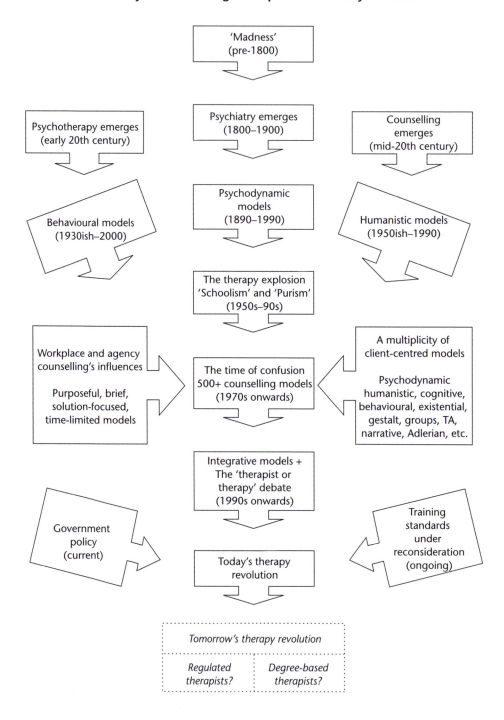

CHAPTER 1

Counselling & psychotherapy –
the opening story

CORE KNOWLEDGE

- The explosion in the demand for personal therapy after the Second World War led to the emergence of many hundreds of therapy types.
- Historically, the development of counselling and psychotherapy has depended on three main theoretical 'schools':
  - psychodynamic
  - behavioural
  - humanistic.
- Modern counselling theories have evolved to include:
  - cognitive-behavioural ideas
  - integrative methods.
- Counselling and psychotherapy are based on extensive research-based evidence. The talking therapies are now established professional disciplines.
- Counselling and psychotherapy are likely to become statutorily regulated professions.

TO BEGIN AT THE BEGINNING

The tale of personal or psychological therapy, which is also the tale of psychotherapy and the tale of counselling, is as old as the story of the human race (Cushman, 1990; Hollanders, 2000a). Humans have long tried to make sense of themselves and their worlds (Bettleheim, 1983). That is why people have always used therapists, be they priests, gurus, wise ones, philosophers, doctors, good friends, or in fact just about anybody prepared to listen, as sounding boards and as guides to help to try to bring some order into their inner and outer worlds. In other words, the role of the talking therapist goes back to the dawn of humanity (Ehrenwald, 1976). However, in terms of what we today would recognise as the discrete discipline (or disciplines) of counselling and psychotherapy, it is probably the profession's developmental history over the last 100 years or so that interests us most (Freedheim, 1992). Of course, personal therapy has come a long way since its early days.

However, before we get too far into exploring therapy's story, let us clear up one important source of confusion. There are many terms used to describe professionals who get involved with helping people who have emotional, psychological or mental health problems. Titles such as counsellor, psycho-therapist, psychological therapist, psychoanalyst, psychologist and so on are all used, sometimes apparently at random. Naturally, people are often puzzled about how to understand the differences between all these professionals. The practical reality is that, historically, these different titles have probably owed more to the inbuilt prejudices learned during early therapeutic training than they do to actual differences in professional practice. After all, many authors (Duncan et al., 1992; Fiedler, 1950; Wosket, 1999, etc.) give us reason to suppose that experienced therapists are far less worried about therapeutic style-boundaries than are the less experienced practitioners. Therefore, the answer to the 'what's in a name' puzzle (as far as this book is concerned anyway) is simple: there are NO differences. If you are a professional – and that includes all the personal therapists – who is trying to help somebody with emotional, personal or mental health problems, then you are a psychological therapist and practising what today are often called the talking therapies. Of course, in these more enlightened times these therapies increasingly include a lot more treatment methods than just 'talking the talk'. Today's psychological therapists work with action therapies, treatment plans, practical activities, psycho-education and many other interventions; they 'walk the walk' as well. In other words, today at least, the choice of which professional therapist title to use to describe your practice is yours to make. However, it is very important to note that the current (July 2009) proposals to officially regulate counsellors and psychotherapists may result in these two callings becoming separately registered. This might happen perhaps from about 2014–15 onwards and may possibly even involve different levels of training. Nevertheless, in this book, all the talking therapy titles will still be used interchangeably.

There is one important exemption to the blanket definition of psycho-logical therapist (or any other title that you prefer) that was given above. It is an iron-clad rule that all psychiatrists must be qualified medical practitioners. Psychiatrists are doctors who sometimes prescribe medical treatment for those suffering from mental distress. Therefore, their pro-fessional title is legally protected. It is theirs alone. However, having said that, wise counsellors and psychotherapists will not allow the high-level professional status enjoyed by psychiatrists to lead them into automatically awarding superior professional status to the medically qualified. Psychia-trists are our respected colleagues and valued co-workers at the psycho-logical coalface; they are not the mine owners.

Whatever we call them (counsellors, psychotherapists or any name you like), what we really need to know is: What is it that they actually do? Well, that is a tale that is long in the telling. This book will give you one take on the therapy story. Perhaps by the end of this book you might have some stories of your own to tell about the psychological therapies.

So, let us think again about the core question that this book will be exploring. What indeed are counsellors and psychotherapists for? What do they do? Do they really sort out people's minds? Surely treating the mad is a job for doctors? Well, historically that might have often been true (except, of course, when the priests claimed their share of the action!). However, we will begin our exploration of counselling's story by considering how madness has been viewed throughout history.

HISTORICAL EXPLANATIONS OF MADNESS

From the earliest of times, humans have struggled to understand mental distress. A brief history of some of these earlier explanations is shown in Table 1.1.

When/who	Cause	Treatment
Prehistoric	Evil spirits/ pressures in the brain	Trepanning
Early Egypt	Loss of status or money	Talking it out; religion or suicide
Old Testament	Despair/incorrect thinking	Faith
Aeschylus	Demons	Exorcism
Socrates	Heaven sent	None – it's a blessing!
Aristotle	Melancholia	Music
Hippocrates	Natural medical causes	Abstain from excesses; diet and exercise
Celsus	Madness is madness	Entertaining stories, diversions, persuasion
Galen	Functions of the brain	Confrontation, humour, exercise

Table 1.1: Historical explanations of madness.

As time progressed, however, the idea that the mind was the source of madness began to predominate and with it the conviction that the sufferer was to blame. Possession by evil spirits, moral weakness and similar 'blame the patient' explanations placed the responsibility for both the disease and its cure on the resulting outcast victims themselves. They were locked away and shut off from society so that 'decent' people could forget all about them. That way the mad were not a problem as they no longer existed.

In these institutions, the mad were cruelly treated. They were whipped, beaten, starved and treated like animals. No differentiation was made between the mentally ill, the criminally insane or the socially disruptive. For example, women were committed for wanting to leave their husbands; men were committed for sedition; and children were committed for being deformed. The mentally ill were accused of having abandoned themselves to the devil and to evil sorcerers and they were considered to be wilfully sinful. They were persecuted without mercy.

REFLECTION POINT

Have our views about either the cause of mental dysfunction or the treatment of the mentally disturbed really altered so much since those early days?

During the eighteenth century, conditions for the insane started to improve, and hospitals and asylums began to care properly for the mentally ill. In 1752, the Quakers opened the first ever hospital that tried to treat the insane kindly, even constructively. By the mid-1800s many institutions were genuinely trying to 'cure' the mentally afflicted. It is important to note that, by the end of the nineteenth century, the medical profession had attained a monopoly in the treatment of the mad. This meant that all psychological disturbances were believed to have medical or biological explanations and so discovering a sufficiency of correct biological cures was the ultimate goal of the doctor-therapists.

PSYCHOTHERAPY IN THE NINETEENTH CENTURY

Medicine's monopoly quickly led to the emergence of specialist doctors (eventually known as psychiatrists) to treat these new illnesses. In the late nineteenth century, the term 'psychotherapy' began to be used to describe a new psychiatric subdivision – one that was based on attempts to 'cure the body by the mind, aided by the impulse of one mind to another' (Van Eeden, 1887, cited in Ellenburger, 1970, p765).

Of course, it is acknowledged today that the great psychotherapist of that period was Sigmund Freud. This 'greatness' is certainly true in terms of his overwhelming and long-lasting influence on the psychotherapy profession. Whether it is true in terms of scientific rigour and honesty, or practitioner integrity, is quite another matter and we will look further into these issues in Chapter 3. However, Freud's ideas were not his alone. Like all trendsetters, his work was very dependent on a number of widely held, pre-existing theoretical concepts and attitudinal beliefs. For example, as McLeod (2003) tells us:

- *Early nineteenth-century biological theories already included the concept of a unitary life-force or libido.*
- *Many nineteenth-century theorists were already debating the possibility that emotions and psychological disturbances had (at least in part) sexual origins.*
- *By the early eighteenth century, the possibility that humans had both conscious and unconscious minds had already begun to be investigated. During the nineteenth century, psychiatrists such as Charcot or Janet began exploring how to tap into the assumed curative powers of the unconscious. Interestingly, even at this very early stage in its development, psychotherapists were aware of the importance of establishing a good rapport between doctors and their patients. In other words, good working alliances were essential.*

Then along came Freud. Although he did not invent psychological therapy, what he did do, and did very well, was to bring all the already existing ideas together and take them forward into an innovative, even pioneering, and certainly extremely well-organised theoretical model of human personality development. The heuristic value of Freud's model has so far stood the test of time. However, its true curative powers remain a matter of intense debate. Freud's model underpins what is generally known in today's psychotherapeutic world as the psychodynamic tradition and, even today, psychodynamic modelling provides useful metaphors to help us understand what makes someone tick. It offers us a comprehensive theory of human development. This is because the Freudians claim that all of us – the mad, the bad, the sad and the glad – are the products of our inner psychological conflicts and our instinctual drives.

PSYCHOTHERAPY IN THE TWENTIETH CENTURY

Real changes in how we viewed the 'mad', and started to wonder more about the 'sad', began to occur as the twentieth century dawned and progressed. Looking back, we can now see the importance of Freud's theories to the evolution of the counselling and psychotherapy trade. However, it took time for his ideas to permeate society to the point where today they are prevalent, even inherent, in everyday language and activities, even when people are unaware that they are being 'Freudian'. It took much of the first third or so of the twentieth century for Freud's ideas about the origins of psychological disturbance to permeate the Eurocentric world. Two big developments in particular influenced people's thinking:

- During the First World War it was noticed that large numbers of soldiers were incapacitated by emotional problems and it was plain to see that not just the few, but the many, developed apparently 'abnormal' thinking and behaviour. It was argued that, if extremely traumatic situations such as combat could cause such widespread mental distress, then it was reasonable to assume that lesser traumas, although perhaps occurring more frequently throughout society, could produce similar effects. Further, if trauma could be seen as often merely being the impact of some of life's ordinary events, then psychological dysfunctions could be identified in the apparently 'normal' population and, it was hoped, eventually treated.

- Another big change came about as it became generally realised that Freud's ideas also apparently applied to people engaged in everyday, routine human activity and not just to the interestingly neurotic. For example, the psychodynamic explanation of interpersonal dislike in the everyday world suggests that it is not simply a rational response to an apparently unlikeable person. It is, some Freudians claim, an unconscious, unregulated, negative response to an unfortunate whose apparent behaviours or appearance remind someone's unconscious of an earlier problematic relationship.

Of course, Freud was not a lone theorist; he was not the only psycho-therapist of his era. Other practitioner-theorists were investigating ways of responding to a new and growing demand for treatments for the mentally dysfunctional. The dying nineteenth century and the first half of the twentieth century was the time of some of psychotherapy's supposedly 'great thinkers': Jung, Adler, Klein, Bowlby, Fairburn and many, many other famous names. However, it would generally be true to say that, at least up until the end of the Second World War, much of the psychotherapeutic world was dominated by the psychodynamicists, many of whose adherents were also medically trained. This was particularly the case in the USA, where analysis was exclusively the province of doctors (Mulhauser, 2008). Interestingly, Freud himself believed that medicine and psychoanalysis were two different topics (Freud, 1986) and argued that training pro-grammes should include non-medical analysts, prominent among whom was his own daughter, Anna. When Ernest Jones brought Freud's ideas to England in 1913, he too promoted the value of lay analysts (Jones, 1959/1990). However, all these practitioners, medical and non-medical alike, were required to undergo extensive and costly training. Therefore, psycho-therapy was inevitably an expensive process and, inevitably, it was largely restricted to the privileged few who alone had the time or the money to be neurotic. The poor just got on with life the best they could.

It seems that, up to the mid-twentieth century at least, psychotherapy was not for the masses. However, two major insurrections were unfolding, quietly and slowly at first and then gradually gathering momentum.

INSURRECTION NUMBER ONE – THE BEHAVIOURISTS

At the same time that psychodynamic theory was becoming increasingly accepted as an explanation of human personality and development, some very important alternative theories were being developed by pioneering psychologists. Two such theories are of significant interest to today's therapists. Both are concerned with deliberately imposed (or obviously overt) learning and its effects on human development. In both cases, human personality is considered to be, at least in part, more or less dependent on automated or routine reactions. Such theorists argue that personality is derived from learned, often automatic, responses to stimuli – the trumpet blows; the old soldier holds himself erect!

The behaviourist explanation

The first of the 'personality comes from learning' models is the behaviourist explanation of human activity, which originated with the work of Pavlov (1927). Pavlov proposed the concept of the *classically conditioned response*. He believed that someone's reactions to certain stimuli are first learned and then become automated. For example, think about how you react to the smell of your favourite food or the mention of your greatest fear. The behaviourists would say that your reactive behaviours actually come from a learned, automatic set of responses. Behaviourism assumed a more modern, more sophisticated form with Skinner (1971), who proposed that even very complex behaviours could be learnt and, much more importantly, deliberately changed, by *operant* or *instrumental conditioning*. To illustrate this, think about a child finding out how to talk to some adults. Suppose the child says something rude but something that's also unintentionally amusing. The adults laugh and the child is pleased and will probably say the rude word again and then go on to say similarly naughty words. As long as the adults show their approval by laughing, the child will carry on. However, as soon as the adults start to disapprove and stop laughing, the behaviour will slow down and eventually probably stop. Every time the adults reverse their approval response, the child will reverse its naughty-to-good behaviours. This type of behaviour/response modification is also known as *behaviour shaping*. It is interesting to note that, although the behaviourists usually decried Freud's concept of the unconscious and its impact on personality, in effect behaviourism too relies on a sort of unconscious, as it depends on the individual being unaware of the psychologically manipulated influences on personal actions and thoughts.

The cognitive explanation

The second of the 'personality comes from learning' models is the cognitive explanation of human activity. This, in part, originated with the work of Ellis (1962), who proposed that irrational beliefs interposed themselves between stimulus and reaction, and Bandura (1977), who proposed that thinking (cognition) plays an important part in learned behaviour. For example, Beck (1963, 1964) argued that depression arose in people whose thinking processes had, in part, become dysfunctional. These, and similar, developments have culminated in a general viewpoint that considers emotionally or psychologically dysfunctional people as being the victims of their own incorrect or negative thinking. However, at base this dysfunctional thinking is learned behaviour. Therefore, a 'cure' will come about if the sufferers can learn how to correct such unhelpful thinking and to replace it with more constructive belief systems. However, in this case, 'incorrect' or 'negative' are not judgemental terms measured against 'proper thinking', but merely describe maladaptive thoughts (cognitions) that have an adverse effect on the patient's psychological well-being.

Various therapists have experimented with various combinations of the overall ranges of the behavioural and cognitive approaches to therapy (Freeman and Simon, 1989; Persons, 1993, etc.). These usually preplanned and personalised individual treatment programmes underpin the currently increasingly popular cognitive-behavioural therapy (CBT) approach to counselling. CBT is usually a quick therapy, often taking fewer than six sessions (in other words, it is cheap). It is also claimed to have easily identifiable and very measurable outcomes. Therefore, it has naturally become extremely popular with healthcare providers both in the UK and in America (McLeod, 2003). CBT's official popularity, at least in the UK National Health Service (NHS), is now enshrined in official governmental policy (Layard, 2005). Unsurprisingly, now that the Government plans to invest £170 million in the provision of CBT, the traditional antipathy that many counsellors have routinely felt for CBT and its practitioners is rapidly fading away.

INSURRECTION NUMBER TWO – THE HUMANISTS

Although the humanist tradition includes many great thinkers (Moreno, Spinelli, Maslow and Perls, to name but a few), for most modern psychotherapists and counsellors the name that stands above all others is that of Carl Rogers. Rogerian (or person-centred counselling) was very much the child of its time. The Rogerian ethic of limitless self-development, together with its emphasis on respect and freedom for the individual, very much resonated with the social ethos of the latter half of the twentieth century. It was seen as a self-liberation therapy for the freedom-conscious, baby-boomer generation. Person-centred therapy offered a sort of cheaply provided mass-production counselling therapy – one that was essentially simple to understand and simple to apply to an increasingly emotionally troubled post-Second World War population (McLeod, 2003). Expensive psychiatrists or psychoanalysts were no longer needed. The therapy had another great appeal – it was apparently testable and quantifiable (Gendlin, 1981; Truax and Carkhuff, 1967, among many others). In other words, customers knew what to expect and what it was likely to cost (essential requirements for any mass-produced product, from baked beans to luxury cars).

The core of the humanistic approach is based on the notion that the therapist's task is to help patients find their own solutions to their own problems. It differs from the psychodynamic approach in a number of significant ways, but the most vital one is this:

The psychodynamicists view their client's current relationships as being effectively unconsciously driven repetitions of previous events and reactions to previous experiences. Their clients are relating to the therapists and to their own worlds as if certain emotional constructs are really true; as if their memories of previous events are accurate or factual. For example, a client perceiving the therapist as a disapproving or judgemental figure may be seeing the therapist as if he resembled a disapproving parent. However, the therapist is not that parent and so *the client/therapist relationship is UNREAL.*

However, the person-centred therapist works with the client on the basis that both the client and the therapist are real figures who exist in the reality of the immediate situation. The therapeutic relationship is therefore not imaginary or 'as if', but immediate and actually happening in the here and now. Therefore, *the client/therapist relationship is REAL.*

Of course, it follows, at least for the Rogerians, that clients are effectively the true experts on their own inner selves. Therefore, the therapist's role must be respectful and not judgemental or directive, and the therapy must be client-led. This is because the therapist is trying to enter the client's world and not trying to coax the troubled client into the psychological haven of any given therapy school's concept of the psychological ideal. Or so they tell us.

Person-centred counselling, often claimed to have originated with a speech given by Rogers to the University of Minnesota in 1940, crystallised into its modern form during the 1950s and 1960s (see Rogers, 1961, 1980 and many others). It certainly met the needs, in terms of availability anyway, of the emotionally troubled members of society in the 1950s, 1960s and onwards. Person-centred therapy, with its emphasis on promoting the needs of the individual over the demands of the established society, can very much be seen as being dependent on the socio-political era from which it originated. It clearly echoed the deconstructivist liberation philosophies that permeated the Western world during the latter half of the twentieth century. This psychotherapeutic child of post-war America was brought to Britain in the early 1960s (Thorne, 2007), mainly through the auspices of the National Marriage Guidance Council (now Relate) and the Facilitator Development Institute (later renamed as Person-Centred Therapy: Britain). From the 1970s onwards, person-centred therapy became the primary intervention method taught to most trainee counsellors and social workers in the UK. If cognitive-behavioural models can be loosely seen as the psychologists' approach to psychotherapy, then humanistic therapeutic models, including the person-centred approaches, could loosely be described as the counsellors' approach. However, at least in academic circles and at training college level, humanistic counselling approaches are beginning to lose some of their primacy (Aldridge and Pollard survey, 2005).

THE THERAPY EXPLOSION – A TIME OF CONFUSION

Although it is true to say that the three main models of counselling and psychotherapy discussed so far (psychodynamic, CBT, person-centred) have dominated the UK therapy scene, it is also the case that they are far from being the only styles of therapy available. Today's therapy customers face an overwhelming choice menu, including gestalt, existential, psychodrama, cognitive-analytic, systems theory, brief intervention, solution-focused, feminist, transpersonal, narrative, etc. – the list appears endless. Each competing therapy model, or school, has its own fierce defenders who try to ensure that their own brand of therapy remains purist and unadulterated by allegedly non-counselling contaminants, such as having pre-set targets or commercial limitations. In fact, although it is not generally known, probably the most widespread approach to psychotherapy (at least in terms of its total client numbers and worldwide availability) is to be found in the various 12-step models as practised by Alcoholics Anonymous and its many spin-offs. This form of mass psychotherapy is likely to be seen by many purists as being so contaminated that it is often even provided by non-counsellors. This may well be the reason why the existence of the 12-step approaches is rarely acknowledged in therapy circles and they are rarely taught and rarely researched, even within the specialist addictions market. In effect, for many counsellors, 12-step therapy is an elephant in the room – we all know it is there but nobody talks about it; somehow it is one of our unacknowledged open secrets.

Since the 1960s there has been an explosion in the types and numbers of therapy models being made available. In 1986, Karasu found over 400 allegedly distinct models and so it is reasonable to assume that, by the end of the last century, there were probably 450 to 500 or more on the market.

Doubtless there are even more today. Clearly such a proliferation of personality theories, therapeutic models and treatment delivery systems has served to create a time of confusion for practitioners and clients. This confusion is deepened by the enthusiastic evangelism that each counselling school's adherents exhibit for their own models, the level of which is usually only matched by the deep antipathy that they express towards all the other schools.

If, as Evans and Gilbert (2005) suggest, there are almost as many therapy models as there are practitioners, the therapy trade must answer two vital questions:

1. What sort of therapy should clients be looking for?
2. What sort of training should student therapists elect to undertake?

Finding sensible answers to these two questions is essential if counselling in particular wants to emerge as a profession that is taken seriously in society. What sort of responses can the talking therapies offer?

It would seem to be a commonsensical way forward to simply test out the various therapies on offer, find out which one is best, and then to concentrate the profession's efforts on promoting therapy's latest 'best buy'. Of course, some practitioners have fundamental objections to the notion of testing therapies, seeing therapy as an art form that cannot be analysed against criteria such as effectiveness, usefulness and value for money. Despite these objections, research into all these areas has long been undertaken and it is worth spending a little time looking at the specific history of counselling research because, unsurprisingly, that too is a vital part of the story of the talking therapies.

THE HISTORY OF COUNSELLING RESEARCH

If counselling is to mature into a socially desirable, politically supported and academically respected profession, it has to justify itself as being a worthwhile activity that society should support. There are three core questions that those advocating counselling as a serious response to a number of personal and social issues must have ready answers for:

1. Does it work?
2. How does it work?
3. Is it cost-effective and how can we best provide it?

The history of counselling research is essentially the history of attempts to answer these questions. It can be helpful if we view this narrative as having evolved over four phases.

Phase one research – 1940s to 1960s

Does counselling work?

Can we measure some worthwhile benefits that the clients have received as a result of coming to counselling? If we can't identify and quantify such benefits, why are we offering people psychotherapy? The core question for the phase one researcher was: Does psychotherapy work?

Eysenck (1952, 1992b) famously claimed that about 65 per cent of all neurotics who were treated by non-behavioural psychotherapy improved substantially over a two-year period. The problem for counsellors and psychotherapists is that he also found that untreated control groups apparently recovered equally well. This suggests that time was actually the primary curative factor and not the psychotherapeutic interventions. As with all psychological research, argument rages over whether or not Eysenck's studies really did show what Eysenck claims they showed.

Eysenck claimed (with apparently good reason) that psychotherapy doesn't work.

However, many modern-day researchers believe that they have answered Eysenck's devastating attack. More modern researchers (see Lambert, 2004) have concluded that spontaneous remission rates in Eysenck's control groups were greatly overstated and that his therapy-based recovery rates were understated. This controversy rages on.

Phase two research – 1960s to 1980s

How does counselling and psychotherapy work?

Phase one research was largely characterised by the 'uniformity myth'. This myth supposed that all the clients treated with a particular therapy would respond in the same way. In other words, the treatment method was more important than who delivered it or to whom it was delivered. No attention was paid to differences in clients' or therapists' qualities. So, as Paul (1967) phrased it, the core question for phase two researchers was: What treatment, by whom, is most effective for this individual with that specific problem, and under which set of circumstances?

Is one kind of counselling more effective than another? The evidence is that most therapies delivered by most therapists to most clients have similar outcomes (Lambert, 2004). In a well-known early study, Luborsky et al. (1975) found no differences between the various therapies in terms of their outcomes or effectiveness. They famously called this finding the Dodo Effect – *Everybody has won and all shall have prizes.*

Phase three research – 1980s to date

Is counselling and psychotherapy cost-effective? How can we best provide it?

In today's managerial climate (Inglis, 1989), society usually demands that these two questions should be answered authoritatively. Put simply, if we as therapists want society to allocate a share of its limited resources to our cause, the core question is: Are we are giving value for money?

On the surface, it would appear to be a sensible quantitative approach to investigating these two questions if we simply measured the effectiveness of some 'super-therapies' that allegedly integrate the core beneficial qualities of all the apparently useful therapy methods. This has been done largely on a trial-and-error basis with quantitative researchers measuring change against baselines – see Evans and Gilbert (2005) for a useful review of such investigations.

Taken overall, these studies suggest that psychological therapies are generally beneficial (Lambert, 2004). There is also evidence that counselling by any method, even when provided by means of a limited number of sessions, is cost-effective (Department of Health, 2001b). However, these sorts of findings are very much based on bean-counter research into quantitative changes in behaviour, prescription take-up, sick time and so on. Studies of long-term versus short-term therapies seem to show that much of the benefit occurs in the first few sessions. This is usually demonstrated by measuring quantitative behaviour changes, such as reduced alcohol usage or a lessening of offending behaviour. However, in cases where clearly the clients have benefited from long-term therapy, it may be that the change processes are too slowly achieved to be noted by researchers using quantitative approaches. In such cases, maybe a qualitative investigation might be a better way of finding out what's really going on.

Phase four research – current and future

What sort of help should be provided for the emotionally troubled?

This asks counsellors and psychotherapists two questions:

1. Does modern thinking still agree that counselling and psychotherapy work?
2. Is counselling and psychotherapy superior to other forms of treatment, such as general practitioner (GP) care or psychiatric medication?

Modern studies, such as Stiles et al. (2007), still routinely find that there are no significant outcome differences that can be found between any of the models of psychotherapy. However, another consistent finding is that psychotherapy is routinely helpful and effective (Wampold, 2001). This has led to researchers asking a third important question:

3. Can we find a way of treating the emotionally troubled that is cheaper than psychotherapy?

There seem to be two general findings in this area. First, when compared to other forms of treatment such as the medical help on offer from GPs, psychotherapy and medical interventions appear to be equally effective over the long term (Stiles et al., 2007), although it might be that psychotherapy is more effective in the short term (Ward et al., 2008). Whether medical treatment is cheaper is an open question, although of course some patients might find taking pills more convenient than attending psychotherapy sessions. It is worth noting, by the way, that the routine guidelines issued by all the drug companies in respect of their antidepressant and anti-anxiety medications nearly always recommend that patients using their drugs should also be undergoing some form of psychotherapy. So, it seems even those with a vested interest in promoting the medical model of emotional dysfunction prefer pills + talk to pills alone.

When comparative therapy studies are carried out, anyone overviewing the literature will see that CBT is often included as one of the therapy models being evaluated. The fact is that, although CBT is usually shown as being very useful, it is also routinely shown as being no more effective than any other form of therapy. CBT is not a 'super-therapy'. One advantage that it does have is that it is a rapid form of treatment and so it is very appealing to the patient. Furthermore, it is allegedly easy to train people to deliver CBT (they don't even need to be first trained as psychotherapists). In other words, CBT is cheap.

WORKPLACE COUNSELLING – ANOTHER 'OPEN SECRET'

Rather like 12-step addictions counselling, workplace counselling is also one of the therapy world's open secrets. This may be because, as Kinder (2005) suggests, many so-called purist counsellors appear to be distrustful of any therapeutic activity that is dependent on commerce and so they rather suspect that workplace counselling is 'not proper counselling'. Nevertheless, workplace counselling in the UK is a high-volume therapeutic activity and its pre-registered client base is extensive. Anyone enrolled on that client base is entitled to demand free help from an appropriately allocated workplace counsellor. Exactly how many potential clients are registered and eligible is difficult to gauge accurately due to commercial sensitivity. However, what is known is that, by the beginning of this century, some five million-plus UK employees and their dependants were entitled to workplace-provided counselling services (Beer, 2003). Given the usual likely take-up rate of between 2 and 5 per cent of those entitled (EAPA, 2008), clearly a very large number of workplace counsellors were needed to service such a potentially immense client demand. It seems that workplace counselling is yet another of counselling's elephants in the room – lots of counsellors do it but they don't seem to like to talk about it very much! However, its importance is such that, by the 1990s, some of its practitioners were arguing that its prevalence was ensuring that 'the centre of gravity of the counselling universe is moving inexorably to the workplace' (Reddy, 1993, p47).

Historically, it appears that the roots of modern workplace counselling provision can be found in the workplace welfare schemes that began to emerge in the early years of the twentieth century (Coles, 2003; Grange, 2005; Tehrani, 1997). In the UK, workplace welfarism began with the industrial philanthropists of the eighteenth and nineteenth centuries (Ward, 2001) and the first UK dedicated industrial welfare workers were Clara Heath, who was appointed by the Boots Company in 1893, and Mary Wood, who was appointed by the Rowntree Company in 1896 (Coles, 2003). In parallel, in North America industrial welfarism first emerged from early twentieth-century attempts to maximise industrial output by promoting the social welfare of workers in the newly emerging mass-production industries and later to address the ever-present problem of alcoholism among employees (Steele, 1989). Like psychotherapy generally, until the mid-twentieth century, workplace psychological services were largely the province of the psychiatrists. For example, Carroll (1996) tells us that the Metropolitan Life Insurance Company appointed an industrial psychiatrist in 1922, as did the RH Lacey Company in 1924. However, an early forerunner of what today might be recognised as workplace coun-selling can be found in the setting up of an Employee Welfare Counselling Service by the Ford Motor Company in 1914 (Carroll, 1996).

Like counselling therapy generally, workplace counselling began to expand from the 1950s onwards. This was when the person-centred movement started to sweep through the workplace welfare services at the same time as it coursed through local authority social services and similar public and voluntary welfare agencies. The time of the workplace counsellor had arrived (Reddy, 1997).

The birth of employee assistance agencies

In the UK, employee welfare provisions have evolved from these early beginnings and spread throughout the world of employment. For the last 20 years or so, much of this welfarism has been provided in the form of workplace counselling services (Claringbull, 2006). By the end of the last century, workplace counselling's UK provision had grown such that up to 75 per cent of medium and large organisations made some sort of counselling available to their staff (Carroll and Walton, 1997; Oher, 1999). Workplace counselling's apparently continuing inexorable rise in the UK was further charted by Coles (2003), and there is good reason to believe that this explosion in workplace counselling provision is a worldwide phenomenon (Australian Bureau of Statistics, 2003; EAPA, 2004). Indeed, it seems that in recent years workplace counselling's growth has been exponential (Hopkins, 2005). By 2006 in the UK, there were at least some six and a half million employees and their dependants who were provided with psychotherapeutic counselling services by employee assistance agencies (Claringbull, 2006).

ACTIVITY 1.1

- Make a list of the activities that you think 'proper' counsellors should be involved with.
- Make another list of the activities that you think 'proper' counsellors should avoid.

Modern employee assistance agencies currently try to offer more than psychotherapeutic assistance to troubled workers (Grange, 2005). As well as considering workplace counselling's current status, other investigators (Carroll, 2002; Grange, 2005; Ryan, 1998; Wright, 2001, etc.) have also speculated about its future status and have discussed the modern workplace counsellor's potential to deliver a much wider range of organisation-based psychological interventions than has hitherto generally been the case. In recent years a number of workplace counselling practitioner-theorists (Claringbull, 2003, 2004a, 2004b; Cullup, 2005; Jamieson, 2004; Orlans, 2003) have proposed a series of major expansions of the scope and breadth of the range of the interventions and help programmes that today's modern workplace counsellor could, and perhaps should, offer their corporate clients. These include a wide spectrum of psychological interventions (management consultancy, coaching, mentoring, etc.) and organisational assistance programmes (training, stress surveys, awareness enhancement, etc.), which can combine into a comprehensive package of service provisions targeted at enhancing overall employee well-being (Carroll, 2002).

Apart from providing extensive employment for therapists, workplace counselling has also impacted on counselling generally in another important way. Because it is commercially driven, workplace counselling is goal oriented and it also has to be seen to be financially worthwhile. Companies investing in workplace counselling services want a return for their money – they want 'added value'. This means that workplace counselling has, at base, two powerful drivers. The first is its underlying purpose of helping employees to recover or retain their employability. The second is that workplace counsellors are required to work within finite financial boundaries. The effect of these two forces has been to ensure that workplace counselling is, by necessity:

- solution-focused and goal-oriented;
- time-limited – usually to some four, five or six sessions.

For many purist counsellors and psychotherapists, the tendency for workplace counselling to be solution focused and time-limited supports their belief that, rather than being another arm of psychotherapy, workplace counselling actually conflicts with the supposedly traditional, non-directional, counselling values. This may be why Kinder suggested that workplace counselling is often unacknowledged by the counselling community generally because they do not see it as being proper, mainstream counselling (Kinder, 2005). It may be different, but is it still counselling? The debate continues. Table 1.2 below explores some possible differences between mainstream and workplace counselling.

Traditional counselling	Workplace counselling
Client-led	Multiple leaders (client, counsellor, employer)
Seeks to explore/correct personality	Seeks to explore/correct behaviour
Has undefined aims and goals	Has specific outcome targets
Benefits clients	Benefits clients and other interested parties
A core client activity	Only part of the client's life
Model-based	Whatever works, works

Table 1.2: Traditional vs. workplace counselling.

TODAY'S COUNSELLING REVOLUTION – THE INTEGRATIVE MOVEMENT

Historically, traditional therapists have associated themselves with the various individual models of therapy (psychodynamic, humanistic, etc.) and so have tended to remain purist adherents of their various counselling and psychotherapy schools. However, these allegiances are breaking down, some say already broken, as the evidence mounts that client 'cure' rates are consistent across the schools and that it is unlikely that any particular therapy model is better than its rivals (Elliot et al., 2008; Stiles et al., 2006; Ward et al., 2008). It is also becoming increasingly clear that the 'who' of the therapist is just as important (possibly even more important) as the 'how' of the therapeutic methodology that is being employed (Blow et al., 2007; Project MATCH, 1997). These developments have underpinned the emergence of integrative approaches to counselling therapy.

In fact, modern integrationalism is not really so very modern. French was writing about the claimed therapeutic commonalities between behaviourism and psychoanalysis in 1933, as was Rosenzweig in 1936. In 1950, Dollard and Miller published an innovative attempt to bring together the then known psychotherapies. Collectively these, and many other writers, were starting to explore the idea of a common factors approach to psychotherapy. This is the idea that certain therapeutic factors are common to all therapeutic treatments and so can be identified in all psychotherapeutic approaches. Therefore, by isolating these commonalities and by focusing on providing them, therapists could maximise the help that they can give their clients. Nevertheless, probably up to the 1990s, single-therapy allegiances remained rife throughout counselling and psychotherapy and they are far from dead today.

The end of the schoolist approach?

However, the schoolist approach to counselling, prevalent in much of the last century, was not to remain supreme. By the latter part of the twentieth century a revolution was already quietly under way. For example, Wolfe and Goldfried (1988) continued to explore the common factors approach; Wachtel (1977) began to propose theoretical methods of combining, or integrating, the therapeutic theories; and Bordin (1979) started to wonder if the quality of the client–counsellor relationship was of more importance in terms of therapeutic outcomes than the supposed benefits of the particular therapy model being employed. In 1975, Egan published the first of his still extremely popular *Skilled Helper* series, which emphasise the need to assess clients' purposes in engaging in counselling encounters and then go on to prioritise the systemic ways in which counsellors might help their clients to achieve these purposes. In 1986, Norcross published his *Handbook of Eclectic Therapy*, which by 1992 (in collaboration with Goldfried) had become the *Handbook of Psychotherapy Integration*. By 1983, the Society for the Exploration of Psychotherapy Integration had been established and today attracts many internationally respected and well-known counsellors, psychologists and psychotherapists. The age of the integrative counselling therapist had arrived.

Integrated therapy today

So what is integrative therapy's position among today's therapeutic practitioners and just what is it anyway? Well, it is now the case that integrative counselling is increasingly becoming the dominant model and this is demonstrated by noting that, by 2008, it was being taught on over half of the British Association for Counselling & Psychotherapy's accredited training programmes. However, currently the only real answer to the second part of the above question – what is integrative therapy? – is that there is no answer. What are its most important factors? Is it therapeutic technique or the person of the therapist that is the dominant agent? As Barkham (2007) has remarked, 'it all depends on who you ask'!

The integrationists are, of course, trying to find an overarching model of psychotherapy – one that forms a comprehensive umbrella for a theoretical framework within which all the other therapeutic approaches can be found a place. Currently, there are a number of integrative models of counselling therapy that might prove to be useful steps along the road to the ideal of psychotherapeutic unity. These include the Cognitive-analytic Theory (Ryle, 1990), the Five Relationships Model (Clarkson, 1995, 2003) and the Relational-developmental Model (Evans and Gilbert, 2005). These models are further explored in Chapter 6.

It is probably true to say that, at the end of the day, adopting an integrative approach to counselling is far more than learning a set of overarching theories or acquiring techniques for maximising the potential benefits of the various aspects of the client–counsellor relationship. As Hollanders (2000b) puts it:

> *integrative goes hand in hand with a philosophy of life and work that is truly pluralistic in its vision.*

He goes on to say that it:

> *means being committed to the whole project of therapy rather than to a particular approach.*

In other words, in its ideal, it is quite likely that integrative therapy is just that which each experienced counsellor makes it to be. It is about finding ways that fit the needs of any particular client at any particular time. It is even possible that integrative counselling might eventually prove to be 'model free'.

TOMORROW'S COUNSELLING REVOLUTION

As we have already noted, for all talking therapists, 'times, they are a-changing'. Statutory regulation of the counselling and psychotherapy profession seems inevitable and probably due by 2011 or 2012 (Clarke, 2008; Pointon, 2008). In addition, the Government's significant investments in the NHS *Improving Access to Psychological Therapies* initiative are likely to accelerate the conquest of the therapeutic world by evidence-based practice. Therapists' outdated single-school allegiances are dying out. As we know, modern research increasingly tells us that no particular therapy model works faster, better or cheaper than any other (Elliot et al., 2008; Stiles et al., 2007, 2008). The impacts of these powerful mega-drivers seem certain to fuel an unstoppable revolution in the counselling and psychotherapy profession and an inescapable transformation in the educational needs of its practitioners.

Degree-based counselling

One major revolutionary change, and one that is almost certain, is likely to be the evolution of counselling into a degree-based profession. The British Association for Counselling & Psychotherapy (BACP) anticipated this inevitability and so established a Core Curriculum Consortium to explore what this change will mean for the future of counsellor education. The Consortium's 2007 draft report stated:

> *inspection of the generic core competencies indicates . . . counsellors . . . need to study to at least at Honours level . . . Need . . . an understanding of a complex body of knowledge . . . analytic techniques and problem-solving . . . [Need to be] able to evaluate evidence, arguments and assumptions . . . reach sound judgments.*

So, will tomorrow's entry-level counsellors eventually need generic counselling degrees?

Such proposals, mainly concentrated on counsellor-training quality assurance issues, have been made before and they certainly have attracted screams of anguish from some sectors of the counselling community. Spirited defences of the 'anti-formal training' viewpoint can be found, for example, in the online *Ipnosis* journal (Postle, 1999–2008). There is a powerful lobby within the counselling profession (e.g. Musgrave, 2007 and many others) that has grave doubts about the feasibility of teaching counselling in any sort of an objective or measurable sense. A quick perusal of the Readers' Letters pages of such professional magazines as *Therapy Today*, or attendance at any of the counselling conferences and seminars, will provide many instances of such viewpoints being powerfully put forward. Counselling is a highly individualised, personal and special activity, the anti-educators claim, and so they say that it is a way-of-being to be acquired or assimilated; it is not a measurable set of skills that can be adapted to meet measurable targets. The basic counter-argument to such a purist viewpoint is to note that, whether or not such noble ideas are actually tenable, this is just not how the world works. Today's taxpayers and investors want value for their money. Counselling's clients, too, need to know if their personal investments in counselling (time and/or fees) are likely to pay off. It seems that sometimes counsellors forget that clients always have the choice of alternative strategies for resolving their problems. For example, depression might be tackled by medication; anxiety might be relieved by meditation. Should clients with relationship difficulties go to couples therapy or visit an Ann Summers outlet? At the end of the day, clients are consumers and, if counsellors and psychotherapists do not provide them with what they want, they will simply go to the shop next door.

Choosing the best therapy

Clients have yet another major difficulty in trying to decide if counselling and psychotherapy is likely to offer a 'best buy' way of resolving their problems. This arises from their difficulties in choosing between the multiplicity of therapy types, methods and modalities currently on offer. A quick glance at any local Yellow Pages will confirm the confusing cornucopia of practitioners and practices vying for custom. Browne (2008) tellingly describes the trials and tribulations of five typical clients who were simply trying to find a therapist who fitted their needs. After all, if therapists themselves cannot decide which is the 'best' therapy, how on earth can their customers make informed choices? Therapy is a curious profession. First, its practitioners don't have to be qualified and it is arguable that this fact, if widely known, would shock a public that is accustomed to its high-level professionals having degrees. Second, it is the only profession wherein its trainees select their career path specialities before they start training. They often need to choose between humanistic, person-centred, psychodynamic, relationship therapy, group work or any other specialist area of practice before they can possibly know enough about counselling to be able to make anything like informed career choices. All the other professions teach a basic generic form of their discipline at undergraduate level to begin with. They then require extensive hands-on supervised practical training before the first-level practitioner qualifications are awarded. Postgraduate-level specialist training programmes follow after.

It is a tried and tested training method; why should counselling training be any different?

The demographics of the therapy trade

If counselling does eventually become a degree-based profession, apart from such a development's huge impact on the training needs of counsellors, there is also likely to be a seismic change in the demographic of the therapy trade. Currently, counselling is almost exclusively entered by very committed mature students who want to train on a part-time basis. Indeed, many training courses set a minimum age of 30 years for their recruits. However, the economics of higher education (HE) in the UK favour full-time undergraduates who usually come from sixth forms or further education (FE) colleges. This demand generates undergraduates who are mainly 18–21 years old and who may, or may not, be committed to their particular fields of study. Today's typical counsellor is probably female, 40 and fully committed. Tomorrow's counsellor might well be metro-sexual, maturity-light and multipurposed – another therapeutic revolution?

REFLECTION POINT

- Can counselling be taught or is it an attitude to life?
- Do counsellors need degrees?
- Can young people be effective counsellors for the entire client age range?

CONCLUSION

Counselling and psychotherapy have come a long way over the last 100 years. Counselling started to separate out as an emotional health-enhancement discipline before the First World War with the inclusion of an early form of counselling into industrial welfarism. Dependent initially on psychiatry and the psychoanalytic approaches to psychotherapy, counselling later began to have a major impact on society as it gradually absorbed the thinking of the humanistic and behavioural psychologists into its practices. Over the years, therapy's theoretical and treatment bases have changed a great deal from the twentieth-century models that were (and to a certain extent still are) rigidly dependent on the traditional, single-school approaches to counselling and psychotherapy. Modern theorists are exploring how far the integrative paradigm models might help them to suggest some possible unifying general theories of counselling and psychotherapy that might better underpin the therapy trade. It seems that the talking therapies can now claim to be independent, academically sound, evidence-based, professional practice – one with its own defined specialist subject area and its own independent discourse. These developments, together with current Government policies, are likely to establish counselling and psychotherapy as a core profession (or professions) within the provision of emotional healthcare services in the public domain.

An important outcome of these events has been to cause the therapy profession to start to reconsider how it should train its practitioners. Given the widely accepted public expectation that HE plays an essential role in professional practices, it seems that the argument that counselling is likely to evolve over time into being a degree-based profession is indeed a very supportable one. However, in this uncertain, and ever-changing, counselling world, one thing at least seems certain. The typical counsellors and psychotherapists of tomorrow will be a very different breed from the typical counsellors and psychotherapists of today.

ACTIVITY 1.2

- What sort of a therapist do you want to be?
- Make a list of the qualities and knowledge levels to which you would like to aspire.

SUGGESTED FURTHER READING

Dryden, W (2007) *Dryden's Handbook of Individual Therapy*, 5th edition. London: Sage.

Very readable and set out in convenient 'bite-sized' chunks. Super chapter on research methodolgy.

McLeod, J (2003) *An Introduction to Counselling*, 3rd edition. Maidenhead: Open University Press.

If you only ever buy one counselling book, buy this one. Essential reading; comprehensive and set out in an easy-to-follow format. Chapter 1, 'Introduction to Counselling', is an excellent point from which to begin your learning. It's all you need to know.

Woolfe, R, Dryden, W and Strawbridge, S (2003) *Handbook of Counselling Psychology*, 2nd edition. London: Sage.

An excellent source book, although perhaps of more interest to those with a psychology background. Part 5, 'Different Contexts', helpfully tells you a lot about various aspects of clinical practice.

PART 2

WHAT DO THERAPISTS DO?

INTRODUCTION

The talking therapies sometimes seem to be rather a 'funny old game', not least because often it seems that its practitioners do not do or say anything very much apart from throwing in the occasional 'mmmm' or 'I see'. Well, at least that is how it might appear to anyone from outside any of the psychotherapeutic professions who happened to sneak a peek into a therapy session. After all, most counsellors and psychotherapists do not usually 'do' anything to their clients, not at least in any active meaning of the word (Nelson-Jones, 2008; Sanders, 2002 and many others). They do not generally give their clients any imposed treatments; they do not often counsel them in the sense of giving specific advice; they certainly do not try to take control of their clients' lives. Even in the case of the cognitive-behavioural therapists, although they undertake active treatment planning and management, it is still the client who has to do the work. The usual thing in most treatment situations is for the therapist to respond to, or work with, whatever it is that the client brings into the therapy session, rather than to actively lead or direct the therapeutic process. In other words, on the surface at least, therapy looks like quite a passive sort of a job and not one that seems to demand much effort from its workforce. Perhaps this is a more widespread view than we realise. As one counselling teacher I know once told her colleagues:

> I'll never forget interviewing an applicant for a training place at
> my college. 'Why do you want to be a counsellor?' I asked her.
> 'Well,' she replied, 'it's a sitting-down job.'

Of course, some therapists might claim that actually they are quite active. For example, counsellors and psychotherapists working with traumatised clients or substance misusers might sometimes decide to be quite directive or purposeful. Others, for example many cognitive-behavioural therapists, would certainly claim to be active in the sense that they assess and diagnose their clients, and then suggest experimenting with ways to try to resolve some of their problems. Nevertheless, it remains arguable that, even with these apparently more action-based psychotherapies, therapy might still be considered to be more of a passive activity than an active one. After all, even with the active therapies, the therapeutic task is often really more one of helping clients to discover for themselves what sorts of new and advantageous ways of being they might want to adopt. It is not usually the therapist's job to actively direct clients towards allegedly beneficial, officially 'therapist approved', lifestyles.

Yet other practitioners might suggest that therapy is at least an active (or perhaps an 'activist') profession in the socially aware sense, because they believe that it inevitably encourages certain attitudes to life, such as supposedly being non-judgemental and anti-authoritarian. It has even been suggested, on the one hand, that counsellors and psychotherapists are inevitably active agents for serious social change (Bennett, 2005), and some therapists (feminist practitioners, for instance) might well sympathise with such an argument. On the other hand, some might claim that the therapy trade is very much the 'non-action-dependent sector' of the so-called 'caring professions'. So, if the talking therapies really are such a 'funny old game', and their practitioners do not seem to have to do anything very much, it seems reasonable to wonder why training programmes are so extensive and demanding. Would therapists perhaps be better employed if they just got on with doing something useful, such as emotionally repairing their clients?

Repairing people

Actually, many counsellors and psychotherapists, from all sorts of backgrounds, would object strongly to the idea that therapists ought to repair people. They would argue that it is wrong to assume that, as psychological counsellors, we know best about how people ought to be; about how people ought to live their lives; about how people's lives should be 'mended'. Indeed, it is likely that most therapists would passionately declare that it is the clients' exclusive privilege to choose the directions that they want their therapeutic experiences to take. Practitioners such as these (probably the majority of the profession) might well argue that psychotherapists and counsellors cannot 'repair' their clients because, quite simply, they were not broken in the first place. Instead, rather than describing psychotherapy as being a form of people-repair, many of today's practitioners (again probably a majority) would most likely describe it as being an emotional development process that is somehow centred on the clients' personal explorations of their own inner selves. This means that, for many practitioners, counselling and psychotherapy is essentially a client-led process. For them, it should not be therapist led; indeed, it must not be therapist led. Choice, they say, is a matter for clients; it is not a matter for their therapists. These sorts of apparently non-directional, non-judgemental views are held by very many practising counsellors and psychotherapists.

However, it is worth spending a moment to consider if, in fact, what therapists claim (and probably genuinely believe) is the proper purpose and value of therapy actually matches the realities of the consulting room. This is because it is arguable that, when a therapist subscribes to a particular model of therapy, then that practitioner is, in effect, also subscribing to some specific ideas about how people develop emotionally over the years. If this is the case, whether or not counsellors and psychotherapists are aware of so doing, by adopting a particular therapy model they are also implicitly giving their support to certain associated beliefs about how people's psychological beings ought to grow, about how they do grow, and about how this process might go wrong. This inevitably leads to therapists having ideas (acknowledged or not) about ways in which troubled people can be helped to become untroubled. In other words, the term 'counselling and psychotherapy', as practised, implicitly contains the concept that therapists have some notions about how to assist their troubled clients to put things right in their lives. All this strongly suggests that even the most ardently non-directional practitioners are inherently a lot more directional, and a lot more dominated by psychological theory, than they either realise or than they would be prepared to admit.

How do we repair people?

Although many practitioners would disagree, it seems to be potentially arguable that, whether or not it is their overt or covert intention, therapists are actually (at least in part) engaged in people-repair. If this is so, it seems reasonable to propose that, before we can put something right, we need to know how it went wrong and (if possible) how it ought to have worked in the first place. Of course, this same pragmatic rule can apply to any of life's mishaps. After all, it does not seem very likely that you could mend anything at all (your lawnmower, your car, your relationship, your life) until you find out how it came to be broken in the first place. This general, 'diagnose first/repair second' principle is equally true for counselling and psychotherapy. As therapist-repairers, we too need to find out what has gone wrong, only in our case we want to know what it is that has gone wrong for our clients. In order to do this, we need to know something about what sort of a person it is that our client has now become and how they came to be that person. We then need to compare what they are to what sort of person our client could have been, might have been, or might want to be.

All this suggests that we might feel a bit more confident in our therapeutic work if we could achieve an understanding of how it is that people become people. In other words, we need to find out what it is that makes some-one tick. These are really all questions about how it is that someone's personality develops, how someone's personality ought to develop, and how that development can become distorted. If we can answer those questions, perhaps we can find out how to 'repair' a 'wrong' personality. At this point we also need to remember that self-reflection is also an important part of any therapist's everyday professional practice. Therefore, as we wonder about how our clients became who they are, we are also making some guesses about how we too became who we are.

This means that, in order to be able to at least make a start helping their clients (and evaluating themselves), it seems clear that:

Counsellors and psychotherapists need to understand people.

Or to put it another way:

Counsellors and psychotherapists need to understand personality.

Of course, finding out about what makes someone tick (what personality is and how it grows) is only the first part of the puzzle. Working out the specifics of what it is that makes a particular client tick is only the assessment (diagnosis) part of the therapist's task. The second part, possibly the major part of the task, is deciding what to do about what has been found. What sort of therapeutic methods will we choose to use? What were the alternatives and why have we rejected them? In order to be able make sensible choices about treatment methods, it is clearly necessary that:

Counsellors and psychotherapists need to know the 'people theories' (personality theories) that underpin the various treatment styles.

The essential point being made here is that practitioners who provide therapy without appreciating the supporting theoretical backgrounds are, in effect, fighting with one hand tied behind their backs. That is why all counsellors and psychotherapists would find it very illuminating to ask themselves:

What makes people tick? (What is personality?)

Our answers to this question lead on to an even more difficult, but absolutely vital, question:

When we know what makes people tick, what are we going to do about it? (What sort of psychotherapy should we offer them?)

REFLECTION POINT

- If counsellors do not repair people, what exactly do they do?
- Is it always wrong for counsellors to know better than their clients?
- Think about one of the therapy models. Can you justify it without referring back to an underlying theory about what makes people tick?

CHAPTER 2

Repairing people – the tales begin

CORE KNOWLEDGE

- Counsellors and psychotherapists will be better practitioners if they know something about:
  - what personality is;
  - how personalities develop.
- For many practitioners:
  - counselling and psychotherapy is about change;
  - counselling and psychotherapy is about choice.
- Much of counselling and psychotherapy theory and practice is based on the psychodynamic, behaviourist and humanistic explanations of how people become the various sorts of individuals we all are. Modern theories include the biological, social and genetic explanations of personality development.
- Put simply, therapists who want to work with people, who want to try to help people, need to understand people.

UNDERSTANDING PEOPLE

This story begins with an assumption. Just for now, let us assume that counsellors and psychotherapists do try to find ways to either 'repair' their clients or at least help their clients to become their own 'do-it-yourself' therapists. So, if we feel that something is emotionally or psychologically 'wrong' with our inner beings (our core personalities), the implication is that somehow or other there is, or at least in theory there ought to be, an emotional or psychological 'right'. Clearly, if our personalities do not seem to be working properly, if they are not 'right', we want to know if we can do something about it. Can we 'mend' our defective emotions, put right incorrect thinking, change our bad behaviours and eliminate our uncomfortable feelings?

It would be great if we could find an 'official' blueprint that tells us what sorts of people humans ought to be. Then we could compare the supposed 'ideal person' with what they actually are. If we could use such a blueprint to identify any mismatches, we might be able to find out where it is that we are psychologically 'broken'. Then we could decide on a treatment plan (select a psychotherapy method?) and we could try to help our clients put things right. Just as medical doctors and their patients look for physical cures, so too might counsellors look for emotional 'cures'.

Although there are no 'officially agreed' people blueprints, as psychological therapists we do need to try to understand what it is that makes our clients tick. If we do not know that, how can we help them? Sensible therapists will also want to know what it is that makes themselves tick, too. Therefore, as practitioners, or indeed as clients, we need to understand ourselves as people. If we can begin to answer these questions, and especially if we are not particularly content with what we have found, we really need to find an answer to the obvious follow-on question, which is: What sort of person do I want to be? Put another way, we need to understand what our personalities are and how they developed. In order to explore these sorts of issues properly we need:

- some ideas about what personality is;
- some ideas about how personalities develop.

From a therapeutic point of view, having an understanding of human personality and how it develops is a vital first step in deciding what sort of treatment method might be the most helpful in any particular case. Clearly, in practical terms, the way in which you set out to repair something must depend on your ideas about what has gone wrong. Obviously, a mechanic has to find out what is wrong with an engine before deciding which spanners to use to repair it. Similarly, a psychotherapist also needs to find out what has gone wrong with the psychological engine (someone's personality) before choosing the therapeutic 'spanner' (counselling approach) needed to put things right. Therapists' choices about which psychotherapeutic tools to use will depend on their ideas about what human personality is and what it could be or should be. The problem is that there are many competing theories about personality and personality development. Which one should therapists choose? What if their choice is wrong? After all, if counsellors and psychotherapists are wrong in their theories about how personality develops, it is possible that they are also wrong in their ideas about how to carry out effective counselling. Clearly, if they are wrong about what is amiss with the psychological 'engine', they might choose the wrong therapeutic 'repair' tools.

WHAT IF WE MISUNDERSTAND PEOPLE?

It is arguable that the various counselling and psychotherapeutic approaches currently available have all arisen, at least in part, from the personality theories with which they are associated. Therefore, it is likely that mistaken ideas about the psychology of personality development will lead to mistaken ideas about counselling and psychotherapy theory. This means that there are many ways in which practitioners could make some fundamental mistakes when they opt for any particular treatment style. What if their treatment choices actually turn out to be dependent on some false premises? Would such mistaken therapists be delivering inappropriate, even harmful, therapeutic inputs? The following are some examples.

A psychodynamic error?

Generally speaking, the psychodynamic theory rests on the idea that personality develops and exists as an unconscious process. Suppose we could prove that the concept of a core unconscious is false. Where would that leave those adherents of the various psychodynamic schools of counselling who depend on identifying unrealised human emotional exchanges? Would their work no longer have any therapeutic value?

Case study 2.1

Georgina was seeing Herbert, her psychodynamic therapist, because she had been having some embarrassing memory lapses. She was forgetting certain people's names and forgetting some of her important professional appointments with those same people. Herbert wondered if Georgina's forgetfulness might be to do with her admitted reluctance to involve herself with certain organisations and their activities. 'They are all fusspot, cranky outfits, staffed by fuddy-duddies,' she told him. 'I leave all that sort of thing up to my father'!

Herbert decided that Georgina's 'forgetfulness' was actually an unconsciously held psychologically defensive position. He believed that unresolved and unconsciously held feelings about her father meant that Georgina was avoiding reminders of him by avoiding (forgetting) about 'fuddy-duddy' people. They worked together on that premise for several sessions and got absolutely nowhere.

Eventually, Georgina's GP referred her to a psychologist. The psychologist explained that recent research-based discoveries had shown that there was no such thing as the unconscious, but that memory simply existed at several levels, and in different parts, of the brain. It also was the case that sometimes memories held at the deepest level were hard to access and that such a process was regulated by how the brain was hardwired. The areas of the brain where memory was stored had been identified and so the idea that humans had an 'unconscious' was now redundant. In cases like Georgina's, it was usually found that minor faults in the brain's hardwiring had developed over the years and that these could interfere with memory access. He simply taught her some psychological 'tricks' for repairing these faults and making accessing deep memories much easier. Georgina practised her 'brain-mending' techniques and her forgetfulness problem disappeared.

A biological mistake?

Suppose that another of the major personality theories (for instance, the idea that personality is derived from a mainly genetically driven process) is found to be correct. Where would that leave any cognitive therapists whose therapeutic practices depend on the concept that maladaptive behaviour can be changed through learning new ways of thinking? If, for argument's sake, we also assume that learning cannot overcome genetic biochemistry, would the cognitive therapies now become invalid?

Case study 2.2

Elisabeth presented as a very depressed person. She always appeared to be in a low mood and she always seemed to be certain that failure and disaster were her lot in life. Elisabeth was one of nature's pessimists. She was certainly a 'glass half empty' sort of a person.

Her poor levels of self-appreciation and her belief that she could never succeed had led Elisabeth into having an extremely poor degree of self-care, almost at a 'slow-suicide' level. This worried her GP, who sent Elisabeth to see Jim, who is a cognitive-behavioural therapist. Jim concluded that Elisabeth's problems were all due to her having some very negative core beliefs about herself. Jim suggested that perhaps these negative core beliefs were causing Elisabeth constantly to generate negative automatic thoughts about everything that occurred in her life. For a number of weeks, Jim worked at helping Elisabeth to set up some personal psychological experiments that were designed to challenge her apparently ingrained negative views of herself. There were no improvements.

Later that same year, Elisabeth volunteered to be a subject in some genetic research that was taking place at her local hospital. The researchers found that there is a specific personality gene, which, if absent or turned off, causes some people to have negative self-perceptions. It turned out that in Elisabeth's case that gene was switched off. Nothing could be done to switch it back on. Elisabeth could no more be reprogrammed to be happy than she could be reprogrammed to have her natural hair colour change from ginger to brunette. No form of psychotherapy was going to help Elisabeth to cheer up.

Humanists go wrong?

Let us suppose, as some would argue, that the very idea that there might be correct, or even ideal, personality templates is actually a sort of 'anti-therapy' theory. After all, very many counsellors and psychotherapists, especially those from humanistic backgrounds, would claim that it is essential to be non-judgemental. Person-centred therapists would certainly argue that people are what they are and there is no specific right or wrong way to be. Suppose, however, that we discover that some 'approved' personality templates actually exist. Would this mean that judging our clients would move from being a counselling sin to being a counselling necessity?

Case study 2.3

Leah had always been very much a client-led therapist. She never pointed her clients towards any particular form of emotional 'health'. Trained in the 1970s never to judge people, Leah had not forgotten a much respected trainer telling her that there was never any point in asking her clients any questions. 'All you'll get are answers,' she was told and, going with the spirit of the times, these seemed to be very wise words indeed to Leah. Over the years, Leah had become very averse to judging her clients or to telling them what to do. Even just thinking about it made her very uncomfortable. As with many of her colleagues, Leah never came to any conclusions about the effectiveness of her work. Doing so was just not her business. 'It isn't proper counselling,' she always said.

Last year, in order to increase her income, Leah started to take referrals from an employee counselling agency. They required her to complete case progress and case outcome questionnaires for each client. Leah was amazed to find that a client's progress, or lack of progress, could actually be measured. She could ask questions and the answers did matter. This breakthrough led Leah to go on to discover that there were many assessment procedures that could be used to measure a client's personality on a pre- and post-counselling basis. It seemed that, actually, there were rights and wrongs about successful outcomes and about productive ways to counsel clients.

PERSONALITY THEORY AND THE TALKING THERAPIES

On the one hand, it might be that the whole idea that an 'approved' personality template actually exists is wrong. If this is so, we have an even more fundamental problem than that of deciding which treatment method to choose. After all, should it be that there are no such 'ideal' people templates, perhaps nothing in human personality can be judged to have gone wrong and so no repairs are necessary – 'If it ain't broke, don't fix it!'. If this is so, perhaps there is no need for any psychological 'fixers' and so maybe human society does not need psychotherapists. A sobering thought.

However, on the other hand, there are the schools of thought that champion their own ideas about what makes a 'proper' personality template. They know what has gone wrong and so they know what repairs to make – they hope. They know that their adopted psychotherapeutic approach is the right one – again, they hope. Unfortunately, many therapists acquire their allegiance to a particular school of therapy before they learn anything much about personality theory. In any case, counsellors and psychotherapists are not usually concerned with people as a whole or with the broad sweep of ideas about personality development. They are usually only interested in the problems facing individuals or small groups of individuals. So, usually, they just want to focus on what makes specific individuals into the sorts of people they are. Nevertheless, even in specific cases, therapists are still asking: What's my client like? What sort of a person am I trying to help? In other words, thinking about personality is an inevitable part of the psycho-therapeutic process, whether or not the therapist acknowledges that this is so. Overtly or covertly, directly or indirectly, personality theory is an implicit factor, even an inherent one, in all therapeutic relationships.

REFLECTION POINT

- Are there emotionally 'incorrect' people – what, if anything, is good about them?
- Are there emotionally 'correct' people – what, if anything, is bad about them?
- Should counsellors 'repair' troubled people?
- Can counsellors 'repair' damaged people?

Later in this book, we will be looking at the various ways in which psychotherapy is delivered. In order to do this we will first explore the particular personality theories behind each treatment approach and then we will consider how these psychological 'parents' have impacted on their therapeutic 'children'. In other words, as well as asking what it is that makes people tick, we will also be asking what this tells us about therapy. We will be asking what therapy is really like – what is it all about?

WHAT IS THERAPY?

As we have already noted, to the casual observer counselling and psycho-therapy might indeed seem to be very much a passive, not doing very much at all, sort of profession. After all, the clients do all the talking and the therapists just do the listening – quite an easy sort of job really. However, is this really the case?

- Is therapy really an easy job?
- Easy or not, what do therapists actually do?

If we think about it, we soon realise that there are many different ways of answering these questions and the answers usually depend on what sort of help it is that clients are looking for and on the professional backgrounds of the sorts of therapists that we are thinking about.

The 'Is therapy really an easy job?' question

The 'Is therapy really an easy job?' question is actually quite a complex one to answer. It is, of course, true that some clients are apparently easier to deal with than others. Not that it always seems so at the time. Like many practitioners, I will never forget my first ever client, although in her particular case I have never solved the 'easy or difficult' issue. When you have read about Mrs Harris in Case study 2.4, why not take a break and spend a little time considering the Reflection Point which follows? You might find it interesting to think about what your own answers are to the 'easy or difficult job?' debate.

Case study 2.4

I was still in training, but I had reached the stage when they were at last actually going to let me begin work with one or two real clients. So there I was, sitting in a real counselling room for the first time and waiting for my first ever client. I was desperately hoping that I would be able to remember enough of what I had been taught so far.

Mrs Harris burst into the counselling room – she did not just enter the room, she invaded it, she conquered it, she took it over. She was a lady well into her middle years; she was what used to be called 'of a certain age'. She was certainly a larger-than-life character, both in her person and in her being. With her ample proportions crammed into an uncompromisingly belted gabardine raincoat, her shapeless hat almost nailed to her head, and with a huge, dauntingly black, handbag held before her like a battering ram, Mrs Harris plumped herself down into her chair in a manner that can only be described as taking royal possession. I was barely able to stammer out 'hello' before she started talking. She never stopped talking. Mrs Harris began by saying that she had never been to see a counsellor before, that she did not know what I was expecting of her, and anyway she just knew that she would not be able to say anything much as she had always had difficulty in talking about herself. She was not one to put herself forward, she said, and people were always telling her that she was too quiet for her own good.

Searching my mind for a suitably 'counsellor-ish' response, and trying to fight down my sense of impending disaster, I tried to offer some sort of an appropriate comment. My attempts to speak were about as effective as a fly trying to punch an elephant. Mrs Harris bombarded me into silence with a barrage of sound and I remained pinned to my chair for the next hour. Coward that I was, I soon found myself taking the path of least resistance; I did not really have any other choice and I soon gave up any plans to do or say anything. The truth is that I had no idea what to do anyway and all my training had flown out of the window. What did Mrs Harris have to say? The reality is that I had little idea at the time and even less idea afterwards. When she decided that the session was finished, Mrs Harris gathered up herself and her belongings and emerged from her chair. Her parting comment was, 'you are clever, I feel so much better now; how ever did you manage to sort me out?'. She left the field a triumphant verbal warrior, still talking even as she progressed down the corridor, leaving behind a very dazed, very bewildered counsellor and a suddenly very empty counselling room. I never saw her again.

REFLECTION POINT

- How would you have treated Mrs Harris?
- Is counselling really a nice, easy, 'sitting-down' job?

The 'What do therapists actually do?' question

Thinking about the 'What do therapists actually do?' question usually throws up a lot of possible answers. That is because, in some ways, it could be argued, just as every client–therapist session is probably unique, every treatment session also provides its own unique answer to the debate. Remember, a core theme in this book is that the story of counselling and psychotherapy is actually a whole series of tales, some interlocking and some not; some complementary and some not. As we noted in the Preface, it is also important to keep in mind that these stories can change according to who is telling them, where they are being told and why they are being told. Obviously, other people will have their own individual 'tales from the consulting room' to tell the world about how they work. Of course, the real answer to the 'What do therapists do?' question (at least as far as you are concerned) will eventually be your own answer. After all, a much more interesting question is 'What do I actually do?'. Your personal answer will evolve as you grow as a practitioner and as you tell your own 'therapist's tale'.

The central theme underpinning my own response to the 'What do therapists do?' question is my belief that most clients go to see a therapist because they feel that something is wrong or missing in their lives. Somehow, in some way, clients might feel unfulfilled, disturbed, concerned, worried, threatened and so on, and these uncomfortable perceptions might cause them to feel frightened, puzzled, out of control, frustrated, angry, hurt, grieved or in some other way emotionally distressed. Some clients' problems might appear to be very serious. Others might appear to be petty. Any such distinctions are unimportant. No matter how worrisome (or not) their issues might appear to anyone else, as far as the clients are concerned, their problems are huge or at least sufficiently disturbing to make them want to get some help. So, in a nutshell, what therapists do is to try to help emotionally or psychologically troubled people. That is the 'what' and the 'why' parts of their work. Learning the 'how' part can take a lifetime.

As well as helping individuals with their concerns, counsellors and psychotherapists are also sometimes asked to help worried organisations. These organisations can include employers, government agencies, voluntary-sector bodies or indeed any group of people who believe that psychological difficulties are somehow disrupting their functioning. All of these troubled clients, individuals or organisations are often referred to as the 'clinical population'. Something is wrong and they want it put right.

Of course, it does not have to be the case that therapists only work with emotionally unwell (psychologically 'dis-eased') individuals or dysfunctional organisations. It is not only the troubled who feel a need to see a practitioner. People can (and do) access counsellors to try to find help with all sorts of issues, dilemmas and life choices. Doing so does not necessarily mean that they were psychologically 'sick' to start with. For example, some clients might go to see a therapist to work on their ongoing personal developments or to find ways of increasing their sense of personal self-fulfilment. They might go to a talking therapist to try to find ways of enriching their relationships with other people. In the case of organisational clients, workplace specialists might be asked to help with, or advise on, how to add to or maximise existing levels of corporate emotional health, staff interpersonal relationships and communal/commercial effectiveness. Untroubled clients (individuals or organisations) are often referred to as the 'non-clinical population'. There is nothing 'wrong' with them as such. Individually or collectively they might be sufficiently content or believe themselves to be sufficiently effective. Nevertheless, they still want to see if any improvements are possible. Perhaps they want to see if they can function more productively.

Generally speaking, however, whether clinical or non-clinical, individual or corporate, it is my contention that most clients go to counsellors and psychotherapists because they feel that something is wrong. No matter what their current emotional situations might be, from their various points of view these psychological states do not fit their purposes and so they want to alter them somehow or try to move on in some way. Therefore, put in terms of a very basic proposition, it can be powerfully argued that:

Counselling and psychotherapy is about change.

Furthermore, as it is also part of the therapist's job to aid clients as they work through their change processes, it is also powerfully arguable that:

Counselling and psychotherapy is about choices.

Indeed, it can be claimed that the BACP's own definition of counselling (2009) reinforces such propositions. You can check out their latest definition for yourself at www.bacp.co.uk. The BACP says that:

Counselling takes place when a counsellor sees a client in a private and confidential setting to explore a difficulty the client is having, distress they may be experiencing or perhaps their dissatisfaction with life, or loss of a sense of direction and purpose. It is always at the request of the client as no one can properly be 'sent' for counselling.

*By listening attentively and patiently the counsellor can begin to perceive the difficulties from the client's point of view and can help them to see things more clearly, possibly from a different perspective. Counselling is a way of enabling **choice*** or **change*** or of reducing confusion. It does not involve giving advice or directing a client to take a particular course of action. Counsellors do not judge or exploit their clients in any way.*

In the counselling sessions the client can explore various aspects of their life and feelings, talking about them freely and openly in a way that is rarely possible with friends or family. Bottled up feelings such as anger, anxiety, grief and embarrassment can become very intense and counselling offers an opportunity to explore them, with the possibility of making them easier to understand. The counsellor will encourage the expression of feelings and as a result of their training will be able to accept and reflect the client's problems without becoming burdened by them.

Acceptance and respect for the client are essentials for a counsellor and, as the relationship develops, so too does trust between the counsellor and client, enabling the client to look at many aspects of their life, their relationships and themselves which they may not have considered or been able to face before. The counsellor may help the client to examine in detail the behaviour or situations which are proving troublesome and to find an area where it would be possible to initiate some **change*** *as a start. The counsellor may help the client to look at the options open to them and help them to decide the best for them.*

(* Author's emphasis)

Although we have noted that organisations can also benefit from the talking therapies, in this book I shall mainly address questions about how therapists actually work as seen from the point of view of the individual client. I am also going to continue to assume that individual clients usually go to see a psychological therapist because they want to put something right. Put another way, they want to somehow give their lives new directions or perhaps to find out how to become more comfortable with their existing ways of being. Therefore, we shall be looking at how therapists work by concentrating on investigating how they meet the needs of the clinical population.

In order to get a useful handle on how counsellors and psychotherapists actually help their customers, it might help if we think about how our clients became the sorts of individual characters that they all are. What makes them tick or, put another way, what sorts of personalities do they have? Having done that, we might find it helpful to consider how our ideas about people's personalities might influence how we go about working with them. How do we decide which therapeutic method to employ in any particular case?

ARE THERE TOO MANY THEORIES?

Of course, having read this far, you won't be surprised to learn, given the disputatious nature of psychologists, counsellors and psychotherapists, that there are quite a number of major theories of human personality. Neither will you be surprised to learn that all these theories compete with each other and contradict each other. This leads to some major problems in linking therapeutic practice to the various ways in which we think about what makes someone tick. Which theories should we include and which should we reject? Ideally, we would find a way to link all these personality theories together, but of course that is outside the scope of this book. However, we do need to at least think about how the various personality theories might be linked together. This is because, when we explore integrative counselling in Chapter 6, we will be trying to link up the various counselling theories.

However, for our purposes, it's convenient just for now to limit our investigations to the three mainstream psychological theories of personality that underpin what have historically been the three mainstream theoretical approaches to psychotherapy:

- psychodynamic;
- cognitive-behavioural;
- humanistic.

In Chapters 3, 4 and 5, we will examine these three personality theories and in each case discuss some of the various counselling approaches that have emerged from them. After that, in Chapter 6, we will briefly take a note of some of the other main personality theories and go on to consider how some of the more comprehensive, all-inclusive, approaches to personality allow us to move beyond the confines of any one model of psychotherapy. After all, it might be that the future of therapy lies in its becoming free from theoretical model constraints. At least that is what some prominent modern theorists seem to be suggesting (Palmer and Woolfe, 2000, and many other authors).

SUGGESTED FURTHER READING

British Association for Counselling & Psychotherapy (BACP) (2008)
How to Get the Best Out of Your Therapist. Information Sheet C1 (Roxburgh, T).

British Association for Counselling & Psychotherapy (BACP) (2008)
What is Counselling? Information Sheet C2.

British Association for Counselling & Psychotherapy (BACP) (2008)
Am I Fit to Practise as a Counsellor? Information Sheet P9 (Gale, H).

All the above are available as free downloads from www.bacp.co.uk (accessed Summer 2009) – they are good entry-level introductions to these topics. Information sheet C2 is particularly useful in offering an 'official' definition of counselling (as the BACP sees it at least).

CHAPTER 3

The psychodynamic story

CORE KNOWLEDGE

- Some psychodynamic theorists believe that the evolution of human personality is powered by instinctual drives. Others claim that social and environmental factors also play a part.

- Psychodynamicists also believe that important parts/powerful factors of and in human personality lie in the unconscious.

- Psychodynamic theorists argue that personality has three components:
    - the *id* (the original mind)
    - the *ego* (the rational mind)
    - the *superego* (the conscience).

- Human personality development is a psychosexual process – Freud.

- Human personality development is a psychosocial process – Erikson.

- Psychodynamic theory suggests that some of present-day life's interactions are influenced at an unconscious level by some of life's previous interactions. When this is happening at an unconscious level, this phenomenon is sometimes known as 'transference'.

FREUD'S PSYCHOSEXUAL THEORY

The important place of Sigmund Freud (1856–1939) in our current thinking about the story of human personality cannot be overemphasised. Of course, whether or not Freud's ideas will continue to be important as the twenty-first century unfolds is an as yet unanswerable question. There is a huge library of texts that tell us much about Freud's life and career (Gay, 1998; Jacobs, 1992, 2003, and many, many others). A cultured and gifted man who originally trained as a medical doctor, Freud's early negative professional and personal experiences as a Jewish physician in anti-Semitic, nineteenth-century Vienna forced him to work in private psychiatric practice and then to go to Paris in order to undertake further study. In Paris, Freud worked with the eminent psychiatrist, Jean Charcot, who was investigating the place of the unconscious in human nature (personality) and ways to access any unconsciously stored mental experiences by the use of hypnosis. Upon his return to Vienna, and in collaboration with Joseph Breuer, Freud began to explore further the properties of the unconscious mind by using a technique that he called 'free association', which, he claimed, allowed his patients to express their allegedly deeply buried emotions, memories and supposed childhood sexual experiences (Hall et al., 1997).

Freud initially claimed that sexuality is a central factor in the development of human personality. It is a major mark of Freud's outstanding personal and intellectual rigour that he was prepared to make such a claim in what was a notably prudish period in European history. Of course, all theorists should be evaluated in terms of the contexts within which they work and this is equally true for Freud, who always was, and in many ways still is, a controversial figure in the psychotherapeutic world and beyond. The reality was that, as a Jew in nineteenth-century, notoriously anti-Jewish Europe, Freud would have been widely perceived as being a so-called 'inferior citizen'. Therefore, to tell his alleged 'social betters' in nineteenth-century Catholic Vienna that, according to his theories of human development, they probably either had sex with their children or their children fantasised about having sex with them, indicated that Freud had amazing personal and intellectual courage. Indeed, some of his admirers might even say that Freud had *chutzpah* (an appropriately Yiddish term meaning admirably 'cheeky', 'audacious' or 'impudent').

The basic premise of the psychoanalytic view of personality is that of mind/body dualism. This means that the mind and the body are mutually interdependent. According to the dualism premise, the mind (personality) is constructed (developed) in response to the needs of the body. These needs are represented by primal or primitive instincts, such as urgent infantile demands for food or comfort. It is how we learn to deal with these instincts as children that makes us into the sorts of people that we are as adults. Therefore, these primitive instincts are the very foundations of our personalities. Each of us builds upon those foundations in various ways and that is what makes us into the varied and various individuals that we become.

Freud identified two main instinctual drives.

- One is the power of the Life Force (Eros or libido), which includes sex (love), but which was eventually defined by Freud as including most forms of pleasurable bodily experiences (Bettelheim, 1983).
- The other, according to Freud, is the opposite of Eros and is the power of the Death Force (Thanatos), which drives us towards the supposed relief from the tensions of Being (anger, fear) that it is claimed comes from personal extinction or the end of existence (Perelberg, 1999).

According to many psychodynamic theorists, a human infant's mental existence is nothing but instinct. They believe that a growing child has to learn to subjugate those powerful instinctual drives for all sorts of survival-dominated reasons. For example, it would be dangerous for someone to display too much uncontrolled or uncontrollable instinctual anger in later life as this might well lead to self-destructive behaviour, such as attacking someone who is too strong to be defeated. The psychodynamicists argue that much of the process of learning to accommodate these primal or primitive needs takes place in our early years. Therefore, it follows that our personalities must clearly be largely the product of our childhood experiences. For example, according to McLeod (2003), psychodynamicists might suggest that a mother who responds too quickly to an infant's instinctual demands for food may be teaching her child that it needs to make very little personal effort in order to get fed. In such a case, the child might grow into a rather selfish adult who is easily frustrated if any demands are not immediately met. Alternatively, if the mother only responds after the hungry child has engaged in extensive crying or has had a temper tantrum, that child might grow into an adult who believes that needs are only satisfied by becoming angry or aggressive. (Any mothers reading this are probably wondering why everything is always their fault! – The answer is, because the Freudians say so!)

However, Freud did much more than simply claim that childhood experiences underpin adult personality. He also claimed that these underpinnings occurred in some specific ways, which means that he certainly believed that there is an 'official' personality developmental blueprint to be followed. Freud's proposed human developmental processes are based on one of his basic premises. He claimed that our conscious minds are influenced by the workings of our unconscious minds. He believed that the human mind has three developmental levels and these are usually described, as follows, by various interpreters of Freud (such as Hall et al. (1997), Lemma (2007), etc.).

- Level 1 – the *id*: This is the original mind that is present at birth and is a container for the primal instincts or drives that eventually motivate our personalities. As we have already noted, this instinctual psychic energy is derived from the two core drives of life/love (Eros or libido) and extinction/death (Thanatos). The id is irrational and only exists to achieve self-gratification at any cost. Put simply, the id says, 'I want my cake! – Gimme now! – Don't care how! – Don't care about what you want!' The id is a monster, self-centredly demanding immediate wish-fulfilment and exclusively concerned with self-pleasure.
- Level 2 – the *ego*: This develops out of the id and is the rational and conscious part of the mind. It evolves as the infant begins to discover that primary mental images such as 'food' or 'warmth' are represented in the real world by actual objects or sources. Therefore, a plan is necessary to obtain the required item. This is the beginning of the

higher mental functioning that plans, executes and tests the processes, thoughts and actions that are necessary for obtaining personal gratification from the adult world. The primary role of the ego is not to frustrate the id but to help it find ways of getting satisfaction and, at the same time, satisfying the demands of the environment. It is a sort of psychological ambassador. The id says, 'Yes, you might want some cake but you will improve your chances of getting some if you play the game their way.' The ego is a realist – amoral and goal-oriented.

- Level 3 – the *superego*: This develops last and is the conscience or rulebook that sets out the boundaries of our personalities. It is the internal, mental representation of the supposedly correct values and ideals that a child learns from family and society. In Freudian theory, the primary sources of this learning are the parents, who implant their own ideals into the child by a series of punishments and rewards. Psychodynamically, the superego has three purposes:
  - to curb the excesses of the id;
  - to inculcate a sense of morality in the ego;
  - to cause the person to strive towards perfection.

  As the superego forms, parental control is gradually replaced by personal control. Internalising this control helps us to create some important qualities in our personalities. So, if we rely on firm, even unquestioned beliefs such as 'lying is wrong' or 'never be late', according to the Freudians, we can be sure that our superegos are hard at work. The superego says, 'Yes, you do want some cake and the ego will show you how to get it. However, you must also share it because that's the right thing to do.' The superego is an idealist – moral and altruistic.

Clearly, the psychodynamic theorists argue that most personality development occurs in a person's early years. Because the Freudians claim that those early years are mainly concerned with bodily satisfactions, they go on to argue that personality development is a *psychosexual* process. During the early part of a person's emotional growth the psychodynamicists claim that there is a clash between the desires of the primal instincts and a need to survive in the world as it is. In other words, human personality development comes about as a result of a series of psychological conflicts between the growing child and its environment. In particular, these psychological clashes occur between children and their parents, or indeed anyone else who is primarily significant in their upbringing and control. Each clash, or episode of conflict, and the manner in which it is resolved, contributes towards the way in which someone's emerging personality grows and develops. For example, it has been argued (at least by the Freudians) that adverse infant experiences during toilet training could lead to the adult becoming the sort of obsessively tidy person often referred to as being 'anally retentive'. (Yes, it's mother's fault again!)

WAS FREUD RIGHT?

The idea that human personality development emerges as a result of an early-years psychosexual process was very revolutionary in its time and remains the subject of heated debate and fierce dispute even today. Indeed, there are some powerful counter-theorists who denounce Freud as a failed person, as an inadequate researcher and as a misguided thinker (Masson, 1992; Shlien, 1987, and many others). Even Freud's own granddaughter, Sophie, went as far as calling him a 'false prophet' (Freud, 2002, cited in Evans and Gilbert, 2005, p9).

It is also the case that some of the alternative, and equally powerful, theories of personality development essentially dismiss psychodynamic explanations of what makes each of us who we are. This dismissal is in part due to the fact that psychodynamic theory is very difficult (many say impossible) to test by accepted scientific methodologies. Of course, the defenders of psychodynamic theory will probably argue that their theories are better supported by clinical practice than by scientific study. They claim that extensive investigations of case study reports show that their theories are valid because, they claim, their patients get better. Their opponents counter-argue by saying that there is no proof that any such improvements (if they really do occur) result from psychoanalytic therapy. After all, it might have been that the patients were going to get better anyway. For example, many depressed patients do spontaneously recover, often quite quickly (NICE *Guideline 23*, 2004). For all these reasons, Freud's opponents argue that his psychoanalytic theories of human personality have no evidence base.

ACTIVITY 3.1

Consider the following:

Mary saw her psychodynamic therapist regularly once a week. After two years she found that her depression had lessened a great deal. Jim saw a clinical psychologist once but did not get on with him, so he never went back. Two years later he, too, found that his depression had lifted.

- Why would there be such similar results from such different experiences of treatment?
- Are these outcomes really the same?

Case study 3.1

Alfred was a very touchy sort of a chap; everybody knew it and everybody stayed clear of him when he was in 'one of his moods'. That was strange really because Alfred saw himself as a very easygoing chap, nice to everyone and kind to animals.

One fateful day, Alfred's employers held a training afternoon. The training role-play was videoed and played back to the trainees. Alfred was horrified to see himself engaged in what he thought had been a helpful and constructive interchange between himself and a colleague. The supposedly 'nice Alfred' was being played by someone who seemed to be in a fury. 'That's not like me,' he said. 'Oh yes it is,' said everybody else.

What Alfred could just not understand was that he could be such a scary guy and yet be totally unaware of it. By now even Alfred wasn't too fond of Alfred. Alfred went along to see his firm's counsellor. After hearing Alfred's story, the counsellor asked Alfred, 'What are you angry about?' 'Nothing at all,' said Alfred. However, as he spoke his features tightened and a scowl appeared on his face. The counsellor pointed this out and again asked Alfred what was bothering him. 'Off the top of your head, without thinking about it, who do you dislike the most in this world,' he was asked. Without any hesitation Alfred replied, 'I could never stand the man who has lived next door to my parents since I was a small child – he touches small boys and I could never tell my Dad.' Then Alfred said something very interesting. 'Do you know,' he said, 'I haven't thought about him for years.' 'Are you sure?' asked the counsellor.

THE PSYCHODYNAMIC 'PEOPLE-MAP'

For now, however, we are going to continue to explore personality development on the assumption that the psychodynamic explanation of it as being a psychosexual process is, at least, a useful working theory. From a psychotherapeutic point of view, it is very important to note that the psychodynamic theorists go much further than merely arguing that personality development is a psychosexual process. They go on to claim that the emerging personality evolves according to a set of rules – a sort of developmental template. There are fixed stages to this development, they say, and if something goes wrong during these early-years processes, this creates psychological and emotional tensions that lead to problems in later years. Therefore, according to psychoanalytic or psychodynamic therapists, improvements in your emotional or psychological well-being will arise if you can identify these developmental errors, locate them in your unconscious and bring them into the light (your conscious).

For the psychodynamicists, each of the psychosexual evolutionary stages has three important components. These are:

1. *a physical focus*: where the child's emotional energy is targeted and how gratification is obtained;
2. *a psychological theme*: directs and balances both the child's internal bodily needs and the demands of the external world;
3. *a resultant adult character trait*: which lies along a 'too much–too little' continuum; if a person remains fixated or stuck at any given stage and has related, unresolved issues, psychological problems may arise.

Generally speaking, Table 3.1 shows how the psychodynamicists claim that personality evolves.

Age (years)	Stage	Physical focus	Psychological theme	Typical adult character traits
0–1	Oral	Mouth, lips, tongue (sucking, food)	Narcissistic; Dependent (only me)	Aggression vs. passivity Impatience vs. serenity
1–3	Anal	Anus (withholding or giving up faeces)	Self-control; Obedience (conflicts with parents)	Controlling vs. subservience Boundaried vs. disorganised
3–6	Phallic	Penis Penis absence Clitoris	Morality; Sexual identity Love for same sex parent Fear of other sex parent	Promiscuity vs. sexuality Re-enacting childhood relationships vs. rejecting them
6–14	Latency	Dormant	Peer relationships	Socially integrated vs. anti-social
14–20	Genital	Sex	Maturity; Procreation; Life-enhancement	Balanced and mature Supportive and nurturing

Table 3.1: The psychosexual development of personality.

It is important to note that, no matter how vigorously it is defended by its proponents, at base the psychodynamic explanation of personality is an inferential one. We cannot see the unconscious operating. We cannot measure the id, examine the ego or dissect the superego. Neither can we prove that children really do have fantasy sexual interactions with their parents or that newborns are essentially narcissistic. The best that we can do is to say that close examination of the ways in which people behave and relate to each other and to themselves gives us grounds for believing that it is *as if* the psychodynamic process is at work. The essential element in the original psychodynamic explanation of personality is the idea that people are unknowingly driven by their sexual instincts. In other words, it is an animalistic theory of personality. Some theorists, Erikson for example, would argue that the initial psychodynamic theory of personality development is too simplistic.

ERIKSON'S PSYCHOSOCIAL THEORY

Erik Erikson (1902–94) was born in Frankfurt of Danish parents. He eventually came to study and teach art in Vienna, where he subsequently underwent psychoanalytic training supervised by Freud's daughter, Anna, and eventually graduated from the Vienna Psychoanalytic Institute in 1933 (Welchman, 2000). Like his mentor Freud, Erikson too was Jewish, and so he was also forced to emigrate, first to Denmark and then to America, where he was able to spend the rest of his life developing his theories.

Erikson always considered himself to be a Freudian. Like Freud, Erikson believed that childhood is very important in personality development. Also like Freud, Erikson was an ego psychologist. He accepted many of Freud's theoretical concepts, including the id, ego and superego, and Freud's belief in infantile sexuality. However, Erikson rejected Freud's attempts to describe personality solely on the basis of infant sexuality and so (very much unlike Freud) he came to believe that personality continued to develop significantly well beyond childhood. Erikson considered that social factors were as important as sexual factors in the development of the human personality. He therefore proposed a *psychosocial stage theory* of personality development (Stevens, 2008).

Erikson's version of ego psychology theory holds certain beliefs that make his ideas quite different from Freud's (Erikson, 1965, etc.). Essentially Erickson believed that:

- the ego is of the *utmost* importance;
- part of the ego is able to operate *independently* of the id and the superego;
- the ego can *adapt* to situations and is a powerful agent in promoting mental health;
- *both* social and sexual factors play a role in personality development.

Erikson's theory is much more comprehensively whole-life than Freud's, and included information about alleged 'normal' personality as well as supposed neurotic, 'abnormal' personality. He argued that personality development is more than merely sexually driven. Erikson claimed that it is also driven by social and cultural forces. However, like so many of the earlier personality theorists (including Freud), Erikson's work does not have a robust, research-based underpinning. Indeed, like Freud, his theories are mostly unprovable. As with many psychodynamic theorists, Erikson's proposals give us a working explanation of personality. They give a plausible description of a possible process, but not an explanation that can be verified by testing any actual, specifically identified, causative mechanisms. This is because Erikson's theories all essentially depend on the proposition that personality develops *as if* psychosocial/sexual drives are at work. Proving such a proposition is quite another matter.

All of personality's developmental stages in Erikson's psychosocial theory are present at birth, but they unfold according to an innate plan. For Erikson, human personality development is 'epigenetic'. This means that it unfolds over time rather like a tulip develops from a bulb. It's all there from the beginning, but it has to grow and evolve. Each stage builds on the preceding stages and paves the way for subsequent stages. For humans, each stage in personality development is characterised by a *psychosocial crisis*. Each crisis arises in accordance with the associated age-related or body-related development and conflicts with the demands then put on the individual by parents and/or society. Ideally, the psychosocial crisis in each stage should be resolved by the ego at each stage. This allows the development of the next stage to proceed correctly. All this implies that, just like the developing tulip, the equally epigenetic human personality can unfold in a proper form. It can also unfold in an improper (distorted) form, or the unfolding can even be brought to a halt. According to Erikson, it is quite possible that, at any given growing stage, someone's psychosocial developmental needs might be incorrectly processed and so distort later stages and eventually deform the emerging adult personality. However, Erikson also claimed that emotional deformities can be corrected. He believed that:

> *developmental stage outcomes are not permanent. They can be altered by later experiences.*

The importance of this concept for therapists is the possibility that one of those later, possibly corrective, experiences might be provided as part of some form of reparative psychotherapy. Realising this helps us to better appreciate why understanding human personality development is so vital for all therapeutic practitioners. It might be that properly understanding what makes people tick could help us to discover some useful ways of doing psychotherapy.

Erikson proposed that everyone's personality is a mixture of the various traits that become paramount at each developmental stage. His theory is based on the assumption that someone's personality development can be considered successful if an individual has more of the 'good' traits than the 'bad' traits. Clearly, the 'ideally developed' personality will only consist of 'good' traits. Table 3.2 overleaf sets out Erikson's theory of personality development on a stage-by-stage basis.

Erikson's model perhaps can be better appreciated if we compare it with Freud's psychosexual model. Jacobs (1998, p10) has produced a useful comparison table, which is reproduced in a slightly modified form in Table 3.3.

Clearly, Erikson's model of human personality is more comprehensive than Freud's because it takes more factors into account. It includes inputs from a person's entire life and not just their early years. It is useful because it acknowledges that humans are more than merely the products of their instinctual drives as modified by life's experiences. Social influences are important too. Therefore Erikson's theories offer us some significant steps towards the modern ideas about human personality. Today, many theorists see personality as being a complex combination of biological, sociological and environmental factors. However, it must not be forgotten that Erikson's theories, attractive as they are, and as useful as they can be when applied in the therapy room, are at best well-argued, intellectual propositions; they are not fact.

THE EGO AND PERSONALITY

Both Erikson and Freud were ego psychologists. This means that they believed that personality (the self) develops as maturing individuals react to the forces in both their inner and the outer worlds (Mitchell and Black, 1995). The danger of conflict (and scary potential chaos) is always present. Therefore, a means of controlling the process, so that its evolution remains orderly, is required. This controller, according to many psychodynamicists, is the ego. It is rather like a combination of programme manager and match referee. Therapists have long found the ego to be a useful theoretical concept when considering how to manage their clients. Whether it is enough is a question that will continue to puzzle practitioners. You might understand some of these ideas a bit better if you try out Activity 3.2.

Stage (years)	Psychosocial crisis	Significant relations (social factors)	Psychosocial attributes	Positive psychosocial assets	Negative psychosocial assets
1: Baby (0–1 yr)	Trust vs. mistrust	Mother, primary carer	To get, to give in return	Hope, faith	Sensory distortion Withdrawal
2: Toddler (2–3 yrs)	Autonomy vs. shame and doubt	Parents, carers	To hold on, to let go	Will, determination	Impulsivity Compulsion
3: Infant (3–6 yrs)	Initiative vs. guilt	Family, significant others	To go after, to play	Purpose, courage	Ruthlessness Inhibition
4: Child (7–12 yrs)	Industry vs. inferiority	Neighbourhood and school	To complete, to make things together	Competence	Narrow virtuosity Inertia
5: Adolescent (12–20 yrs)	Ego-identity vs. role-confusion	Peer groups, role models	To be oneself, to share oneself	Fidelity, loyalty	Fanaticism Repudiation
6: Young adult (20–30 yrs)	Intimacy vs. isolation	Partners, friends	To lose and find oneself in a another	Love	Promiscuity Exclusivity
7: Middle adult (30s to 50s)	Generativity vs. self-absorption	Household, workmates	To make be, to take care of	Care	Overextension Rejectivity
8: Old adult (50s +)	Integrity vs. despair	Mankind or 'my kind'	To be, through having been, to face not being	Wisdom	Presumption Despair

Table 3.2: Erikson's psychosocial theory of personality development.

Stage*	Freud	Aims	Erikson	Tasks
1	Oral	*Feeding*	Baby* (Oral)	*Basic trust vs. mistrust*
2	Anal	*Muscular pleasure*	Toddler* (Muscular-anal)	*Autonomy vs. shame and doubt*
3	Phallic	*Oedipal resolution*	Infant* (Locomotor-genital)	*Initiative vs. guilt*
4	Latency	*Learning*	Child* (Latency)	*Industry vs. inferiority*
5	Adolescence	*Genital expression*	Adolescence	*Identity vs. role confusion*
6	Adulthood	*Love and work*	Young adulthood	*Intimacy vs. isolation*
7	None	*N/a*	Mid-adulthood	*Generativity vs. self-absorption/stagnation*
8	None	*N/a*	Late adulthood	*Integrity vs. despair*

* Author's additions/amendments.

Table 3.3: Freud and Erikson compared.

ACTIVITY 3.2

Ask yourself the following questions and note your answers:

- What sort of a person am I – who in my family do I take after?
- What sorts of very strong feelings do I sometimes have – why and when do I have those strong feelings?
- What's my earliest memory – why do I still remember it?

Find someone who has known you all your life and ask them to answer all the above questions as they think you would answer them.

Try to explain any differences or similarities between your answers to these questions and those that someone has given you.

LATER DEVELOPMENTS IN PSYCHODYNAMIC THEORY

Obviously, there have been many advances in psychodynamic theory since Freud's day. As we know, Freud believed that personality was powered by instinctual drives. Other psychodynamic theorists believed that people and their emotional developments were much more complicated than that. For instance, as we have also already noted, Erikson argued that people's lifelong interactions with their social environments were just as influential as instincts on the ongoing development of personality and the emergence of the self. There have been many other post-Freudian and neo-Freudian theoretical advances. These include: Attachment Theory (Bowlby, 1969, 1973, 1980); the Unitary Ego (Fairbairn, 1952); True-self/False-self (Winnicott, 1965); Psychological Archetypes, the Collective Unconscious (Jung, 1970) and many others. Many of these theoretical standpoints are much more mutually contradictory than they are complementary. The psychodynamic 'schoolists' seem to have been a traditionally disputatious lot!

Over the years, the internal politics, the disputes over theory, and the power struggles in the psychodynamic world have been fierce, vicious even. Freud himself was a difficult figure to disagree with. It was well known that, in Freudian circles, agreement with the Master was expected. Either you were an approved member (approved by Freud, that is) of the International Association for Psycho-Analysis, or you were not. If you disagreed with Freud you were better off not belonging. Those who broke ranks and promoted contradictory views were certainly out. One early defector was Jung, who believed that biologically derived motivational drives are only part of the overall picture of human development. He argued that people also have drives towards the integration and fulfilment of the self and that understanding the unconscious necessitates understanding its spiritual and transcendental components (see Jung, 1965). Ferenczi and Rank broke away because of disputes over the importance of therapeutic technique. Many other eminent theorists were cast out into the non-Freudian 'wilderness'.

Melanie Klein was an important critic of some of the early psychoanalytic orthodoxies and so she too earned the disapproval of the Freudian faithful. Her primary reinterpretation of Freudian orthodoxy underpins what later became known as the Object Relations School of psychodynamic theory (Klein, 1997). It must be borne in mind that in Kleinian psychoanalysis the term 'object' does not mean an inanimate item or thing. It refers to the objects (or targets) of someone's relationships. These may be internal objects (the internalised self); external relationship objects (e.g. people, etc.); external objects that represent relationships (e.g. a child's security blanket); and part-objects (e.g. the nurturing breast rather than the mother herself).

THE 'FREUD WARS'

Melanie Klein originally trained under Freud in Vienna and subsequently emigrated to Britain in 1926. She became a prominent member of the British Psychoanalytical Society, which had been first formed in 1919. In 1938 (having fled Austria with her father), Freud's daughter, Anna, connected with what was already an argumentative British psychotherapeutic scene. In the early 1940s, the tensions between the then prominent (and vigorously competing) British psychoanalytic factions erupted into serious conflict (Rayner, 1990). In particular, there were fundamental disagreements between Melanie Klein and Anna Freud. By 1942, these two formidable women were generating so much tension and rivalry in the British psychoanalytic world that the Society decided to conduct a series of professional debates in order to try and instil peace between the warring factions. This led to the series of famous exchanges that are known today as 'The Controversial Discussions' (King and Steiner, 1991).

Despite the efforts of the peacemakers, the arguments actually became more and more intense and so, in 1946, the British Psychoanalytical Society tried an alternative way of healing some of the rifts. It divided its training function into three groups: the Freudian purists (led by Anna Freud after the death of her father), the Object Relations Theorists (led by Melanie Klein) and a rather loose group called the British Independents. This group, which actually was the largest of the three, included such luminaries as Gillespie, Milner, Winnicott, Bowlby, Rycroft and Balint.

Fortunately, today much of the 1940s/50s factional discord seems to have largely died away and a workable amount of rapprochement has been achieved (Jacobs, 2004). This is certainly true at a training level. Of course, as they grow professionally, psychodynamic practitioners usually develop their own individual styles of working and their own interpretations of psychodynamic theory. Happily, there is now much common ground between the psychodynamic schools about the basic principles that therapists need to bear in mind when working with their clients.

These areas of agreement include some commonly held ideas about the psyche, the unconscious and transference.

THE PSYCHE

Counsellors and psychotherapists do not have to be 'Freud-friendly', or even psychoanalytic 'groupies', to find that psychodynamic ideas sometimes have their uses. For many practitioners (e.g. Jacobs, 2005), 'psychodynamic' is a generic expression that explains the active part that the psyche or inner self (commonly described as a sort of fusion of mind, emotion and spirit) plays in our everyday lives. The actions of the psyche, as envisaged by many modern-day psychodynamic theorists, are supposedly powered by much more complex drives than the simple instinctual forces described by Freud. Today it is believed that the workings of the psyche also depend on the active (dynamic), ongoing inter-relationships that occur between people, or between people and their own interpersonal environments (how people relate to themselves). It is about how our past experiences (internal and external) actively influence (consciously or not) today's activities and interactions. Today's psycho-dynamic practitioners claim that the psyche not only has relationships with people (objects) that are external to the self, but also interacts internally with the self. In other words, the psyche interacts with the psyche; the self interacts with the self. For instance, you might be experiencing anxiety because your 'good self' is in conflict with your 'bad self' over whether or not you ought to eat a bar of chocolate. You might also be worried because your doctor says you are overweight. All this means that, as well as the psyche (self) having internal *intra*-actions with itself (good/bad self), it also has external *inter*-actions with others, such as the doctor. An example of this process could be as follows.

Suppose somebody finds themselves acting out of character; perhaps that person uncharacteristically became frivolous and inattentive when a very serious matter was under discussion. 'That's not like you,' someone else might say (*external inter*-action). The person concerned might confess that 'I'm feeling rather silly today' (*internal intra*-action). The implication here is that today's aberrant, 'improper' self ('Mr Silly') actually has a real self, a 'proper' self ('Mr Sensible'). However, just for now at least, the normal, properly sensible, self has been temporarily displaced by a deviant, silly self. Behind this interchange, there is an implication that there is also a third self present. This is a judgemental self ('Mr Critical'), who decides what is silly and what is not. Perhaps the self-criticism ('I'm being silly') stems from the person having an underlying, unconsciously held belief that frivolity should be avoided.

It seems to be the case that a common article of faith within most, if not all, of the psychodynamic 'churches' is the belief that the psychodynamic process is largely concerned with understanding the present-day effects of someone's past relationships, either with that person's own self (or selves) or with external objects. This means that it is a core principle of psycho-dynamic therapy that the psyche is at work at all times – whether or not the client is aware of this process. Furthermore, the activities of the psyche, both past and present, can be identified from a person's present-day behaviours, relationship patterns and emotional lifestyle. The various ways in which clients present themselves, including their behaviour during counselling sessions, are indicators of their underlying psychological and emotional processes. Therefore, exploring the psyche by means of attempts to interpret these intrapersonal and extrapersonal relationships is a key activity for the psychodynamic psychological therapist (Mander, 2000).

THE UNCONSCIOUS

The difference between the conscious and the unconscious seems at first to be a simple one. You are either aware of what is going on or you are not. However, the reality is not so simple because it appears that there are different levels of awareness and unawareness. For instance, you might think that you remember all too clearly a friend's funeral that took place two years ago. You are very aware of the sorrow you felt when you heard your friend had died. However, you might not remember just how overwhelming your grief and pain really were. That pain is now safely stored away at a deeper level that is too hard to routinely access. Life seems simpler that way.

At one level there are the easily accessible memories. Freud called these the 'preconscious'. For example, it might be that you have forgotten all about a long-lost love, but going down 'memory lane' with an old friend easily jogs your memory. Then at a second, much lower, level there are the deeply buried memories that are so far down in the unconscious that it can be very hard to access them. For example, someone might have feelings of intense, even primal, anger towards a parent figure that cannot be allowed to surface. Possibly that person unconsciously fears that acknowledging such potentially destructive emotions might allow some frighteningly aggressive feelings towards an idealised parental figure to break through.

Locating such deeply buried memories (the true unconscious) can be very difficult, sometimes perhaps even impossible. It is the task of the psycho-dynamic therapist to infer, to explore and to identify these hidden sources of emotional and psychological disquiet. In the ideal therapeutic world, the psychodynamic therapist will help the client to safely bring the unconscious into the conscious, and convert the unaware into the aware. Psychodynamic therapists attempt to foster the emotional growth that can result from breaking the powerfully restrictive, unconsciously constructed, emotional shackles that are holding the client inside a private psychological prison; a prison that has been constructed within the unaware self.

It is a basic requirement in psychodynamic therapy that practitioners should attempt to help their clients to access the unconsciously held experiences, emotions and beliefs that are influencing their current lives. This is done by reflecting on the clients' behaviours in the counselling room and by attending to the ebb and flow of the therapeutic relationship. 'It ain't what you say; it's the way that you say it.' It is also how you behave when you are saying it that is important to the modern psychodynamic therapist.

The hope, of course, is that, by making the unconscious conscious, clients might be able to conduct their lives with more control, with less emotional disquiet and with more fulfilment. No longer must these clients be slaves to the unrealised and therefore uncontrollable forces (psychodynamics) from within the unconscious parts of their own selves.

TRANSFERENCE

Psychodynamic theorists argue that not only are there links between people's inner selves and their external selves, but also there are links between their past experiences and their present-day experiences (see Freud, 1986, etc.). In other words, not only do we conduct our current relationships in ways that are influenced by what is going on inside us, but we also do so in ways that are influenced by our past experiences. Here are two examples.

1. Bob, a normally affable, longstanding member of a social club, has taken an instant dislike to Jim, a new member. This seems irrational as Jim is a nice enough chap. One explanation might be that, even though Bob is unaware of it, there is something about Jim that has stirred up some unconsciously held memories of some of Bob's adverse childhood relationship experiences. Bob might honestly believe it when he says, 'I don't like him – can't stand people with beards.' However, at an unaware level, it might be that Bob is actually saying 'I can't stand reminders of my slob of a father who could never be bothered to shave.'
2. Josephine, usually a placid soul, has started to become grumpy at work. 'What's got into her?' her colleagues might wonder, whereas Josephine genuinely believes 'There's nothing wrong with me – they've all started winding me up.' However, what has actually happened is that a newly appointed office manager is reminding Josephine at an unconscious level of a bossy teacher in her primary school whom she detested. The result is one highly disgruntled Josephine, although she genuinely does not know why.

Because these feelings are held in the unconscious, Bob might genuinely believe that he does not like beards and Josephine might really think that her colleagues are conspiring to annoy her. In both cases, neither Bob nor Josephine is aware of behaving any differently or that they are reacting to the new people as if they were the real-life people whom they disliked at earlier stages of their lives. In other words, Bob and Josephine are unconsciously transferring experiences from their pasts on to the present.

In psychodynamic counselling terms, these earlier experiences, these buried feelings and emotions, are often unknowingly acted out by clients in their relationships with their counsellors. Like Bob and Josephine, clients are unconsciously transferring their pasts on to the present. This is the psychological process known as 'transference'. Of course, transferences routinely occur in everyday life too. Clinically significant transferences (client to therapist) are often encountered during therapy. Such transferences might be representative of psychologically unhealthy transferences that are occurring outside the therapy room.

The client–counsellor relationship often contains many clues and hints about how clients interact with other people out in the wider world. It is the job of the psychodynamic therapist to use the interpersonal processes between the client and the counsellor (the transferences) to the client's advantage. The therapist has to try to help the client to rediscover (and to work through) past relationships in ways that are therapeutically beneficial to current life and current relationships. Therefore, it is a fundamental requirement that psychodynamic counsellors should work with their clients' transferences and help them to explore their feelings about these 'hidden' interactions as and when they emerge during the counselling sessions.

In the everyday world, clients experience many sorts of transferences with many sorts of people. However, in the therapy room there are usually only two people actually present – the client and the therapist. Therefore, the transferences in the counselling room can only be between the client and the therapist. Other people might be 'present' but only as 'ghosts from the past'. In other words, clients bring all their previous experiences with them when they meet their therapists. Sometimes these 'ghosts' are present but unacknowledged (in the client's awareness but not yet talked about). Sometimes they might be present but unrealised (buried in the client's unconscious).

Transference is, of course, a two-way process. Therapists are not immune to the possibility (probability) that their own pasts influence their interactions with their clients. This therapist-to-client transference is known as 'countertransference'.

Bob and Josephine's cases are both instances of *negative* transference. However, many *positive* transferences also occur both in everyday life and in the therapy room. Exploring positive transference can also be therapeutically useful. For example, therapists might choose to build upon any warm feelings that their clients might have towards themselves (positive transference), in order to reinforce the therapeutic relationship in ways that, for example, might help clients to talk about difficult or embarrassing topics. The danger for counsellors is to fall into the trap of believing that transference has a real, a concrete, existence rather than just being a useful metaphor (an error known as 'reification'). For example, some counsellors are reluctant to admit to disliking someone and prefer instead to concede that they may be experiencing 'negative transference'.

PSYCHODYNAMIC THERAPY AT WORK

Case study 3.2

June deliberately chose to see Andrew because, as she told him, 'I always get on better with men.' She wanted to find out why it was that her adult relationships usually failed. June presented herself in an overtly sexual manner. She dressed revealingly and she injected a powerful sexual content into all of her descriptions of her life and her problems.

It was apparent to Andrew (as June cheerfully confirmed) that she routinely tried to seduce the men that she met, previous therapists included. When, during the third session, Andrew made it clear that he was not going to be her next conquest, June became visibly agitated. However, the next time she appeared there was noticeably less sexual tension around.

During later sessions, June found herself telling Andrew about her childhood. Her father had been physically abusive to her and her sisters. When she had grown big enough, June tried to protect them all by offering him sexual gratification in an attempt to defuse his aggression. This did not always work and so June came to believe that his violence was her fault because she was 'not sexy enough'. June eventually found out that offering sex was how she 'paid her way' in life.

In June's case it eventually emerged that she had internalised three 'life rules' into her unconscious: men are scary; their threats can be diverted by offering them sex; and eventually, due to her own inadequacies, her diversion strategies would fail. June was not consciously aware of her three 'life rules' and she was initially oblivious to her overtly sexual behaviour. As far as she was concerned, 'I dress this way because I feel more comfortable when I do and, anyway, men always let you down in the end.' Andrew gained his first, tentative, understandings about June's unconscious processes from his reflections on the possible causes of the overt transferences present in the counselling room (that is psychotherapist talk for 'turning him on a bit'). His suspicions were confirmed when he noted how his rejection of June's advances caused her so much anxiety that she felt reluctant to continue her therapy. It took quite a few counselling sessions before June felt safe enough to examine the true causes of her many failed adult relationships and to trust herself enough to try to relate to someone in a non-sexual way.

REFLECTION POINT

- Do you believe that overt sexuality is really psychological transference or is it just down to hormones?
- In what ways might it have helped (or hindered) June's therapy had she seen a female counsellor? Would the transference/counter-transference have been any different?
- From a psychodynamic viewpoint, could your relationships with your clients ever be non-sexual?

SUGGESTED FURTHER READING

Appignanesi, R and Zarate, O (2007) *Introducing Freud: A graphic guide to the father of psychoanalysis*. Cambridge: Icon Books.

Jacobs, M (2004) *Psychodynamic Counselling in Action*, 3rd edition. London: Sage.

Jacobs is an acknowledged authority on this topic. An excellent introduction to a vital topic for all counsellors.

Jacobs, M (2005) *The Presenting Past*, 3rd edition. Buckingham: Open University Press.

Mander, G (2000) *A Psychodynamic Approach to Brief Therapy*. London: Sage.

A very useful, 'hands on', practical approach and will help you to find out just what it is that psychodynamic therapists do. Chapter 5 is particularly good.

CHAPTER 4

The cognitive-behavioural story

CORE KNOWLEDGE

- Some psychologists argue that how we behave and how we think make us into the sorts of people we are.
- Behaviour can become automated – classical conditioning.
- Behaviour can be shaped or modified – operant conditioning.
- Thinking (cognition) can affect how we react to life's events. Each of us interprets our own world. The ways that we do this makes each of us who we are.
- Cognitive-behavioural therapists believe that emotional difficulties and other forms of psychological problems arise from embedded errors in how people think and act.
- Cognitive-behavioural therapy is a partnership between therapists and their clients in which the clients are encouraged to try to resolve psychological issues by finding new ways of doing things or new ways of thinking about things – or both.

PERSONALITY – THE COGNITIVE-BEHAVIOURAL STORY

The cognitive-behavioural (thinking-doing) explanation of the personality story is quite straightforward. It is an approach that simply connects ideas about how people think in the ways that they do (Ellis, 1962; Kelly, 1955) with ideas about how they act in the ways that they do (Bandura, 1977; Skinner, 1953). According to the cognitive-behaviouralists, the combination of the thinking and doing processes makes the person. That is all it is. That is the cognitive-behavioural explanation of human personality in a nutshell. There are no hidden or unconscious processes going on as personality evolves. Personality growth is plain for all to see. There is no need to follow any hidden or preset personality development plans, because there are no such plans. What you see is what you get.

Clearly, cognitive-behavioural ideas about personality development are in complete contrast to the psychodynamic approach. For the psycho-dynamicists, personality comes about from the workings of an inner psyche and it evolves in certain ways according to certain rules. However, historically Freud's detractors have always claimed that his arguments are inherently weak because the id cannot be seen, the ego cannot be measured and the superego cannot be examined (Shlien, 1987; Thorndyke, 1932; Watson, 1925, etc.). Therefore, they say that Freud's alleged inner psycho-dynamic processes are just that – allegations. They can only exist in theory and there is no evidence that they exist in reality. At best, these critics claim that, even if Freud's ideas are sometimes therapeutically helpful, they are still only myths and can only explain personality on an 'as if it is true' basis (Eysenck, 1990; Shlien, 1987, etc.). The alternative to depending on Freud's apparently unsupported speculations, say the cognitive-behaviouralists, is to find out what really happens when people become people.

The cognitive-behaviouralists argue that our personalities emerge from the easily observable processes that we can see taking place in ourselves as we respond to events in our worlds (to our social and physical environments). Therefore, it is claimed, the cognitive-behavioural approach to personality is based on hard science and factual observation. Because the cognitive-behaviouralist model of personality is allegedly objective, empirical researchers have been inspired to investigate it. An important attraction of the cognitive-behavioural theories is that they are apparently evidence-based.

According to the cognitive-behaviouralists, how you think and how you behave makes you the sort of person you are. However, some behavioural psychologists (see Eysenck, 1967, 1991, for example) also think that our thinking and acting might also be governed, at least in part, by our individual biological make-ups. After all, it does sometimes appear to be the case that some personality traits are more ingrained than others. For example, has someone's deep-rooted stubbornness been derived from long-practised habit or might it have been genetically inherited? Nevertheless, cognitive-behaviourists remain convinced that our personalities are a mix of how we think and how we behave.

If we assume that we are indeed all such personality mixes, then it seems likely that changing any of our ways of thinking, or altering any of our ways of behaving, might cause changes in our characters. For example, suppose that you change your self-perception from 'I always fail' to 'I am competent', or change your behaviour by, say, stopping smoking. From a cognitive-behavioural point of view, making these changes might result in your personality changing in some way as well. The initial changes that you make in your lifestyle or your attitude might be big or they might be small; they might have big effects or they might make little difference. Here, for example, is the story of a big change from a big event:

Case study 4.1

Bill was nearly 50. He had been employed by Mega Bank Ltd for all his working life. Recently he had become anxious, depressed and stressed. His life was getting out of control. That's why he had started seeing his counsellor, Genevieve.

When he came along for his third session of counselling, Bill had some earth-shattering news. During the preceding week Bill had lost both his marriage and his job. On the Monday, Barbara, his wife of 27 years, had simply announced that she had had enough and just walked out. Then, on the Thursday, the bank had made Bill redundant. Bill was in a state of shock. He had financial worries, personal worries and no future. The third session was very difficult and very fragmented.

A very different Bill arrived at the fourth session. He was like somebody whom Genevieve had never met before. The impact of all the events of the last two weeks had awakened a spark long buried in Bill. The worm had turned. He simply announced, 'I'm off.' Bill had decided that, if nobody wanted him, he wanted nobody. He had converted everything that he owned into cash and a round-the-world airline ticket. 'I've only come to say goodbye,' he said, and that's just what he did. Bill disappeared.

Eighteen months later Genevieve happened to run into Bill once more. Bill's whole being had altered. His posture was different, his clothes were different and his attitude to life was completely different. A revitalised Bill was back in the UK and happily living a new way of life. Bill had no security, he had no long-term plans and he certainly didn't have any money – nevertheless he was a happy man.

ACTIVITY 4.1

Consider the following and discuss with a friend or colleague.

- Did events really change Bill's personality or did they simply permit the 'real Bill' to emerge?

COGNITIVE-BEHAVIOURAL THEORY – THE BEHAVIOURAL BIT

For the first half of the twentieth century, the emphasis of the 'non-Freudian' investigations into personality development was mainly concentrated on asking why one person typically seemed to have one sort of personality and usually behaved one way, whereas someone else seemed to be a different sort of person and usually behaved another way. These investigators, famously including Pavlov (1927), Skinner (1953) and Wolpe (1958), among others, came to believe that personality was a result of imposed learning from events. For example, we might get an electric shock from some faulty wiring and so we learn that electricity is dangerous. Unsurprisingly, from then on, we are always wary about touching electrical cables. These investigators also came to believe that, if a particular behaviour was repeated often enough, it would eventually become automatic or ingrained. For example, someone who has learned through many painful experiences that fire burns might automatically, even involuntarily, flinch away from glowing red objects, whether or not they are really hot.

The idea that personality comes from learned behaviour leads us to wonder if personality development is just a mechanical process. If the behaviourists were right, it seemed likely (perhaps worryingly so) that people could be made, unmade and remade as required. What could be simpler? If you need a different sort of a person, simply alter how the human machine works. Just adjust a few psychological nuts and bolts – job done.

The Behavioural Model of Personality, or *behaviourism* (Burrhus F. Skinner, 1904–90), is based on the notion that it is simply our learning from our experiences that makes us do what we do and that makes us who we are. If this is true, if we do not like what we have become, we can simply change ourselves by unlearning or relearning. So if, as therapists, we come across clients who have learned to have some 'wrong' emotional reactions to life, perhaps we can simply help them to 'unlearn' these 'wrong' feelings and to learn the 'right' ones instead. If we really could do this, we might be able to simply get on with actually curing our patients rather than spending hours helping them to agonise endlessly over their 'delicate inner beings' – well, that's the basic idea anyway.

Clearly it would help our enquiries into how personality types come from our learning if we could understand more about how learning works. The learning process is usually referred to as the *stimulus/response mechanism*. At its simplest it works as shown in Figure 4.1.

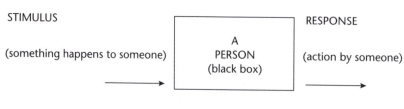

Figure 4.1

In the behavioural case, the way to understand this process is to visualise the person being studied as a sort of 'black box'. We cannot see what is going on inside and actually we do not care. Such a lack of understanding does not matter because it is only the result that counts. This sort of learning is called *associative learning* – it automatically connects stimulus with response – no thinking involved. This is how it works.

Example 1

In this first example, think about having a glass of wine (if you prefer you can think about bacon sandwiches, chocolate bars or whatever you fancy). We will stick to wine.

You go to the cupboard and get out the bottle (there's the clunk of the cupboard door). The bottles clink as you pull one out. You push in the corkscrew and pull out the cork (there's the plopping noise as the cork pops out). You pour out the wine (there's the gurgle as the wine leaves the bottle and falls into the glass). By now you are really ready for that wine; you can almost taste it. This is a *classically conditioned response* (Ivan Pavlov, 1849–1936). Your learning-based response to those noise-generated stimuli is so strong (reinforced) that you don't always need to see what's going on in order to react. Just my describing what happens when wine is poured will get lots of people quite excited. If someone in the next room were to open what was actually a vinegar bottle and then pour the vinegar into a glass bowl, many people would probably show the same 'I want some now!' reaction. This is exactly what happened to Pavlov's dogs when they learned to salivate at the sound of the dinner bell, even when there wasn't any food. Classically conditioned responses are also called *rigid* responses.

Example 2

In this second example, think about a teenager first entering the world of work. At school, peer pressure taught our teenager to wear jeans (learned behaviour 1). However, at work, different social pressures made our teenager feel uncomfortable in jeans and influenced him or her into wearing more formal office clothes (learned behaviour 2). Next, the management decided to promote a more customer-friendly company image and so the employees were encouraged to dress casually. Our teenager then started to wear smart-casual clothes because that was how colleagues began to dress (learned behaviour 3). Clearly, if behavioural change is really this simple, if someone in authority wanted to do so, subtle overt or covert reward/pressure systems could be used to more or less change or manipulate another person's behaviour at will.

These more complex, ever-changing, directed behaviour patterns are known as *operantly conditioned responses* or *instrumental conditioning*. Such responses are also called *plastic* responses because they can easily be bent or distorted. This type of behaviour/response modification is also known as *behaviour shaping* and it is sometimes used in schools, psychiatric hospitals, prisons and similar institutions to encourage appropriate behaviours. The inmates of such institutions are able to obtain various treats and privileges by being awarded points (reward) for being supposedly good. They can lose points (punishment) if they are allegedly bad or non-conforming. Such regimes are often known as *token economies*.

According to the hard-line behaviour theorists such as Skinner, learning is all that there is to personality. We are all effectively automatons whose personalities are made up from the particular mix of learned behaviours that each of us has acquired. At birth we are blank slates (*tabulae rasae*) and life events engrave each of our individual personality patterns into each of our slates. For example, you might have had lots of belittling experiences in your life and so you learned to be an introvert. Someone else has encountered nothing but praise and admiration and so has learned to be an extrovert – we are what we are.

COGNITIVE-BEHAVIOURAL THEORY – THE COGNITIVE BIT

From the middle of the last century, personality theorists more and more came to the view that humans do not just simply react to their environments. Psychologists such as Bandura (1977), Mahoney and Arnkoff (1978) and, of course, many others, claimed that humans don't just respond to events in their worlds, they also try to understand what is happening to them and this understanding determines how they react. For example, suppose someone points a gun at you – that could be frightening if you think it's a real gun or amusing if you think it's a water pistol. In other words, it is how you think about and interpret what is happening that determines how you will react.

Clearly, if our personalities really do depend on how we think, we might be able to change our personalities by changing our ideas. So, rather than depending on an animalistic process, driven by powerful instinctual drives operating outside our conscious choices (psychodynamic), the cognitive theory of personality says that what makes each of us the person that we are comes from our conscious thinking and our conscious choices and from how we actively interpret life.

So now let's look again at that stimulus/response mechanism (Figure 4.2).

In the cognitive case, the person is a 'glass box' and we can try to see (or perhaps just guess) what is going on inside. We want to know something about the cognitive processes that are going on within the person. This sort of interpretations-based learning is called *conceptual learning* – it cognitively connects response with stimulus. Thinking is involved; thinking is essential.

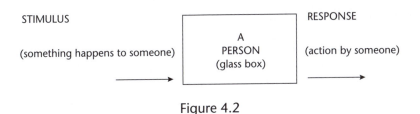

Figure 4.2

Conceptual learning happens when you already have some core beliefs established as part of your view of the world – a sort of acquired mental predisposition. It works as follows.

Suppose you are reading this book sitting in a room somewhere and suppose that I were to tell you that the wall next to you had just been newly painted. Your immediate reaction might be either to draw away from that wall or to be very careful if you get near to it. Such a reaction might come about because you possibly have a core belief that 'I must always be clean and tidy.' Your established ideas help you to link the concept of 'new paint' with 'wet paint' and then to 'wet paint ruins my clothes'. This final link endangers your core belief that being well presented is all-important and so you go to great pains to avoid touching the paint.

Alternatively, my telling you about the new paint might not have bothered you at all. Perhaps your core belief is 'Being clean and tidy is unimportant.' This might mean that getting your clothes paint-stained does not worry you at all and so your reaction to my warning is to dismiss it. The essential question is this: do the two different core beliefs (must-be-tidy/tidiness-does-not matter), as indicated by two different reactions (must avoid/don't care), make two different personalities? Cognitive personality theorists say that they do.

The cognitive theorists believe that personality is based on the idea that people become the sorts of individuals they are, not just because of the way that they react to their worlds, but also because of the ways in which they interpret what has happened to them, or what is, or what might be, happening to them. An individual's personality is therefore mainly generated by that person's characteristic thinking patterns (cognitions). This suggests that, from the cognitive perspective, personality types also emerge from the ways in which individuals organise their thinking and how they manage, integrate and organise the information that they get from the world around them. Therefore, our personalities depend on:

- what we think – how we interpret our worlds;
- how we deal with the incoming information (perceptions);
- the way we self-monitor and self-regulate ourselves by changing or modifying our thoughts as our circumstances and our beliefs about those circumstances change.

COMBINING THE COGNITIVE AND BEHAVIOURAL BITS

By speculating about adding cognitive (*thinking*) explanations of personality to the behavioural (*doing*) explanations, the earlier investigators paved the way for modern theorists (e.g. Scott et al., 1996) to argue that human personality develops as a combined cognitive *and* behavioural process. This is how a lot of theorists (see discussions in McLeod, 2003, and many other texts) say that it works.

Let us suppose that a client comes to see us and, for whatever reason, we have decided to use a cognitive-behavioural method of treatment. Say, for example, that our client has what some psychotherapists might call an obsessive-compulsive personality. This might cause our client to feel a powerful need to continuously tidy, organise and control his or her surroundings. So there are events or actions ('I see a messy room'), and these are followed by disturbing thoughts ('This messiness is bad for me'). This causes distressing feelings ('I don't like this'), which leads to more actions such as some possibly compulsive behaviours ('I have to clean and tidy this room – it must be perfect'). As perfection is impossible, it is likely that our client will feel compelled to keep on repeating his or her cleaning behaviour and, of course, keep on failing to achieve perfection. The psychological conflict between the person's ideal ('It must be perfectly clean') and the person's reality ('I cannot achieve this') might cause the client to end up experiencing a stress reaction that could include physical symptoms (rapid heartbeat, sweating, etc.) and emotional symptoms (anxiety, depression, etc.).

Bearing the previous example in mind, it seems reasonable to assume that all a person's feelings, actions, thoughts and physical symptoms are interlinked in some way. Each person's patterns of linkages combine to create our individual personalities. Cognitive-behavioural theories of personality are often based on such an assumption. The '4 Gates' Model (see Figure 4.3) of how this might work comes from Scott and Dryden (1966, p157). I have slightly modified it.

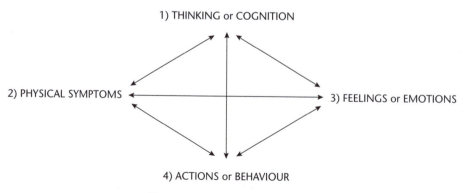

Figure 4.3: '4 Gates' Model.

If we think about the four components of this model as all being possible 'entry-points' or 'gates' into someone's personality, it follows that any of the four entry points might be a suitable starting place for any of our attempts to modify that person's personality. For example, in the case of the obsessive-compulsive client whom we have already considered, we might think about any, or all, of the following treatment strategies.

- Enter at Gate 1: Explore ways to eliminate/change unhelpful thinking and cognition perhaps by suggesting ways to reframe the problem (*some messiness is OK*, etc.).
- Enter at Gate 2: Teach symptoms-management techniques, such as relaxation therapy or engaging in physical exercise.
- Enter at Gate 3: Offer psychotherapy or some other form of emotional diversion.
- Enter at Gate 4: Agree a programme of new actions and behaviours that might help regain personal control (e.g. joining a self-help group; reading a book that explains anxiety, and so on).

Traditionally, psychotherapists have concentrated on accessing personality via Gate 3 (the 'feelings/emotions' gate). This is because that is where they believe the client's most important issues are located. Indeed, many therapists will ignore the other gates and denigrate behavioural therapy as 'only treating symptoms'. It does not help with the 'real problem', they claim. A powerful alternative argument (Beck, 1991) is that emotional disorders are actually only the indicators (symptoms) of cognitive and bodily disturbance. They are not the cause. If this is so, it can be argued that treating the cognitive and behavioural symptoms should actually be the preferred method of helping a client.

ACTIVITY 4.2

Suppose a group of clients are helped in some way by a form of therapy based on cognitive-behavioural ideas about personality. Perhaps they have learned to adopt healthier life–work balances.

- Have they really permanently changed (improved), or are they just feeling a bit better for now?

What is your response to this question?

WHERE WE HAVE GOT TO SO FAR

Cognitive-behavioural ideas about human personality are certainly attractive, at least superficially. They appeal to scientists because they are testable.

They appeal to clients because they hope to gain early relief – after all, most clients probably come along to be cured, not just to talk about cures. They appeal to therapists because they might gain professional and personal satisfaction from being successful helpers. However, it must always be remembered that, at the heart of the cognitive-behavioural theories of personality, lie the 'learning boxes'. We cannot see into the black learning box and we only think we can see into the glass learning box. It may be that we are not yet able to evaluate the cognitive-behavioural explanations of personality. Perhaps when we know a lot more than we do today about what goes on inside the person, we might be better able to come to a judgement. However, that is certainly a story for another day.

COGNITIVE-BEHAVIOURAL IDEAS IN PSYCHOTHERAPY

As the name implies, there are two key therapeutic components in the cognitive-behavioural approaches to psychotherapy.

1. *Cognitive*: First, there are the therapeutic methods that are based on the assumption that cognitions (thoughts, beliefs, self-images, etc.) intervene between the stimulus and the response. One example of this process can be found in the Rational Emotive Behavioural Therapy Model pioneered by Albert Ellis (1913–2007). This therapeutic technique is based on the well-known *A, B, C* principle (Dryden, 2005; Ellis, 2001, etc.). This method assumes that stimulus and response are not directly connected but are modified by belief. For example, I might see someone carrying a gun (*A* – activating event). If my intervening thought (*B* – belief) is that all gun bearers are violent criminals, I might become afraid (*C* – consequence). However, my fear is likely to change to relief if I subsequently find out that the gun carrier is an on-duty police officer who is there to protect me.
2. *Behavioural*: Second, there are the behavioural therapy methods that are largely based on the work of Joseph Wolpe (1915–97). Wolpe, a South African who eventually became an American citizen, taught and researched from 1965 to 1988 at the Temple Medical School in Philadelphia. His subsequent academic years were spent in California, where he taught at UCLA. Wolpe's great contribution to behavioural therapy was his work on *desensitisation*. This is a technique that uses biofeedback to help reduce and/or eliminate the physical and emotional symptoms that usually accompany emotionally distressing, dysfunctional behaviours. For example, a person who is very afraid of spiders might be taught how to use relaxation techniques to reduce any associated anxiety symptoms, such as sweating, increased heart rate and so on. This helps the client to reduce any fearful feelings. Lessened fear in turn yet further reduces the physical symptoms and

so on – round and round. Geeks like me would call this a 'positive feedback loop'. The idea is that, eventually, the original anxieties and phobias are either reduced to acceptable levels or are even extinguished (Wolpe, 1976, 1990, etc.). It is important to remember that Wolpe's approach assumes that there is a direct link between the stimulus (e.g. spotting a spider) and the immediate response (e.g. anxiety). There are no intervening processes.

It is arguable that the behavioural theories of personality evolved, in part, as a rebellion against the early dominance of the psychoanalytic view of human personality. By the mid-1950s, some of the more committed behaviourists were arguing that human personality is nothing more than the accumulation of learned behaviours (Skinner, 1953, 1971, etc.). However, by the 1970s there was another rebellion, this time against the extremes of the behaviourist's position. This second rebellion is sometimes called 'The Cognitive Revolution' (see Westbrook et al., 2007, etc.). The cognitive theorists argued that thinking was also an important element in the development of personality.

Cognitive therapy very much depends on the work of Aaron T Beck (b. 1921), who, upon retirement, became Emeritus Professor of Psychiatry at the University of Pennsylvania. Beck argued that mental processes (thinking, believing, evaluating and so on) all contribute to the human psychological condition (Beck, 1999, 1975, etc.). When these processes become unhelpful, people suffer emotionally. When that suffering becomes too much, they seek help. It is the cognitive therapist's task to help clients to change their harmful thinking. For example, someone who believes that they might be about to fail to achieve a promotion at work might also have an underlying general belief that he or she is a person of little value. This poor self-evaluation will probably have been reinforced over the years by that person continually failing in life, usually by giving up trying too soon ('What's the point? I can't win!'). Such people are often said to be setting themselves up to fail. In cases like these, it is the cognitive therapist's task to help such a client to identify, and then to challenge, this negative (and personally destructive) core self-image.

CBT IS BORN

Cognitive-behavioural therapy (CBT) is a term that actually describes a range of therapeutic approaches. These approaches are all based on certain common principles that are mainly derived from investigating the established links between learning, thinking and behaviour (Beck, 1995; Leahy, 2003). CBT is not a single-method therapy – it does not offer a one-size-fits-all therapeutic technique that allegedly suits all clients irrespective of their individual needs. It is a collaborative approach to psychotherapy in which the practitioner and the client mutually agree on a 'tailor-made' treatment programme that best suits each client's particular needs. CBT clients play a very active role in their own treatments.

Behaviour therapy and cognitive therapy very much grew up together and, to begin with, grew in parallel. Initially, the behavioural approaches tended to be used for anxiety-based conditions and the cognitive approaches tended to be used for mood disorders, such as depression. However, over the years, research-based practice has encouraged these two approaches to become one unitary form of psychotherapy. This happened because both therapies were found productively to complement each other and both therapies were found to be increasingly effective across an expanding range of psychological and psychiatric conditions (Westbrook et al., 2007). As the two therapies evolved together and influenced each other, they inevitably merged. Their combination has produced the general model of CBT that is so prevalent in many of today's health service treatment programmes and elsewhere.

SOME BASIC CBT CONCEPTS

- Events (each person's experiences) are not important in themselves; it is how we interpret those events that matters ('A cigar is just a cigar', however for me it is a pleasurable smoke, whereas for you it is a cancer stick).
- How we act influences how we think – as the song says, 'Whenever I feel afraid . . . I whistle a happy tune . . . the happiness in the tune convinces me that I'm not afraid.'
- Nobody has perfect mental health. Most of us muddle about in the middle section of our various emotional continuums (happy – sad, shy – bold, etc.), with occasional trips towards the highs at one end and the lows at the other. We are each affected in our different ways by where we are along our individual continuums – 'One man's meat is another man's poison.'
- It is what is going on for your clients right now that matters. That is where your clients need therapeutic relief. If your house is on fire you immediately call the fire brigade – you worry about whether it was an accident or arson later on.
- Feelings, thoughts, behaviours and bodily symptoms all interact like a sort of psychological cat's cradle – so tweak the bit of psychological string that is nearest to hand or that is easiest to tug at.
- Base everything on empirical evidence. So, do not just claim that in theory your treatment will make your clients better – prove it!
- Cognitions exist at two different levels in the mind:
  - an easily accessed level where thoughts are either at a conscious level or held in very easy-to-recall memories;

– a hard-to-access level where the thoughts are held in an unaware part of someone's being. It can be very difficult to bring such thoughts to the surface.

HOW MISINTERPRETING LIFE'S EVENTS CAN CAUSE PROBLEMS

If we get our thinking wrong (unhelpful or distorted cognitions), we might cause ourselves all sorts of psychological problems. An important job for the CB therapist is to try to help clients to discover how this might be happening in their own individual cases. Only then can they be helped to put things right. Knowledge is empowering. We can get the wrong idea about ourselves or about what is happening to us in two important ways.

1. *Negative automatic thoughts* (NATs): We all have them. They are our stereotypical ideas about ourselves: 'I'm no good at DIY'; 'People don't like me'; 'Whatever I do goes wrong.' NATs are all the putting-ourselves-down ways in which we interpret (often inaccurately) what goes on in our worlds. Like the name implies, NATs automatically frame our existence. Very often NATS are all too plausible and are apparently easily confirmed: 'Maria, would you like to come to the pub with me this evening?', 'Sorry, can't make it tonight.' A negative NAT confirms your interpreting this 'rejection' as yet more proof of your supposed unpopularity. However, the reality might be that Maria actually regrets missing out on spending an evening with you, but she has to work a nightshift. NATs are usually held at an awareness level or at a level that is only just below awareness. One way of defeating NATs is to challenge them. Find the courage to ask Maria if she is free later in the week. You might get a pleasant surprise.
2. *Core beliefs* (CBs): These are the fundamental ideas that provide the bedrock of our views about ourselves. A core belief that 'I am bad' can underpin such NATs as 'People don't like me'; 'I shouldn't join that club'; 'People who say they like me are only pretending.' Core beliefs tend to be buried deeply in our unaware levels and are hard to identify and change.

   Either or both of these cognitive processes (NATs and CBs) contribute to our psychological problems. Their fundamental purpose is to influence how we *interpret* life's events. These interpretations can be helpful or harmful. The following basic model shows us how CBT theorists think NATs and CBs might interfere in our lives.

A BASIC MODEL OF CBT

The CBT theorists tell us that our attitudes to ourselves and our worlds are mainly due to our interpretations of what we think is really going on around us. This suggests that CBT should be a multi-method approach to psychotherapy – one that allows each client's treatment plans to be individually crafted. If we combine this 'interpretation is all' concept with the '4 Gates' Model of personality, we can construct a very useful, generic model of the CBT approach to most psychological difficulties. In this 'combination model', if anything goes wrong at any given location, that is the place where the CBT practitioner starts work. See Figure 4.4 for my suggestion of what such a model looks like.

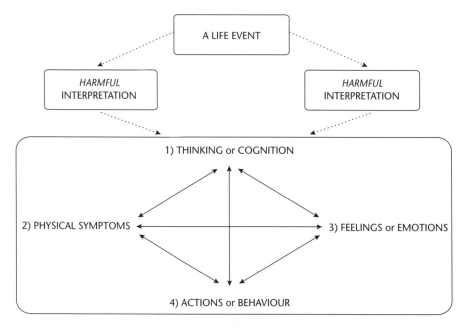

Figure 4.4

Case study 4.2

Bertie's marriage was in tatters. His intense anger with everybody (including his wife) had caused her to threaten to leave him. Bertie was scaring people. He was even scaring himself. He consulted Valerie, a CB therapist, and asked her to tell him how he could regain his self-control and save his marriage. Valerie could see that Bertie was actually physically and psychologically exhausted (physical symptoms + emotions/feelings). Eventually, she discovered that Bertie's problems began every morning at 4 a.m. That was when his neighbour, Tony, started up a huge, noisy lorry and drove off to work. Not only did this wake Bertie up, but his immediate fury due to his neighbour's apparent lack of consideration (cognition 1) made Bertie angry all day long. He lay there every morning fuming (emotion) and could not get back to sleep (behaviour 1). Bertie's days all started badly and got worse.

Valerie questioned Bertie about his thoughts on Tony's lack of consideration (*harmful* interpretation).Were they correct? She suggested that he should try to talk to Tony and so check out what was actually happening. The following week, Bertie reported that he had found out that Tony was being compelled to work far away from home in order to save his job. That was why he had to leave at such an early hour (*helpful* interpretation). Bertie was now feeling very sorry for his neighbour (cognition 2). He had also started to notice that, over the last couple of days, his general anger had started to calm down a bit (behaviour 2). However, he was still losing sleep.

Valerie next taught Bertie some relaxation techniques and encouraged him to practise them at home. He also began to try them out each morning when he was wakened so early (behaviour 3). Bertie soon found that he could nod off again (behaviour 4). After a few weeks of practising his newly learned skills, Bertie no longer even noticed when Tony's lorry started up.

PROBLEM ASSESSMENT

A proper assessment of a client is an essential preliminary before any treatment can be planned or before CBT can begin. A client's whole life should be assessed and not just the immediate presenting problem(s). For example, an attempt to treat a particular client for depression is quite likely to fail if the therapist does not discover that the client also needs to address an alcohol misuse problem. However, once it has been established that a client's problems are indeed of a psychological nature, the specific contributing issues can be identified and their theoretical origins evaluated (diagnosis). Next, the client's problems should be assessed in terms of why obviously harmful behaviours are currently being kept up. In sum, the therapist needs to try to understand not only how the client acquired the problem in the first place, but also why and how that problem is being kept alive. This last issue is vital. We must find out what the client's problem-maintenance behaviours are. If we do not, and if we do not find ways to interrupt these maladaptive behaviours, we will probably find that all our attempts to help our client will get nowhere fast.

For example, suppose that you are scared of getting cancer. Smoking a cigarette might reduce your anxiety in the short term, but doing so will ensure that your fear is kept alive in the long term. There are a number of very common adverse-behaviour preservation processes. They can be very subtle and hard to spot. Very often the client is unaware of acting in such self-defeating ways. Among these problem-maintenance processes are the following.

Playing it safe

A safety behaviour, no matter how apparently harmful, might be maintained because it seems to prevent something else that is even more threatening from happening. For example, someone who is actually healthy but who fears a heart attack might avoid 'risky' exercise and so become dangerously unfit. Someone else who is frightened that people might not like their 'real person' might curry favour by being overly helpful to others, even at the expense of his or her own needs.

Running away

Some people avoid their problems by escaping from them. For example, a person who claims to prefer buying everything online might actually be forgoing the actually preferred pleasures of personal shopping due to an unadmitted, or possibly unacknowledged, fear of crowds.

Withdrawing

This is particularly common maintenance behaviour in depressed people. Depression usually induces a lowered mood in its victims. This might result in someone who is normally quite sociable believing that going out somewhere or perhaps meeting people is no longer worthwhile. This reduction in normal activity, and the resulting reduction in stimulation, leads to increased depression. This in turn leads to even more reductions in activity. The person's mood is thus lowered still further. A downward spiral has been established.

We are all doomed

This involves the client putting the worst possible interpretations on everything. Nothing simply goes a bit wrong; mistakes are always total catastrophes. For example, some people on a diet who eat a piece of chocolate might just see their slips as a bit of a hiccup on the road to their target weights. However, our troubled clients would probably see such a 'sin' as indicating total failure and so give up dieting altogether.

Super-worrying

This is best illustrated by a typical case. For example, a driver who was injured in a car crash might now become automatically, yet unnecessarily, excessively anxious whenever another car gets near – even if that car is being driven quite safely. This over-worrying is also known as *hypervigilance*. Because such clients worry all the time, any little problem at all immediately becomes very scary – a pain in the stomach is not indigestion but cancer of the colon; a cough is a symptom of tuberculosis and not just a mild cold. Even if these misconceptions are put right by a doctor, they still serve to increase that person's physical and psychological anxiety/worry levels and so increase the already established tendency to super-worry.

I told you so

Here is another typical example. A client who fears rejection might become socially anxious and so seem to be a bit hostile to other people. This only serves to make the other people unfriendly too. The original social anxiety increases and so does our client's apparent hostility. Such clients have clearly set up self-fulfilling prophesies – 'I told you they didn't like me!'

There are, of course, many other problem-maintenance behaviours and the hardest of all to spot are the ones that seem most plausible.

ACTIVITY 4.3

Victoria always used a special cream that was 'guaranteed to make her look ten years younger'. 'Those things never work,' her friend claimed. 'They must do,' said Victoria. 'As soon as I put it on I feel so much more youthful and so much more attractive.'

- Explain this exchange between Victoria and her friend using the basic CBT model.
- How many different ways of doing this can you find?

SOCRATIC QUESTIONING

A very important, indeed fundamental, treatment method in CBT is an approach called *Socratic questioning*. In fact, Padesky (1996) called it the essential foundation of CBT. Put simply, and in keeping with Socrates' well-known philosophical style, it is a way of asking our clients challenging questions. The eventual conclusions are, of course, their own. As some theorists tell us (Beck et al., 1979, etc.), in the ideal, CBT clients effectively become their own therapists. Socratic questioning is used to encourage clients to reappraise their current thinking about their situations. It does not encourage clients to have 'correct' thoughts, but it does encourage them to evaluate and, if they find it necessary, to amend their own thinking. Here is an example of how competent Socratic questioning might be used beneficially in psychotherapy.

Case study 4.3

Miranda was convinced that she would fail her degree. Her counsellor, Angus, thought that Socratic questioning might help. It went like this.

Assessment

Angus   When did you first start thinking you will fail?

Miranda Just after I came back to uni last October. It was around about the time that I had to find a B&B in a hurry as my flat-share place had been given to someone else.

A   What goes through your mind when you think about your exams?

M   The college doesn't want me – they want to chuck me out.

Discovering

A   Suppose you were sitting in the exam hall right now, what would you do?

M   I'd open up the paper, see that I couldn't do it and I'd panic and run away.

A   Suppose that what actually happens is that you look at the paper and find that you know the answers?

M   I'd feel safe and feel a part of this place after all – I'd feel wanted.

Challenging

A   How does feeling that you will fail help you?

M   It doesn't really, but it does show that I shouldn't be here.

A   How do you know that you are not wanted at this university?

M   Why else would my flatmates have chucked me out?

A   Does that really mean that nobody else here wants you either?

M   Well, now I come to think of it, the Athletics Club do want me for the competition trials.

Problem-solving

A   How could you make yourself feel more wanted at this university?

M   I could see if anybody would let me join their flat-share. I heard that Pete needed someone.

A   How can you check that out?

M   I'll ask him this evening.

  (*One week later*)

Review

A   How did it go with Pete?

M   I moved in last night.

A   How are your studies going?

M   It all seems a lot easier somehow now – what did you do to me?

A   Nothing – what did you do?

BEHAVIOURAL THERAPY TECHNIQUES

Much of the behavioural modification element in CBT is carried out through a series of client-suggested and client-led experiments (Bennett-Levy et al., 2004). The therapist assists this process by encouraging clients to test their existing beliefs by carrying out behavioural experiments on themselves. The clients do this in order to find out if their beliefs and expectations really do work out in practice. In addition, clients are encouraged to devise, and again to try out, new ways of behaving that might serve to ease their fears. For example, people who are afraid of crowded places might be encouraged to experiment by gradually exposing themselves to increasingly crowded situations. In each case they would arrange the trial so that they had an easily accessible escape route. At the end of each test, these clients would be invited to evaluate their distress levels, say on a score out of ten. As they continue to experiment, they will often find that their distress level scores will start to decrease and possibly even eventually fade to zero. This first process is known as *in situ desensitisation*. It can also be done in the therapy room by inviting the client to imagine the distressing circumstances in a sort of emotional role-play. This second process is known as *vicarious desensitisation*.

There is a third process that is a way of using extreme exposure to rapidly reduce anxieties and eliminate false beliefs. It is called *flooding* or *implosive therapy* (Stampfl, 1973). Do NOT try this at home! Not many practitioners would try it anywhere! The method is surprisingly simple – probably too simple. For example, suppose someone is afraid of snakes. You simply lock them in a room with a large number of non-venomous snakes and leave them there until they discover that the snakes cannot hurt them. The idea is that the person will eventually calm down and the fear will disappear. Well, that is the theory anyway and, when it works, it works at once, miraculously. However, the chances of emotionally scarring someone for life seem pretty high too – client help or client abuse?

COGNITIVE THERAPY TECHNIQUES

A major principle underlying the cognitive element in CBT is the idea that existing thoughts can be reappraised and reframed. This is because, as we now know, if we can change the way we interpret events, we can change the ways in which we react to them. The first thing to do is to discover what the client's thoughts are that are associated with a given feeling. For example, a depressed person might have thoughts about being helpless or having no future (I'm sad; I'm a loser, etc.). A manic person might have thoughts about being invincible or always being safe from harm (Nothing can touch me!). The therapist's task is to nudge the client towards trying to adjust these thoughts or towards trying out different beliefs. The clients are then asked to test out if the new ways of thinking about things are any more appropriate or any more helpful. If they are, it might be that lots of other things could change for that client too, all for the better – we hope. Here is an example.

Case study 4.4

Jessica just could not stop herself verbally harassing her partner, Frank. It had become so bad that he had felt compelled to move out, although he did not really want their relationship to end. She very much wanted him back home and so, in desperation, she consulted Gerald, who is a CBT counsellor. Jessica's story went like this:

> 'Frank and I were on a dream holiday in the Caribbean. It was the time of the World Cup and Frank had been keeping up with the football via the TV in the hotel bar. On the Tuesday, it was the big final and it was also the first anniversary of our getting together. We had booked a super-romantic dinner at a superb restaurant to celebrate. During the morning of our big day, Frank remembered that the Cup Final was on that evening but he told me that he would miss the match and go out with me instead. During the meal I just couldn't stop having a go at him. It was a horrible evening.'

Gerald asked Jessica, 'When you were shouting at him, what was going through your mind?'

Jessica replied, 'I just knew that he couldn't love me because, if he did, he would never even have thought about watching that match.'

Gerald asked Jessica just to test out what would happen to her feelings if she tried, just for now, to deliberately change her thinking to, 'Yes, it's true that Frank would have liked to see the match. However, the fact that, despite all that, he still decided to be with me anyway actually proves just how much he really does love me.'

Jessica tried out this new way of evaluating Frank's actions. 'It feels weird,' she said. 'It's like a light has switched on inside me – I do feel strange.' By 'strange', as Gerald eventually discovered, Jessica actually meant 'less angry'.

WHAT CB THERAPISTS MIGHT ALSO BE DOING

CBT has an enviable track record of proven efficacy (Roth and Fonargy, 2005). The current state of the research strongly suggests that it is a very helpful treatment method for:

- generalised anxiety disorder;
- health anxiety;
- obsessive-compulsive disorder;
- panic disorder;
- agoraphobia;

- post-traumatic stress disorder;
- social anxiety;
- specific phobias.

However, there is also mounting evidence that CBT can also be usefully delivered by alternative methods. These include working in groups, self-help programmes such as reading suitable texts or using the internet, and working with couples. In addition, CBT is also starting to appear in some interesting variants. These include *compassion-based therapy* (Gilbert, 2005); *mindfulness-based cognitive therapy* (Segal et al., 2002); and *behavioural activation* (Martell et al., 2001). Westbrook et al. (2007) offer a useful review of a number of these very modern CBT techniques.

One direction that CBT is certainly going in will be to remain as the NHS's preferred model of psychotherapy for the foreseeable future (NICE, 2004). Counsellors currently in training, or counsellors currently considering furthering their existing skills, would be well advised to bear this in mind.

REFLECTION POINT

- CBT only deals with symptoms and doesn't address the 'real' problems. Is this true? Does it matter?
- CBT practitioners tell their clients what to do in order to get better. Is this always true? Is it ever true?
- What, if anything, could counsellors and psychotherapists add to the practice of CBT? Alternatively, could the use of CBT diminish counselling practice?

SUGGESTED FURTHER READING

Westbrook, D, Kennerly, H and Kirk, J (2007) *An Introduction to Cognitive Behaviour Therapy*. London: Sage.

A good 'entry-level' book. Chapter 4, 'Assessment', is a vital read.

Wills, F (2008) *Skills in Cognitive Behaviour Counselling & Psychotherapy*. London: Sage.

Wilson, R and Branch, R (2006) *Cognitive Behavioural Therapy for Dummies*. Chichester: Wiley.

CHAPTER 5

The humanistic story

CORE KNOWLEDGE

- Humanists believe that personality is powered by the so-called 'soft drivers' – *creativity, love, growth, self-actualisation, autonomy, etc.*

- The main humanistic personality theories include:
  - the person-centred approach;
  - the existential approach;
  - the gestalt approach;
  - the hierarchy of needs approach.

- The basic unit of personality is the self and the basic purpose of existence is self-actualisation.

- Early-years personality development is largely fuelled by a need to love and be loved. This need, when fulfilled subject to parental sanctions and control, establishes a person's developmental 'conditions of worth'.

- Person-centred, or Rogerian, therapy was one of the most important developments in the talking therapies during the second half of the twentieth century.

- Person-centred therapy is more a way of being (as evidenced by the therapist's own personal qualities) than it is a way of working, a therapeutic technique or a set of applied treatment 'rules'.

INTRODUCTION

The humanistic accounts of what makes people tick, when collected together, are usually called the 'Third Force' in personality theory. This Third Force came to the fore in the second half of the twentieth century as psychologists tried to move beyond the psychodynamic and behaviourist ideas about personality that, up until then, had been 'the only two kids on the block'. In general, it seems that humanistic theorists prefer explanations of human development that include the so-called 'soft' personality drivers, such as creativity, love, growth, self-actualisation, autonomy and so on (the list can be as long as you care to make it). Some of the more well-known innovators in humanistic psychology include Fromm, Horney, Rogers, Maslow, Allport, Moustakas and many others.

The basic principle that underpins the various humanist explanations of personality is deceptively simple. People are just what they are right now; what they are today; what they are in the here and now. There are no ideals, no hidden blueprints and, therefore, there can be no failures because there is no way to measure success. Humanists say that understanding people does not need the hard science of behaviourism; it does not need the supposed advanced skills of the psychodynamic movement's specialist, guru-like psychological interpreters. All we have to do is to listen to what people are really telling us. If we want to know what makes someone tick, all we have to do is to really hear the stories that lie behind the words. Understanding people does not need experts; it just needs good listeners.

The key element in understanding humanistic ideas about personality is the concept of the 'self'. This is because humanistic psychologists believe that each of us continues to develop our individual selves as we reflect on life's ever-occurring experiences. In other words, the self is a lifelong 'work in progress'. Humanists argue that maximising and optimising the growth of our individual selves (*self-actualisation*) is the ongoing, core purpose of personality development. In other words, self-actualisation is the ultimate purpose of the human being. There are a number of ways in which human-ist theorists explain how this might come about. We will now explore four of the main humanistic approaches to the understanding personality. These are:

- the person-centred approach;
- the existential approach;
- the gestalt approach;
- the hierarchy of needs approach.

THE PERSON-CENTRED APPROACH

The person-centred approach has been largely attributed to the seminal work of Carl Rogers (1902–87). Of course, many other theorists (Carkhoff, Gendlin, Greenberg, Elliot, Truax, etc.) have also made, and in many cases are still making, significant contributions to the development of person-centred theory (Lietaer, 1990). However, Rogers has probably been one of the leading figures (if not *the* leading figure) in humanist personality theory and psychotherapy over the last 50 years. Like those of many great thinkers, his ideas have permeated general society. It is not hard to see that many Rogerian concepts (e.g. refraining from judging people; emphasising/

respecting individuality, etc.) are readily identifiable as integral elements in the moral and philosophical foundations of many twentieth-century, liberal, social structures. For many people, Rogerian/humanistic beliefs have become part of their everyday language and shared attitudes. For example, there is often a socio-political presumption that maladaptive behaviour (violence, criminality, substance abuse, etc.) should be understood more and condemned less. In other words, society's liberals tend towards being non-judgemental about anybody, and respectful towards everybody. This includes those who allegedly deviate from society's assumed norms.

Carl Rogers grew up in a Midwest rural community in America, where the Protestant religion played a central role in everyday life. Indeed, he intended to become a church minister until exposure to other cultures during a trip to a Christian conference in China, together with his early experiences in theological college, led him to break away from the rigidly religious background of his family upbringing. He then returned to his original love of science and went on to study psychology at Columbia University. After graduating, Rogers started out on what became his extremely successful career in clinical psychology. Rogers spent much of his career in academia, first at the University of Chicago (1945–57) and then at the University of Wisconsin (1957–63). Over time, Rogers became more and more dis-illusioned with higher education's internal power politics. As a result he left Wisconsin for California in 1963, where he became very involved with the Encounter Group movement. He also became a Resident at the Centre for Studies of the Person in La Jolla. Rogers' major innovative contributions to person-centred therapy had been mostly completed by the late 1970s and in his final years he became interested in worldwide conflict resolution.

Although he abandoned his early-life plans to enter the ministry, Rogers continued to believe in many of the fundamental moral principles of his religious background, such as respect for individuals, the importance of offering people unconditional love and the personal benefits of offering forgiveness to others. Rogers also believed in self-redemption – that everyone is unique and that we are all constantly struggling towards self-fulfilment (self-actualisation). Much of Rogers' person-centred research concentrated on investigating ways of exploring, enhancing, perhaps even rediscovering, these qualities in each of us. Rogers believed that such morally high-level attributes are at least inherent in all of us, even if they are not always actually present in any obvious ways. These beliefs can be seen as persistent threads running through all of Rogers' work.

Throughout his career, Carl Rogers' principle interests, and indeed the core of his life's work, were centred on developing his innovative theories about psychotherapy. Because Rogers was mainly interested in therapy, his views on personality evolved more as by-products of his work as a pioneering counselling theorist and practitioner. His eventually emerging model of personality was based on certain fundamental beliefs. For example, Rogers believed that human behaviour is 'exquisitely rational' (Rogers, 1961, p194). He also believed that 'the core of man's nature is essentially positive' (Rogers, 1961, p73), and that 'man is a trustworthy organism' (Rogers, 1977, p7).

Rogerian theory

Roger's approach to personality is based on the concept of the 'self'. The self, according to Rogers, is the sum of all of a person's experiences that are available at any given time (Rogers, 1959). Therefore, the self must be the product of a person's interactions with other people and that person's awareness of being. This means that people's perceptions of their individual selves are 'the organised set of characteristics that the individual perceives as being peculiar to himself/herself' (Ryckman, 1993, p106). Another way of putting this would be to say that our self-perceptions are how we, as individuals, would each describe our own personalities. Equally, other people's perceptions of us are how they would describe our personalities from their own points of view. Note the word 'perception'. We are talking about how people perceive or interpret events. We are not talking about absolute or objective fact.

Clearly, 'self-ness' is the key to personality in the Rogerian universe. If someone's experiences lead them to say, 'I am an xyz sort of a person', then 'xyz-ness' is probably a significant part of that individual's self-identity or personality. The Rogerian approach to personality (the self) is based on his argument that there are two basic developmental drives. These are:

1. the need for self-actualisation;
2. the need to be loved and valued.

Self-actualisation

According to Rogers (1959), people have an 'actualising tendency', which is an implied drive towards fully developing and satisfying all their emotional capacities and physical needs. Actualisation is a directional (onwards and upwards) process that is ever-present. It can only be suppressed and never destroyed (Rogers, 1977). Ideally, the actualising tendency will promote satisfactory mental and bodily growth. Put another way, in its psychological form, actualisation is an essential function of the emerging self. This means that actualisation can be seen as the power behind ongoing attempts to experience the self in ways that are consistent with people's own established views of what makes them tick (their self-perceptions). Therefore, this type of actualisation is usually known as *self-actualisation* (Maddi, 1996).

The need to be loved and valued

In terms of personality development, Rogers believed that a strong need to be loved and valued exists from early childhood. Children, he argued, will naturally seek love and approval from their parents. If that love is given unconditionally, children are able to freely express inner feelings and are able to attain their full potential. However, when obtaining that love is possible only if the child behaves in ways approved by the parents, that love is said to be 'conditional'. In other words, obtaining love and positive valuations depends on the child accepting the parents' own values. Rogers called this shaping of the child's personality by giving and removing parental approval the 'conditions of worth' process of personality development.

The conditions of worth, an apparently innocuous phrase, actually summarises the whole of the Rogerian understanding of child development. This is because he claimed that childhood experiences have an enduring influence on someone's whole life if they become internalised values and self-concepts. At first glance, it seems that Rogers is agreeing with Freud. Are not his internalised values and Freud's superego simply different words for the same process? Humanistic theorists would argue that there is actually a huge difference between the two concepts. They claim that, for Rogers, the internalised values are the person's own values; they are personal qualities. For Freud, the internalised values are symbolic representations of other people who have been significant in a person's early years. In that sense, the Freudian internalised values are not personal qualities but images of someone's childhood 'lawgivers'. The humanists also go on to argue that there is another and much more important difference. They claim that, for Freud, much (if not most) of personality is fixed in childhood, whereas, for Rogers, personality development is a lifelong process.

According to person-centred theory, personality does not depend on the unconscious re-enactment of previous experiences (Rogers, 1961). Unlike the psychodynamic position, there is no place in the person-centred world for the unconscious. Nevertheless, some humanistic theorists (e.g. Mearns and Thorne, 2000, etc.) do suggest that there is an area of the self wherein the client experiences mental activities that are at the edge of awareness. However, for Rogerians, personality is wholly dependent on the individual consciously understanding or interpreting the self 'as I am now' and the self 'as I would like to be'. In Rogerian thinking, the fully developed person (the 'personality ideal') is the fully functioning individual. Such a person is fully congruent and able to accept feelings as guides to actions. Unafraid of feelings, comfortable with emotions and open to experiences, the actualised self is autonomous and independent of the approval of others.

In sum it can be argued that, like many other humanistic psychologists, Rogers, too, was a child of his socio-political time. He proposed a very individualistic, 'me-focused' view of society and of how individual personalities might develop in such a culture. The world is, of course, ever-turning and it might be that individualism will be replaced by collectivism in the likely overcrowded, resource-scarce world of the future. Rogers will not reign for ever.

ACTIVITY 5.1

Person-centred humanism: is it properly self-concerned, self-respecting, self-valuing and self-developing, or just self-centred, self-obsessed and selfish? You decide.

THE EXISTENTIAL APPROACH

Existentialists believe that the mind/body debate, which is so important to the Freudians and the behaviourists, is actually irrelevant. Their argument is that all the information about someone's inner self and someone's external world can only exist in that person's consciousness. There is only me (or from your point of view – only you); there is nothing else. A more academic way of putting that is to say that observers, and that which they are observing, are just different aspects of each other – they are all one (Husserl, 1997).

This means that humanists argue that people's personality traits only come into existence when their experiences give them good reason for coming to believe that they have certain qualities in their individual personalities. What they see outside themselves and what they see inside themselves is all the same thing. For example, suppose that a series of abusive interchanges between a worker and a manager over time result in the worker feeling a bit second-class. Suppose also that all this unpleasantness has caused the worker genuinely to believe that he or she really is an inadequate person. Now it might be that, if you or I met that particular worker, we might think that this negative self-assessment is completely wrong. We might think that the worker is good at all sorts of things. However, our external, supposedly objective, opinions do not matter. In the worker's world, observations of self and reflections on personal experiences are the same thing. In his or her own eyes, the worker has become a second-class person. From their point of view this is an existential fact and it does not matter what anyone else says.

All this suggests is that we have no existence, no substance (no personality), apart from that which comes from our 'being-in-the-world' (Cooper, 2003;

Heidegger, 1962; Spinelli, 1996, etc.). The world cannot exist without us and we cannot exist without the world. It is a mutually dependent inter-relationship. In other words, our entire substance (including our per-sonalities) comes from our individual interpretations of our interactions both with each other and with our wider worlds. The universe is not 'out there'; each of our universes is inside each one of us. If this is true, each of our individual existences (our personalities) depends on our own unique experiences and our interpretations of those experiences. There cannot be any 'approved' or 'finished' personalities because each individual's personality is both a one-off and, at the same time, also in unending development. Personality therefore comes from the individual ways in which each of us makes meaning out of our existences and that is what puts the 'existence' into existentialism and the 'human' into humanistic. The inference here, of course, is that the whole of creation only exists in our individual consciousnesses. This means that, if there is no 'us', there is no 'universe'. Some people might find this idea to be more of an excessively finely tuned, philosophical theory than a useful definition of reality. Are we really our own creators? You tell me!

The existential explanation of personality becomes important for human-istic psychotherapists when our attempts to create meaning for ourselves, to interpret our worlds, go wrong. After all, if 'meaning' in our individual selves and our worlds only exists in our individual consciousnesses, outside of ourselves there can only be 'meaninglessness' (or nothing). In existential terms, meaninglessness is non-existence (or death). This is, of course, a very scary idea (van Deurzen-Smith, 1988, 2002). Therefore, if we encounter a significant conflict between how we think we have made our world meaningful and our actual experiences, our very existence is threatened and we become frightened (Spinelli, 1994). This is the disturbed psychological state that existentialists call *angst*. In theory, at least, we can get rid of our angst by either recreating ourselves or by recreating our worlds. From an existentialist point of view it does not matter which we choose – it is all the same thing. Here is an example of how all this might work.

Case study 5.1

About ten years ago, Bill was a rail-crash victim. He was badly injured and this resulted in his losing a leg. He was in hospital for a long time and that was where he met his wife. She was one of his nurses. They have been happily married for ten years and they have twin daughters.

Before the crash, Bill had been a soldier, but the loss of his leg meant that he had to be invalided out of the army. Bill never seemed to get over this major disruption in his lifestyle. His overwhelming anger with the railway company was preventing him from moving on and making what he might even have agreed was a success of his new life. He went to see a counsellor. Bill spent much of the first session grieving for the life he might have had. Over and over again, Bill kept on repeating, 'If only I could turn the clock back to five minutes before the crash. I'd quickly change carriages and escape unhurt.'

'OK,' said the therapist. 'Suppose I could give you a magic button, one that will let you remake your world. Press it and you will go back to just before the crash. Change carriages and you won't be injured. Of course, that would mean that you never went into hospital, you never met your wife and you never had any daughters. So, it's up to you – are you going to press the button?'

Bill went very quiet!

THE GESTALT APPROACH

For many people, *gestalt* psychotherapy is essentially based on the work of Fritz Perls (1893–1970) and his wife Laura (1905–92). Like many others in psychotherapy's history, they were refugees from the Nazis. They eventually settled in New York, where they were prominent among the devotees of the 1940s–1950s avant-garde culture in the arts, drama and radical politics. Fritz loved the theatre and Laura was an accomplished musician. Fritz's own style of therapy-delivery tended to be confrontational and often involved getting the client to act out life's experiences in order to discover their real meanings. He tended to despise academic theory, which he famously used to refer to as 'over-intellectualised' and as being mostly 'bullshit' (Ginger, 2007).

In common with most humanistic ideas about people, gestalt beliefs about personality are also based on the celebration of individual freedom and creativity (Perls, 1948; Perls et al., 1951). The word 'gestalt' is a German one and its definition includes such concepts as 'pattern', 'shape' and 'wholeness of form'. Gestalt psychologists believe that, as people grow and develop, they organise their experiences and thoughts into patterns and this is how they try to understand their worlds and themselves. This will make sense if you think about the vast amount of information impacting on all of us at any given time. There is far too much data coming in from all directions to keep it all at an overt level in our minds. If you also add all the inputs that we have received since birth into this huge incoming-data stream, it can clearly be seen that we are in serious danger of information overload. One way to control this information onslaught is to organise it into clusters (patterns, or 'gestalts'). We can then group these patterns into sections and file them into a sort of internal mental catalogue. It will then be much easier to call up the relevant catalogue sections when the need arises and then to search within them for the exact item that is required. The supposed alternative to such a gestalt-based, organised internal information catalogue is chaos.

Gestalt psychology addresses the person as a functional whole. This is why gestalt-based personality theories are considered to be 'holistic'. They look at the person in the round and do not separate out the constituent parts. Completeness, in personality terms, comes as someone strives towards ever-higher levels of personal integration or self-actualisation. Therefore, gestalt personality theory is principally one of growth and education, with the focus on health and not on psychological 'dis-ease' (Latner, 1986).

It must be remembered that these organisational patterns (gestalts) do not spring into existence in a complete or finished form. They need to be built up over time. This means that a fully developed personality is made from integrating the required completed patterns or 'wholes' as they emerge. Therefore, if there are any incomplete personality patterns, this is an indication that more growth or development is either needed or is yet to come. However, if there is stalled or unintegrated growth in the development of someone's personality patterns, that person might be experiencing distressful emotional conflict. In order to be fully functioning, people need to construct 'whole' patterns of thinking and being. Fully functioning people have 'whole' personalities.

The concept of wholeness is a very important concept in gestalt psychology (Crocker, 1999). This is because, in order to construct the completed overall patterns of being that make up someone's personality, all of that person's experiences must be properly integrated and fully interconnected. Therefore, when everything in the personality is fully interrelated and interconnected, clearly the resultant whole (the 'rounded' person) is something that is much more complex than merely being a collection of various separate personal qualities or traits. We can use a computer as an example.

Think of the individual components of a computer. Individually they can perform various limited functions. It is possible for the hard drive to be connected to an external modem and so receive data independently. The CD reader could be connected up to a sound system and so produce music by itself. However, it is not until these two parts, and all the other necessary bits and pieces, are put together and connected up that the computer can function as a computer. In gestalt terms, once the pattern that we call 'computer' is complete, it then becomes much more than just a box containing lots of individually useful electronic gadgets. It becomes a very complex tool with many yet to be discovered uses. In other words, the 'completeness' of the assembled computer is something to be striven for.

Gestalt theorists say that this means that, when completeness is achieved, 'the whole is greater than the sum of the parts'. Therefore, again we come to the gestalt view that personality is essentially a holistic proposition.

THE HIERARCHY OF NEEDS APPROACH

Abraham Maslow (1908–79) was the sixth son of Jewish immigrants flee-ing Russian persecution. In accordance with his parents' fervent desire for their children to better themselves, Maslow set out on his road to self-improvement by studying law in New York, but later transferred to the University of Wisconsin, where he studied psychology. He spent the remainder of his academic career at Columbia University, where in 1943 he published his theories about the place of *actualisation drives* in human personality development. Maslow was a strong critic of the psychodynamic and behaviourist theorists and their views on personality. He argued that most of our learning and personality acquisition takes place at a conscious level. According to Maslow, it is interference from negative elements in our environments or our life experiences that obstructs our psychological developments. Therefore, if we could overcome these barriers by gaining a greater understanding of ourselves and increasing our acceptance of our worlds, we could all achieve higher levels of psychological growth (per-sonality development) or *actualisation*.

Although Maslow argued that actualisation was the driving force behind human personality, his greater contribution was to place actualisation into a supposed hierarchy of motivations or drives. Self-actualisation is the highest drive, but before a person can attend to this need, he or she must satisfy other, lower, motivations such safety or hunger. Maslow's actualisa-tion hierarchy (Maslow, 1943), as Figure 5.1 on the next page shows, is based on five levels of need.

Once one level of need has been dealt with (for example, the need for the basics of life such as food and water), the person can move on to the next level (the need for safety and security). As Figure 5.1 shows us, the highest need for a human being is self-actualisation and this, according to Maslow, can only be dealt with when all the lower needs have been sufficiently met. However, in times of stress or psychological discomfort, some people might find it easier to deal with any resulting unpleasantness by regressing (perhaps only temporarily) to a lower motivational level. For example, an attack at the 'esteem' level, possibly by feeling personally rejected, might cause someone to regress to a lower level and so concentrate on satisfying bodily requirements, perhaps by engaging in comfort eating (I've been dumped – munch a large cream cake?).

However, Maslow went further than just providing us with a motivational theory of personality. He also tried to describe what might constitute a healthy human personality and how it might grow (Maslow, 1962, 1973). Unfortunately for him, at the time that he was exploring these ideas, the only available biographical case material came from clinical reports of

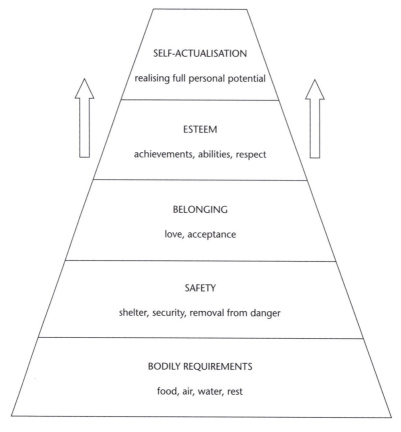

Figure 5.1: Maslow's hierarchy of needs.

troubled patients. This meant that there were not very many examples of apparently truly healthy personalities to choose from (always assuming such paragons ever exist). Like many counsellors and psychotherapists, a lack of evidence did not stop Maslow. Undeterred, he used supposed historical 'greats', such as Abraham Lincoln, Albert Einstein, Eleanor Roosevelt and so on, as his role models. His hypothesis was that, because such people were apparently super-successful, they must therefore be fully functioning and emotionally super-healthy. You may wish to question Maslow's assumptions. His studies of these 'greats' led him to argue that psychologically healthy people – properly self-actualising people – have:

- awareness and acceptance of themselves;
- openness and spontaneity;
- the ability to enjoy work and to see work as a mission to fulfil;
- the ability to develop close friendships without becoming overly dependent on others;
- a good sense of humour;
- the tendency to have peak experiences (spiritual/emotional satisfaction).

It should be noted that Maslow viewed the drive for self-actualisation as being an essential human need. For Maslow, it is not optional. At its highest level, self-actualisation means being completely comfortable with the self; having a full understanding of the self; knowing who you are. The self-actualised person feels a unity with society and has moved beyond guilt, shame and hate. Maslow's detractors might say that, in some cases, it could be hard to spot the difference between 'highly self-actualised' and 'smug'.

Probably most of us find ourselves on the downside of self-actualisation. Because all too often our personal needs are necessarily focused on the lower drives as we struggle to survive in the world, we lose focus and concentrate our being on the lesser needs (as Maslow rates them). Therefore, we cannot properly move towards personal growth. In Maslow's terms, we are deficient. It would appear that, if we want to become truly self-actualising, we need to have all of our lower needs fully taken care of. It is only then that people can devote their energies into fulfilling their potentials. However, coming back to real life, it does not seem very likely that many of us could enjoy such a privileged existence and so very few of us can ever be fully self-actualised. Even Maslow thought that this happy state was only achievable by about 2 per cent of the population. Some might think even this is far too high a figure.

SUMMING UP HUMANISTIC IDEAS OF WHAT MAKES PEOPLE TICK

In sum, it should always be borne in mind that all four of the humanistic personality theories discussed above are just that; they are only theories. This is also the case with any of the other humanistic personality theories that you might come across. Until fairly recently, there has been a scarcity of supporting evidence apart from clinical reviews. However, this lack is starting to be made good. In recent times, there has been significant expansion of the supporting evidence, particularly in the case of the person-centred approaches to therapy (Elliot et al., 2008; Gurman and Messer, 2005; Patterson, 2007, etc.). Nevertheless, the humanistic approaches to personality theory have been, and certainly still are, very influential throughout psychology, psychotherapy and even across the wider reaches of general society. Many influential psychologists and other thinkers agree that, at least in personality terms, a person's subjective experiences arguably outweigh objective reality. In other words, it is not reality as such that is important. What is important is how each of us interprets the apparent realities in our individual worlds. Such a constructivist-deconstructivist attitude can be seen as permeating modern intellectual society. For many people, the old certainties are disappearing and everything seems to be up for debate. Whether such views will remain tenable in the light of further advances in our learning and knowledge is yet to be seen. For example, we are increasingly discovering genetic markers for some personality traits. Might it be that our personalities will eventually be found to depend more on biochemistry than psychology; more on physics than philosophy?

It is possible to claim that the humanist personality theories were, and perhaps still are, the 'children of their time', both psychologically and socio-politically, at least in some parts of the world. It might even be that, in the foreseeable future, their time will be over. However, whatever the future brings, it has to be acknowledged that the importance of humanistic thinking in our ever-evolving understanding of what makes us all tick is undeniable.

REFLECTION POINT

- Did the humanistic thinkers of the second half of the twentieth century grow out of their times or did they help to shape them?
- Outside the world of psychotherapy, where else would you find humanistic ideas prevalent in society?
- The humanist theories concentrate on empowering the individual rather than concerning themselves with collective needs. Does this mean that they are only relevant in social systems that are based on individual freedom?

Humanistic approaches to personality theory have given rise to a large number of approaches to counselling and psychotherapy. The list includes transactional analysis, encounter groups, psychosynthesis, psycho-drama, transpersonal and many other therapy types and sub-types (Cain and Seeman, 2002). The common factor in them all is that they tend to concentrate on the 'here and now' experiences of the client rather than overly concerning themselves with either past events or predictions about likely future activity (Schneider et al., 2002). However, probably the best known humanistic approach internationally, and almost certainly the most widely practised, is *person-centred therapy*. In the UK, person-centred counselling has probably been the most widely available counselling approach available from the late 1970s onwards. Although imminent developments in NHS psychotherapy provisions are likely to challenge person-centred therapy's dominance, it is likely to remain as an important therapeutic style. Therefore, the remainder of this chapter will concentrate on exploring the person-centred approach to counselling and psychotherapy.

PERSON-CENTRED THERAPY IN PRACTICE

Person-centred therapy, also known as 'client-led', 'non-judgemental', 'Rogerian', 'non-directive', 'experiential' and so on, is of course usually accredited to Carl Rogers (see pages 87–9). However, as we have already noted, many other eminent theorists (Gendlin, etc.) have been involved in its development. At its root is the proposition that therapists and their clients are inherently trustworthy and well intentioned (Thorne, 2002). Person-centred therapy emphasises the place of individual choice and creativity in our lives (McLeod, 2003), so it naturally incorporates a humanistic view of society. Rogers (1942) put forward an apparently simple idea. He argued that the proper role of the psychotherapist is to help clients to find their own solutions to their problems. According to Rogers, clients' problems usually arise when they do not adequately attend to what his notion of personality theory suggests are people's two basic developmental requirements. These requirements are, as we have already noted, the need to self-actualise and the need to be loved and esteemed by others (see pages 90–1). In both cases, clients grow towards psychological health when these two needs (drives) are satisfied.

Person-centred therapy and self-actualisation

Remember, self-actualisation is the psychological process that motivates individuals to initially secure the practical necessities of life and then move upwards and onwards towards satisfying their emotional needs. At its higher, more spiritual and creative levels, self-actualisation enables clients to make helpful or beneficial judgements about the whole of their existences (Mearns and Thorne, 2000). Therefore, a vital task for the therapist is to help clients to explore the mechanisms and qualities of their individual self-actualisations. Clients do this in order to better fulfil their individual potentialities and maximise their emotional health and growth. Of course, in the therapy room, the process of self-actualisation is constrained by reality; by the necessary compromises that life forces on to all of us. However, this does not mean that clients should refrain from being ever spurred on to attempting the personal ideal; towards achieving their own individual uniqueness. In person-centred counselling's theoretical world, it is the ultimate job of the therapist to encourage the emergence of fully self-actualised clients (should such human perfection actually be attainable). These 'flawless' people would naturally be in complete harmony with their own inner beings and with their individual surroundings.

The self

In contrast to these 'flawless' people's perfections, for the rest of us the real self, especially the 'self-as-is', can be a far from harmonious state of existence. Unhealthy or negative self-concepts can, and do, clash with any desires for improved self-actualisation. Put simply, we might not like what we are. Being so might make us uncomfortable, but we cannot necessarily find a way to stop being that way. Of course, it is also possible that we might be completely unaware that we currently exist in some sort of unfulfilled, diminished emotional state. In either case, realised or not, the result is personal disharmony and potential psychological ill-health. In both cases these are the points in our lives at which we might seek or need help. These are the places in our lives, in our individual developments, where the person-centred therapist might choose to intervene.

In Rogerian therapy, the emphasis is on an individual's here and now. It is the 'self-as-is' that is important, not the 'self-as-was' or the 'self-as-ought-to-be'. People who are highly dependent on the judgements of others might well be experiencing conflicts between their own inner values and externally imposed values. This introduces the possibly of another form of the self – the 'self-others-expect'. In Rogerian theory, emotional disturbance also results from the intrapersonal disquiets that can arise when a person contrasts the self 'as I am now' with the ideal self 'as I would like to be' or with the self 'as judged by other people'.

Congruence

Clearly, helping clients to explore their current self-concepts is a key function for person-centred therapists. This is because self-concepts are how their clients define their essential selves. Rogers argued that our self-concepts (both clients' and counsellors') might be generated either by imposed external values or by our inner feelings about ourselves. He believed that conflicts (incongruency) between our internal value systems and our actual activities and experiences are the fundamental causes of emotional disquiet (Rogers, 1961). If these self-definitions conflict with real-life experiences, psychological disharmony is a possible outcome. Suppose, for instance, that you usually see yourself as a strong person. If you behave accordingly, all is well. You are being psychologically congruent. However, if instead you were to behave in a way that you perceive as being weak, you might well become disturbed by some inner psychological conflicts. You would be emotionally incongruent.

If there is a match (congruency) between a person's self-perceptions and their actions or their realities, all is well. For example, if people who would define themselves as being nurturers encounter someone in difficulty, those people may well get a sense of personal fulfilment out of consoling or helping that troubled person. They have attained congruency. However, if those same people encounter someone else in apparent need who nevertheless rejects their offers of help, congruity may not be possible and psychological discomfort might then arise. One way of relieving this discomfort (attaining congruency) would be for the helpers to reframe the rejecter as being ungrateful. An alternative, which for example might require the helpers having to reframe themselves as being unnecessarily interfering in other people's lives, might be much less comfortable (much less congruent). So, if congruence (a match between feelings and actuality) underpins emotional good health, incongruence (a mismatch between feelings and actuality) indicates emotional ill-health.

The core conditions

Rogers believed that the purpose of person-centred psychotherapy is to help the client to move towards becoming a 'fully functioning person'. By this Rogers means a person who is unafraid to experience the totality of emotion, who is open to inputs from all sources, and who is fully engaged in self-actualisation, living in the here and now and fully self-aware. The emphasis is on personal autonomy rather than dependence on others. This idealised self-state (some might say, not so much 'self-actualised' as 'self-satisfied') is facilitated therapeutically when certain allegedly 'necessary and sufficient conditions' are present in the counselling relationship (Rogers, 1957). Slightly amended by me, these five core conditions are as follows.

1. Client and therapist must be in productive psychological contact.
2. The client is in a state of incongruence and feels vulnerable and anxious.
3. The therapist is congruent or integrated in the relationship.
4. The therapist experiences unconditional positive regard for the client.
5. The therapist has an empathetic understanding of the client, which is, to a sufficient extent, communicated to the client.

In everyday person-centred counselling terms, the normal emphasis is on the need for the counsellor to be genuine, empathetic and accepting ('accepting' is also known as 'unconditional positive regard'). However, it is worth noting that fulfilling condition 1 ('. . . in productive psychological contact'), which is another way of saying that an effective client–therapist working alliance must be in place, is quite often considered to be the primary therapeutic task by many modern therapists. This is because modern research recognises the fundamental importance of the therapeutic relationship. Indeed, for some theorists (Constantino et al., 2002; Safran et al., 2002, etc.) it seems that the working alliance might almost be the 'all' of successful psychotherapy. In other words, for some counsellors and psychotherapists, there is only core condition 1 – the rest are irrelevant.

REFLECTION POINT

Think about the following as they might apply to you.

- Can therapists really be non-judgemental? If they cannot, can they ever be truly congruent?
- In person-centred terms, when does therapy actually stop? When should it stop?
- Does the Rogerian therapeutic aim of maximising individualistic self-fulfilment more represent a 'liberal/progressive' view of society than it depicts a useful therapeutic construct?

How Rogerian therapy works

In Rogerian therapy, personal growth and emotional health emerge as the therapist helps the client towards becoming open to the full range of life's experiences. The ability of clients to discover how to increasingly (and better) relate to both their inner and outer worlds is, according to Rogers, a stage process. Rogerians claim that, at the beginning stages of therapy, clients are focused outwardly and present themselves as being impersonal, unable to acknowledge their own feelings or to relate to others. Such people are very much dependent on the judgements of other people. By the final stages of therapy, these tendencies have been reversed and the clients increasingly trust their inner selves and other people, and are comfortable with feeling the real immediacy of their here and now. The client's self-worth assessments now depend on self-judgements; the client's important values are now self-evaluations. This newfound confidence in the self and openness to experience, which is facilitated by the therapist's empathy, acceptance and genuineness, allegedly permits the emergence and nurturing of new and more fulfilling ways of being.

Case study 5.2

Sally was an outwardly successful woman, although inwardly, as she told her counsellor, Harry, she felt a total wreck. Throughout their first counselling session Harry sensed an underlying vulnerability in Sally and he had a feeling that she was on the edge of a major emotional collapse. There was something about Sally – a sort of brittleness that made Harry feel uneasy.

During the first two sessions, Sally focused on her apparently successful professional and personal life. She expressed herself in terms of other people's judgements: 'My girlfriends all think I'm a bit of a laugh' or 'My manager always trusts me to get on with things.' Sally talked freely, but only about what she had been doing a few days ago or what she might be doing during the coming weekend. She never seemed to be fully present in the here and now of the counselling room.

Harry believed that the fact that Sally had come to therapy strongly suggested that she was actually looking for something. So what was Sally avoiding? Early in the third session Harry decided to take a chance. He told her that he felt that she wanted something important from him and that behind her outward air of confidence he sensed a vulnerable and frightened person. Sally became very angry and told Harry that he was completely disrespecting her. She threatened to leave on the spot. Harry remained calm. He told Sally that, if she did decide to walk out, he would still be there for her at their routine appointment time the following week. Harry was paying attention to two person-centred counselling principles. He was showing Sally that emotions do not have to scare people and that he still wanted to help her. Harry was not responding to Sally's aggression by being becoming judgemental and his empathy was not diminishing. Sally spent the remainder of the third session in an aggressive mode. Harry remained unfazed.

Sally did come along for her next session and, at last, she seemed to be able, hesitantly at first, to talk more about how she was feeling in the here and now of the counselling room. She told Harry that she had been very surprised by his controlled reactions to her outburst the previous week, but that somehow he now seemed to be the sort of person she could really talk to. 'You feel safe,' she said. 'Do you know, for the first time in ages I don't feel like running away.' Sally had at last arrived in the counselling room as a real person.

Person-centred therapy in progress

Despite apparent evidence to the contrary from many counselling skills training courses offered by many therapist training agencies, there is no recognised, official set of therapeutic techniques that support person-centred therapy delivery. In other words, there is no 'proper' way to 'do' Rogerian counselling. Rogers himself vehemently rejected the idea that the delivery of person-centred therapy could be reduced to fixed processes and techniques (Thorne, 2002). Essentially, person-centred therapy relies on therapists who can somehow engage with their clients in ways that help the clients to acquire self-knowledge and self-acceptance. Therapists need to be able to transmit their own Rogerian values to the client, especially those values that focus on the innate goodness and trustworthiness of the individual. However, this must be done in ways that respect and value the client. For Rogerians, the therapeutic process is client-led and not therapist-directed. It is because each client is unique (as is each counselling session) that none of these therapeutic tasks can be achieved by relying on the application of a 'one size fits all' technique. Put in very basic terms, person-centred psychotherapy is so much more than just repeating what the client has just said or, from time to time, offering summaries of what the counsellor believes has been going on in the therapy room. Mearns and

Thorne (2007) suggest that client growth during person-centred counselling sessions takes place in three stages.

1. During the first stage, clients are helped to develop *trust* in themselves, their counsellors and the counselling process.
2. In the second stage, the therapist and the client develop a beneficial level of *intimacy*, such that clients feel increasingly able to reveal what is really going on inside themselves (mind and body) and become willing to explore their own experiences.
3. During the third stage, there is a high level of client–therapist *mutuality*, at such a level that both therapists and their clients are comfortable with self-disclosure. This last stage, although presumably very rewarding for the therapist and self-fulfilling for the client, is clearly one that would appear to require a great deal of skilful management. Careful attention must be paid to professional and ethical boundaries.

Person-centred practitioners would certainly argue that none of these stages is likely to be adequately facilitated by a simplistic application of therapeutic technique.

REFLECTION POINT

- Self-disclosure – a therapist's dream or a therapist's nightmare?
- Is counselling training in techniques that complement the theory possible?
- Are the higher levels of self-actualisation really relevant to Third World societies?

SUGGESTED FURTHER READING

Cooper, M, O'Hara, M, Schmid, P and Wyatt, G (eds) (2007) *The Handbook of Person-Centred Psychotherapy and Counselling*. Basingstoke: Palgrave.

A helpful book, particularly the theoretical introduction given in Chapter 1 and the explanation of actualisation set out in Chapter 5.

Mearns, D and Thorne, B (2007) *Person-centred Counselling in Action*, 3rd edition. London: Sage.

An easily read 'starter book'. The 'hands-on' approach to the core conditions (Chapters 4, 5 and 6) are very much worth reading.

Tudor, K and Merry, T (2006) *Dictionary of Person-centred Psychology*. Ross-on-Wye: PCCS Books.

CHAPTER 6

Personality and therapy – today's story

CORE KNOWLEDGE

In addition to the psychodynamic, cognitive-behavioural and humanistic explanations of personality (see Chapters 3, 4 and 5), modern personality theory includes the following.

- Trait Theory
  - Eysenck's three dimensions of personality:
    1 introversion/extroversion;
    2 neuroticism/emotional stability;
    3 psychotic/non-psychotic.
  - McCrae and Costa's 'Big Five' personality dimensions:
    1 extraversion: excitability, sociability, assertiveness;
    2 agreeableness: positive social qualities;
    3 conscientiousness: thoughtfulness, achievement focus, purposefulness;
    4 neuroticism: emotional instability, anxiety, moodiness;
    5 openness: insight, emotional intelligence, wide interests.

- Bio-genetic Theory – personality depends on internal biochemistry or genetically inherited qualities.

- Interactional Learning Theory – social pressures affect personality development.

Complex personality theories attempt to integrate all the known influences on personality development. Such processes underpin some of the integrative theories of counselling and psychotherapy. Integrative theories include:

- Ryle's Cognitive-analytic Theory – integrates psychoanalytic theory with cognitive methodology;

- Clarkson's Five Facets Theory – argues that the therapeutic relationship is fundamental and divides it into five modalities: working alliance; transferential; reparative/developmental; person-to-person/real; transpersonal;

- Evans and Gilbert's Relational-developmental Theory – includes all the client's relationships both inside and outside the therapy room.

TODAY'S STORIES ABOUT PERSONALITY

The ever-ongoing story of how humans have tried to make sense of what it is that makes us all tick is probably a tale that will never end. In this book so far, we have been focusing on exploring the psychodynamic, the cognitive-behavioural and the humanist aspects of personality theory (the traditional 'Big Three'). We have also been exploring how and why these three theories have been so important to psychotherapists. As we now know, much of counselling, as practised to date, has been largely based on what the 'Big Three' psychological theories tell us about what makes people what they are. However, times change and so too do fashions in psychology generally and personality theory in particular. Just as fashions in personality theory change, so too do fashions in psychotherapy. As a consequence, partly in parallel with modern revisions in psychological theory and partly independently, the true values of the traditional therapies are currently being extensively reassessed. This means that counsellors will need to continually update themselves about developments in personality psychology because any such changes might well have implications for future developments in psychotherapy practice. In any event, today the 'Big Three' personality theories are far from being the only players in the game. There are many other modern ideas about what makes people tick (see Schustack and Friedman, 2007), indeed far too many to include them all here. Among the many additional, currently popular, personality theories that are around, some of the following might be of particular interest to counsellors and psychotherapists.

TRAIT THEORY

Trait Theory is a fairly modern approach to personality theory, although its origins can be traced back to some much earlier ideas. Way back in 1936, Gordon Allport claimed to have found over 4,000 words in just one English dictionary that he thought described all the supposed personality traits. He grouped them into three levels (Allport and Odbert, 1936):

1. *cardinal traits*: such as 'narcissistic', 'Machiavellian' and so on;
2. *central traits*: general qualities such as 'intelligent', 'cunning', 'honest' and so on;
3. *secondary traits*: appearing only in certain circumstances, such as 'anxious', 'frightened', 'impatient' and so on.

Some 30 years later, in 1965, Raymond Cattell regrouped Allport's list into 16 key personality traits, which he claimed were the fundamental building blocks of human personality. These are:

warmth	social boldness	apprehension
reasoning	sensitivity	openness
emotional stability	vigilance	self-reliance
dominance	abstractedness	perfectionism
liveliness	privateness (*sic*)	tension
rule-consciousness		

At about the same time, Eysenck was starting to produce a different three-dimensional model of human personality traits (Eysenck, 1992a). This model proposes that someone's personality can be defined by its positions along three continuums:

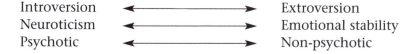

Introversion	⟵⟶	Extroversion
Neuroticism	⟵⟶	Emotional stability
Psychotic	⟵⟶	Non-psychotic

Modern trait theories of personality tend to concentrate on what is popularly known as the 'Big Five' (McCrae and Costa, 1997). Generally speaking, this theory proposes five broad categories of personality trait.

1. *Extraversion*: excitability, sociability, assertiveness, etc.
2. *Agreeableness*: positive social qualities, such as trust, kindness, altruism, etc.
3. *Conscientiousness*: thoughtfulness, achievement focus, purposefulness, etc.
4. *Neuroticism*: emotional instability, anxiety, moodiness, etc.
5. *Openness*: insight, emotional intelligence, wide interests, etc.

It seems reasonable to suggest that many, if not most, people can be described in terms of any of the above lists of relatively easily observable personality traits (Cattell's 16 traits, Eysenck's three continuums or McCrae and Costa's 'Big Five'). The difficulty, of course, is how to decide which set or subset of traits to select. Doubtlessly, debate about the numbers and types of traits to be best employed will persist. In any case, it is arguable that most of these trait lists are little more than common sense and so, basically, 'you pays your money and you takes your choice' – your ideas are just as good as anyone else's. They are certainly as good as mine.

Another major problem with Trait Theory is that it often has poor predictability. It tells us what sort of a person you have been up until now, but it does not necessarily tell us how you will be in five minutes' time. Sometimes the worm turns. We are all familiar with situations in which someone's behaviours in one set of circumstances are nothing like that same person's behaviours in a similar set of circumstances or on a different occasion. A difficulty with Trait Theory, as far as therapists are concerned, is that it tells us a lot about where someone has got to but very little about how they got there. It tells us even less about where they are going. Perhaps the theory only labels people without really explaining them.

BIOLOGICAL AND GENETIC THEORIES

Like much in personality theory, many of the current biology-based explanations about what makes us the sorts of individuals we are, are actually modernised versions of quite long-held ideas and beliefs. Many earlier theories about the physiological explanations of personality types went out of fashion in the last century but have now been resurrected in the light of modern-day advances in biological knowledge.

For example, in 1848, a railway worker called Phineas Gage incredibly survived having an iron bar driven through his head by a mistimed explosion. It appeared that his personality was irreparably changed by his injuries. This and many similar discoveries (see Lishman, 1996, etc.) led the then contemporary theorists to begin to argue that personality must have a biological (physiological) dimension. Nevertheless, from a psychological standpoint, interest in the physiological constraints/determinants of personality seemed to fade into the background as twentieth-century theorists emphasised individual freedoms and psychological choices. However, many modern investigators now claim to have discovered (or perhaps rediscovered?) biological drivers in personality development. For example, Eysenck (1990) suggested that high cortical arousal indicates introvertism, whereas low cortical arousal indicates extrovertism. Other modern advances in neuroscience appear to be locating numerous physiological processes that indicate differing brain activities that are associated with differing personality types (Yager, 1999).

Furthermore, according to the popular press at least, today we are apparently witnessing discoveries in DNA science that claim to be identifying genes that are supposedly associated with certain personality traits. Doubtlessly, there are many such discoveries yet to be made. As far as the biological explanations of personality are concerned, it is very much a case of 'watch this space'. Clearly, this could be an ethical minefield. Will we want to redesign our personalities by making chemical adjustments to our brains? If we can, society might no longer have any need of psychotherapists. Chemists would probably be able to do our job quicker and more cheaply – Huxley's 'Brave New World' indeed.

SOCIAL INTERACTIONAL LEARNING THEORY

Traditional learning theorists (Pavlov, Skinner, etc.) viewed personality development as being little more than a mixture of qualities that are acquired as people interact with their environments and learn how to respond to life events (Carver and Scheier, 2000). Later theorists (Funder, 1997; Rotter, 1981, etc.) have argued that this learning process is more than just stimulus and response. They say that it is actually a much more complex phenomenon and they claim this is because learning appears to be strongly influenced by social pressures. This, they argue, is demonstrated by the observation that, although many people might experience similar events, they seem to produce varying responses, possibly due to their living in a variety of mini-cultures. For example, not everybody who survives a particular disaster is equally traumatised. Not everybody who grows up on a 'sink estate' becomes a social misfit. This would suggest that the development of learning-based personality qualities is, at least in part, socially or culturally determined.

There is a further important difference between simple stimulus response learning and social learning. It seems that social learning can take place without being reinforced by any obvious reward (Rotter, 1982). This suggests that some people can altruistically learn behaviours and develop various personality qualities (reward-free learning). Others might do so in accordance with how they assess the value of intangible or deferred benefits (reward-postponed learning). This concept is not dissimilar to Sullivan's (1953) view that a sufficient reward for adopting a particular behaviour might only be an internal 'feel good' benefit. However, Sullivan argued that such rewards usually involve relief from internalised anxiety (immediate reward), whereas Rotter's argument allows the possibility that the reward for altruistic behaviour might simply be an eventual increased sense of personal worth (reward deferred).

It might seem at first glance that the Social Interactional Learning view of personality is one in which individual development becomes quite a complicated process – a product of many internal and external forces and drivers. Perhaps truly understanding people is too complex a task for anybody to even begin to tackle.

EMERGING FROM THE THEORY MAZE

Clearly, having a grasp of personality theories is essential for any counsellor trying to decide how best to work with any particular client. As always, the basic dilemma for therapists is deciding which personality theories to work from – which ones to choose; which ones to reject? One way out of this dilemma might be to avoid making fixed or specific choices. If we take the view that personality is dependent on a number of factors, counsellors need only deal with whichever of those factors seem important in any individual case. Like so much else in psychotherapy, the answer to the 'Which personality theory; which counselling method?' question depends on when it is asked and on who is asking it. In any case, it is quite likely that the answers will change as the therapeutic process unfolds. Therefore, it might be helpful to consider personality as resulting from a combination of theoretical positions, and that from time to time any one (or more) of these might become more useful or more influential. Figure 6.1 on the next page will give you a better idea of what I mean. For convenience I have split the psychodynamic position into two separate parts (classically psychoanalytic and psychodynamic therapies) and the cognitive-behavioural approach into its cognitive and learning components.

REFLECTION POINT

Think about someone you know who is now 'a very different person'. What caused that change – is it permanent?

- What about you?
- Who are you today?
- Who were you ten years ago?
- Who do you think you will be in 20 years' time?
- Why is all this so?

MODERN STORIES ABOUT THERAPY

Today, anyone thinking about investing time or money in counselling and psychotherapy faces a bewilderingly extensive list of treatment options. How can the customers (or indeed their therapists) possibly know which of the many, many therapies to opt for? Which is the best? Which is the most likely to work? The reality is that nobody knows, although it does seem that some particular therapies can be shown to be usually effective in some specific situations (Cooper, 2008). However, this does not mean that other therapies cannot help too, or in many cases probably work just as well.

What we do know is that many investigations indicate that the mainstream psychotherapies are all more or less equally effective with 'cure rates' in the 62–65 per cent region (Stiles et al., 2007; Wampold, 2001, etc.). Such findings are not new. Similar studies have found similar results throughout counselling and psychotherapy's history (Dollard and Miller, 1950; French, 1933; Luborsky et al., 1975; Project MATCH, 1997, etc.). Some theorists explain this apparent consistency by suggesting that there are certain 'curative' factors that are common to all the therapies (Norcross and Goldfried, 2005, etc.). Ideally, these common factors, when properly identified, could be combined into a sort of super-therapy. Then, in theory at least, an all-embracing overarching therapeutic model should emerge – 'You name it – we'll cure it!' Clearly, the discovery of such an all-inclusive

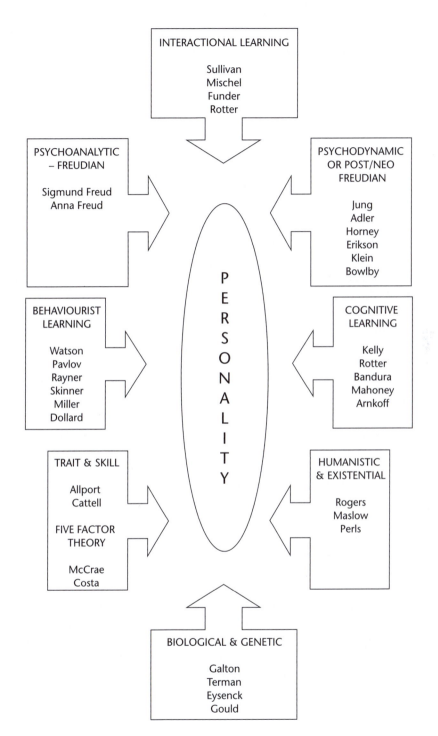

Figure 6.1: Possible influences on personality.

therapy model is a highly desirable prospect. That is why many practitioners are interested in exploring therapy integration. As Roth and Fonagy (1996) suggest (or perhaps hope?), 'ultimately, theoretical orientations will have to be integrated as they are all approximate models of the same phenomenon'.

It seems that, generally speaking, a good-quality therapeutic relationship between the client and the therapist, when combined with a productive working alliance, usually indicates that a positive therapeutic outcome is likely (Castonguay et al., 2006; Hubble et al., 2000; Norcross, 2002, etc.). Therefore, it is not surprising that the current interest in integrative psychotherapy includes a growing appreciation of the primary importance of the client–counsellor relationship. By concentrating on relationship qualities rather that individual therapy qualities, counsellors can choose to ignore the restrictive theory boundaries of the single-school models. Therefore, integrative therapy is typically considered to be 'model-free'. Integrative practitioners are free to import, mix and remix, and generally fiddle about with, any of the elements from any of the entire range of available therapies as circumstances appear to indicate. For an increasing number of counsellors, integrative psychotherapy is emerging as the treatment method that seems to offer the most help to the most clients in most situations.

Currently, probably the three most developed forms of integrated therapy (in terms of being customer-ready) are Ryle's Cognitive-analytic Theory, Clarkson's Therapeutic Relationships Model, and Evans and Gilbert's Relational-developmental Model. Doubtlessly, many other integrative models are in development or about to be launched.

RYLE'S COGNITIVE-ANALYTIC THEORY

Ryle (1990) has attempted to integrate psychoanalytic theory with cognitive methodology. This model uses cognitive techniques to uncover neurotic behaviour patterns that are then allegedly gradually deactivated by the therapist's deliberate attempts to reformulate or reprogramme the client's emotional responses to targeted psychological problems. It could be argued that Ryle's model is not truly integrative as it does not specifically include many important aspects of the contributing psychotherapeutic theories.

CLARKSON'S THERAPEUTIC RELATIONSHIPS MODEL

Petruska Clarkson (1948–2006) based her model on the idea that the therapeutic relationship is the cornerstone of psychotherapy (Clarkson,

2003). She went on to claim that client–counsellor relationships can be described as existing in Five Facets. However, this is not an ordered stage theory because all these facets are always potentially active. The importance of any individual facet keeps waxing and waning as the therapy progresses.

Facet 1 – The working alliance

This relationship is based on a cooperative agreement between therapist and client that they will work together on some agreed therapeutic goals targeted at meeting the client's needs. For example, a therapist working with a client who is misusing alcohol might propose that they mutually agree that the client should become abstinent. The healing power in such a working alliance might come from the therapist saying to the client, 'I won't see you at times when you have been drinking, but I will always be there for you when you are sober.' In other words, the contract sets out the therapeutically beneficial conditions (for the client) that will govern their meetings. In fact, if the client does manage to stop drinking, the psychologically beneficial effects of such an achievement could be so powerful that no further help is required. Indeed, some theorists (see Horvath and Greenberg, 1994) have argued that the working alliance can be powerful enough to be the 'all' of psychotherapy.

Facet 2 – The transferential/counter-transferential relationship

This relationship is 'the experience of unconscious wishes and fears transferred onto or into the therapeutic relationship' (Clarkson, 2003, p67).

Feelings provoked in the client by the client's perceptions of the therapist (transference) might be therapeutically helpful; they might be harmful. Supposedly identifying or interpreting such transferences gives the therapist insights into how a client relates to other people. Counter-transference refers to feelings evoked in the therapist in response to the client's story. Here is an example of how the transferential relationship might be encountered during counselling:

Suppose that a client, who was lonely and frightened when sent away to boarding school as a child, tells her therapist that she feels overwhelming sorrow whenever each of their therapy sessions ends. It might be that this grief comes about because the client is unconsciously associating her therapist with her rejecting parents. Perhaps, somehow at an unaware level, the therapist reminds her of her uncompromising father. This is transference and it might end or become unimportant if the client can accept the realities of her true relationship with her therapist. Doing this might help the client to gain a better understanding of her essential self.

Perhaps it is also the case that, when he heard how his client was bullied by the staff at her hated boarding school, the therapist felt a strong sense of personal anger. Possibly the therapist is unaware that he is taking her story personally and unconsciously connecting it to his own earlier brushes with overbearing authority figures in his own life. In such circumstances, counter-transference can be assumed to be playing a major part in the therapist's relationship with his client.

Facet 3 – The reparative/developmentally needed relationship

This relationship is 'the intentional provision by the psychotherapist of a corrective/reparative or replenishing parental relationship (or action) where the original parenting (or previous experience) was deficient, abusive or over-protective' (Clarkson, 2003, p13).

It includes 'those aspects of relationship which may have been absent or traumatic for the client at particular periods of his or her childhood and which are supplied or repaired by the psychotherapist, usually in a contracted form' (Clarkson, 2003, p13).

Here is an illustrative example:

Suppose that a client deliberately chooses to consult a female therapist in the hope that she will be able to help him to overcome his fear of women. During the counselling sessions it becomes apparent that the client's inability to relate to women is rooted in his poor-quality early-years relationship with a rejecting mother. Her abusive behaviour to him as a child has convinced the client, even as an adult, that male–female relationships are dangerous. The developmentally needed therapeutic element in this particular case might require the therapist to help the client to regress emotionally and to revisit those troubled childhood times. It is here that the therapist might help the client to 'unstick' from any early-years develop-mental 'errors'. For instance, this might be achieved if the therapist offers the client unthreatening positive regard while he works through the missed parts of his early-years personality development. In addition, by also offering a non-judgemental attitude towards her client, the therapist may be deliberately trying to provide him with a reparative relationship – one that allows him to benefit from experiencing some 'safe' contact with a woman.

Facet 4 – The person-to-person, dialogic or real relationship

This is also known as the core relationship or the 'I–You' relationship (Buber, 1970). This relationship encompasses the ordinary everydayness of being human that therapists and clients experience as they relate to each other. This includes the immediacy and mutuality present in 'here-and-now',

'person-to-person' relationships that the client is encouraged to acknowledge and explore during the ongoing therapeutic processes. By this means,
the clients' growing understanding of their evolving, real-time relationships
with the real selves of their therapists are used to promote healing. Such
a relationship is facilitated when the therapist offers clients empathy,
unconditional positive regard, congruence, genuineness and warmth.

For example, consider the following dialogue:

Client (babbling on about anything and everything, looking anywhere
but at the therapist) – *'Blah, blah, blather, blather, nonsense, nonsense'*, etc.

Counsellor (keeping the therapeutic relationship Real and immediate)
– *'Right now, I'm feeling very left out of this session. What I'd be interested
to know is what the issues are that you want us to talk about today.'*

Client (fantasising an Unreal relationship) – *'Sorry, sorry; you must be
getting fed up with me talking about all the wrong things.'*

Counsellor (anchoring the relationship in Reality) – *'No I'm not fed up
with you. I just want to know what's going on for you right now, in this room.'*

Perhaps the counselling can now begin.

Facet 5 – The transpersonal relationship

The transpersonal relationship is allegedly 'the spiritual, mysterious or
currently inexplicable dimension of the healing relationship' (Clarkson,
2003, p18).

Clarkson herself acknowledges that this relationship is difficult to describe
because it supposedly transcends words and reaches into a space that is
allegedly 'above and beyond' the physical. As she says herself, it is 'the
timeless facet of the psychotherapeutic relationship, which is impossible to
describe, but refers to the spiritual, mysterious or currently inexplicable
dimension of the healing relationship' (Clarkson, 2003, p20).

It is clearly not at all easy to find examples of such a hard-to-define way of
therapeutic being. Some theorists believe that examples of the transpersonal relationship might be found in therapeutic interventions that use
some form of creativity, such as play therapy, art therapy, or perhaps even
in therapies that refer to symbols such as Jungian archetypes, mythology
and fairy tales. It is usually considered that the therapeutic focus of the
transpersonal relationship is on fostering the client's awareness of a
spiritual self. The best definition that I ever heard was: 'You know it's
transpersonal when you get goose bumps.'

EVANS AND GILBERT'S RELATIONAL-DEVELOPMENTAL THEORY

Evans and Gilbert (2005) believe that there are self-developmental ('heal-ing'?) powers in all of the client's relationships. These include relationships both inside and outside the counselling room. The attraction of the Evans and Gilbert model is that it clearly recognises that any series of counselling sessions, no matter how intensive or prolonged, will nevertheless only ever occupy a very tiny percentage of the client's life. This raises the possibility that therapists might overemphasise their contributions to their clients' personal developments and that non-clinical relationships are as thera-peutically important, possibly more so. A very brief 'taster' of this particular approach to integrative psychotherapy is set out in the following Case study.

Case study 6.1

Muriel's GP had referred her to Adam, an integrative therapist. 'I don't know why I'm here,' she told Adam, 'I've only come because I was sent.' Muriel saw her main problem right then to be about organising her elderly mother's admission to a nursing home and, as an ex-social worker, she felt quite capable of sorting that out on her own. She didn't need Adam!

Adam's initial reaction was to feel angry with Muriel for dismissing his skills, but that soon changed to a feeling that he might really not be competent enough to help her (transference/counter-transference). He also realised that any attempt to set up a realistic, more open-ended working alliance too soon might actually fatally disrupt their currently fragile therapeutic relationship.

'How's it going with your mum?' he asked. 'Awful,' Muriel replied. 'The old bag is against anywhere that I suggest, usually just because it's me who suggested it, and she is too frail to look for anywhere on her own.' As she said that, Adam saw Muriel becoming more and more tense and there were tears just below the surface. 'Some mothers can be problems,' replied Adam. 'Mine always has been,' Muriel said bitterly, 'nothing I have ever done has been right for her or good enough.' Adam noted that Muriel was describing her mother as an object, the 'I–It' relationship. However, at the same time Muriel seemed to be denying any 'I–You' feeling. Nevertheless, her Real relationship with her mother (who almost seemed to be in the room with her) was certainly powerful enough to make her feel angry and frustrated right there, right then.

'So, how am I doing as a patient?' asked Muriel. 'Will you give the doctor a good report about me? I bet you won't – I've already annoyed you.' 'But I'm not annoyed with you,' said Adam, 'I'm actually feeling that you might be feeling a little bit sad.' This immediacy seemed to unnerve Muriel; 'God, you're just like my Dad,' she replied. 'On the rare occasions that he was around he could make me feel small too.' Adam reassured Muriel and told her that he was not looking down on her. This seemed to cheer her up (reparative/developmental).

CONCLUSION

The future of psychotherapy, as usually practised, is likely to be complex and certainly full of argument and debate. In this sense, it mirrors the likely future of the psychotherapy profession as a whole. However, in terms of being deliverable treatments, the integrative therapies, in particular, are still in their infancy. This remains the case even though they have been a source of controversy and study over the last 25 years or so (see Norcross and Goldfried, 1992). The development (or not) of the integrative therapies lies at the core of the current debate about which is the real curative factor in psychotherapy, the therapist or the therapy. Perhaps that is a tale that, in time, you might want to tell for yourself?

REFLECTION POINT

Think about the following – how might these issues affect you?

- Should the various therapies be integrated – might it be better to have 'horses for courses'?
- How can prospective clients decide which therapy style is best suited to their needs? How do trainee counsellors who study at single-therapy training centres know which one to enrol at?

SUGGESTED FURTHER READING

Clarkson, P (2003) *The Therapeutic Relationship*, 2nd edition. London: Whurr.

Heavy going but essential reading for anyone interested in integrative therapy. Chapter 1 explains just how important the therapeutic relationship is to successful client work.

Evans, K and Gilbert, G (2005) *An Introduction to Integrative Psychotherapy*. Basingstoke: Palgrave Macmillan.

A fairly easy read. Part 2 tells you all about the author's approach to Integrative Practice and gives a vital explanation of Integrative Theory.

Palmer, S and Woolfe, R (eds) (2000) *Integrative and Eclectic Counselling and Psychotherapy*. London: Sage.

A useful handbook, but becoming a bit dated for such a fast-evolving approach to psychotherapy.

PART 3

WHERE DO THERAPISTS WORK?

INTRODUCTION

There are no doubt lots of reasons why the counselling and psychotherapy story has evolved in so many different ways and for so many different purposes. So far we have been considering this tale from a mainly theoretical standpoint. However, there is another powerful force that is shaping the development of the talking therapies. This comes from the need to find practical ways of achieving the purposes and objectives of the various individuals and organisations that deliver real-life psychotherapeutic services to a wide range of clients or groups of clients. Here, I am referring to those who turn the theoretical into the practical – the practitioners who are the stallholders in today's therapy marketplace. Many such services have been set up and developed over the years. They include:

- individual private practices;
- group private practices;
- groups with specific purposes;
- localised groups;
- nationwide groups;
- voluntary organisations;
- public services;
- statutory/governmental bodies;
- commercial agencies.

It seems to be generally the case that many of these services started out pretty much disconnected from each other. Mostly, they seem to have been set up from time to time in order to meet specific, locally or nationally identified needs and purposes (Tyndall, 1993). Despite their often insular beginnings, these various types of counselling and psychotherapy services have still managed to influence both each other and the wider therapeutic world as well. The stories of some of these therapy delivery services are addressed in Part 3 of this book. Therefore, the following chapters will tell you some more of the talking therapy story. However, this time, we will be looking into some of the real-life situations in which real-life therapists meet their real-life customers.

No individual or organisation setting up a therapy service can succeed unless one vital requirement is attended to. It is this – they all need customers or patrons. This essential group includes clients, supporters, funders, referrers or any other interested parties. Quite simply – no patrons, no service! The fact is that all potential patrons are being asked to invest time, effort, money and trust in any of the therapeutic services that are trying (sometimes vying) to catch their interest. Clearly, patrons will only invest if they believe that their needs and purposes are likely to be met. This means that any service that is seeking customers, support or investment has to position itself in the personal therapy marketplace in a manner that will attract trade. As a result, all such services are vulnerable to the influences of the market. Indeed, in order to survive they must often actively conform to the demands of the customers. This is equally true for the most altruistic of the voluntary agencies, the most practical of the government-funded services and the worldliest of the commercial counselling and psychotherapy consultancies.

All therapy services, even those that are free at the point of delivery, demand some sort of personal outlay from their users and investors, even if it is only time and effort. That outlay is, in effect, a potential demand that the services shape themselves in ways that suit the marketplace. This demand will almost inevitably influence the styles of counselling and psychotherapy that these services need to provide. For example, most workplace counselling agencies subscribe to time-limited or solution-focused methods of practice and usually only offer clients a maximum of five or six sessions. Of course, some investigators claim that research shows that modern counselling methods do not need to be, indeed should not be, open-ended (Draper et al., 2002; McLeod et al., 2000). However, does the appeal of today's therapeutic brevity truly have a sound academic base? Is the current tendency towards focusing on short-term therapy simply an inevitable outcome of the intense commercial competition between all the rival agencies?

This all suggests that the direct, the indirect, the overt and the covert interactions between therapists, the organisations that they work for, their client populations and their funders/backers are all likely to have noticeable effects on the style, type, approach, purpose and duration of the various services being offered. Like all shopkeepers, therapy's traders have a choice. They can either adapt their merchandise to the demands of their customers or they can go out of business! Therefore, in order to better understand the counselling and psychotherapy story, we need to understand how the demands of the marketplace have shaped professional practice. How might the various organisational systems and pressures under which therapists carry out their trade affect the ways in which the various counselling and psychotherapeutic treatments they offer are actually applied?

There are, of course, those who believe that counselling and psychotherapy is a purely altruistic undertaking, one that should remain independent of any external attempts to influence it. These therapeutic purists might argue that ethical, client-led, professional practice is an absolute – one that cannot be, must not be, compromised in any way or by any means. Alternatively, there are those who believe that counselling is only a social enterprise like any other and is therefore subject to the needs and requirements of the wider society. These therapeutic realists might well subscribe to the old saying that 'whoever pays the piper calls the tune'. In other words, they would argue that the demands of the talking therapy marketplace will inevitably determine – must determine – which treatment approaches are adopted and control the terms under which they are delivered.

From the standpoint of those managing counselling and psychotherapy services, the purist/realist debate can sometimes appear irrelevant. They have a service to run and limited resources with which to manage it. For these workaday service providers, therapy, if it is to be anything, has to be pragmatic; it has to be purposeful; it has to deliver. Such counselling and psychotherapy services (free or paid for) are major employers/users of large numbers of practitioners (paid or volunteer/honorary). Therefore, we need to hear more about how the evolution of these services has influenced therapy's story. Improving our understanding of the purposes of the individuals, the organisations and the agencies that deliver counselling and psychotherapy to the public is essential if we want to gain a useful appreciation of the overall story of the talking therapies.

The individual chapters set out in Part 3 tell the tales of counselling and psychotherapy as it is delivered in the commercial sector, the educational sector and in the National Health Service (NHS). In each case, the range of the available services is huge and so only a limited number of examples can be given. The commercial sector's tale (Chapter 7) is illustrated by discussion of issues in private practice counselling and psychotherapy and a review of some of the concerns of counsellors engaged with the employee assistance providers (workplace counselling). In the educational sector's tale (Chapter 8), the concerns of counsellors working in schools, colleges and universities are explored. Counsellors and psychotherapists working in the NHS also have their own tale to tell and this is set out in Chapter 9.

There is one obvious omission in Part 3. That is the story of the voluntary sector. This tale has been deliberately left out because it is simply too vast to do justice to in a single book. The voluntary sector offers therapy through a huge variety and range of organisations, from very localised, very small groups to formally organised, nationwide super-agencies. It includes counsellors and psychotherapists who work in many specialities, from locally targeted mini-groups (e.g. women's shelters, youth groups, care centres, etc.) to national and international pressure groups (e.g. substance misuse, specific illnesses/syndromes, prisoner welfare, relationship guidance, etc.). The list is endless. Some voluntary agencies might operate under an informal structure, whereas others might function under strict regulation. Of course, it would be very useful if we had a more comprehensive picture of the various ways in which the voluntary sector works. Unfortunately, however, it seems that research into this area of therapy is currently very limited (Moore, 2006). It also seems that there are relatively few modern texts on relevant theory and core issues available, although Tyndall (1993) and Stimpson (2003) offer some useful overviews. We must hope that other authors and investigators are focusing on addressing this gap in the market.

What follows now in Part 3 are some more of therapy's tales, this time told from the viewpoint of those offering therapeutic services to those who wish to use them. We are now moving away from therapeutic theory and towards the everyday reality of the workaday therapist. These, then, are the stories of some of counselling and psychotherapy's practitioners and the work that they do.

CHAPTER 7

Working in the commercial sector

CORE KNOWLEDGE

- Private practitioners:
  - are free to choose their own ways of working;
  - are only concerned with, or responsible to, one client at a time;
  - are not required to be formally qualified or members of a professional organisation;
  - need to be able to market themselves;
  - need to maintain their professional contacts – they should not become professionally isolated.
- Workplace counsellors:
  - often have to multi-task;
  - usually have a responsibility towards multiple stakeholders;
  - may be sometimes working in ways that are very different from traditional counselling;
  - sometimes need to look beyond the needs of the individual client.
- All commercial sector practitioners:
  - need to be 'business-aware';
  - need to be able to sell themselves.

THE PRIVATE PRACTICE STORY

Some might argue that the story of psychotherapeutic private practice, at least as it might be recognised today, began in 1886 in Vienna, when Freud started working with his psychologically troubled private patients. This was during his early investigative phase (1886–99), when he was experimenting with the application of the new 'science' of psychoanalysis to his psychologically dysfunctional private patients (Mulhauser, 2008). It is certainly the case that most of Freud's so-called 'disciples' and their followers were prominent private psychotherapeutic practitioners during the first half of the twentieth century.

Of course, some of psychological therapy's historians might argue that the proper tale of the talking therapies in private practice really dates from the end of the Second World War. This was when there was an explosion in the demand for psychological therapies from a worldwide population that had been emotionally scarred by conflict-related trauma (Romero and Kemp, 2007). However, irrespective of when the story of private practice therapy actually began, today it is an important part of the working lives of many counsellors and psychotherapists. A quick check of local directories or the internet will show that there is an abundance of available private practitioners in most areas.

Why private practice?

There are probably many reasons why therapists work in private practice and why this is such a widespread activity. For some practitioners, limited employment opportunities in their own particular locale might mean that seeing private clients is essential if they wish to practise at all. Other therapists, many of whom either practise part-time, or work for or with a small portfolio of employers, often wish to reduce their dependency on limited or single sources of employment. Private practice helps them to achieve this and it is also a useful way of better ensuring and/or supplementing their incomes. Yet other counsellors and psychotherapists, such as academics, consultants, practice trainers and so on, might often work in ways that do not take them into regular direct contact with clients. Therefore, for these professional practitioners, including a limited amount of private practice work in their overall employment portfolio is an important way of maintaining their professional skills and satisfying the registration requirements of their various professional bodies. However, irrespective of the reasons why therapists enter into private practice, in most cases it is a commercial activity – they nearly all charge fees.

Generally speaking, although most private counsellors and psychotherapists tend to work alone, a significant minority work in small collective practices. In either case, probably the greatest advantage of private practice is that it provides the therapist with an opportunity to freely apply whichever model or style of therapy seems appropriate for the client and with which the therapist is professionally comfortable. Those who directly employ counsellors (schools, the NHS, voluntary bodies, etc.) often require their employee-practitioners to work to their employers' own particular counselling models. Such employers are also likely to have restrictive practice rules and to demand compliance with specified operating procedures. Private practitioners, of course, are much freer than their directly employed counterparts, although, of course, they do have to comply with their profession's general ethical rules. This freedom allows private therapists to cross professional boundaries at will and to be at liberty to explore all the creative breadths and depths of the counselling and psychotherapy profession. In other words, the private practitioner is free to develop 'a rich tapestry of informed, effective and creative practices that can benefit an increasingly wide range of clients' (Lane and Corrie, 2006). Unlike their directly employed colleagues, private therapists can tell their own tales – their personal stories – because they are able to decide for themselves on such key issues as:

- how many sessions to offer a client;
- how long each session should be and how much to charge;
- how often the client and therapist should meet;
- the counselling approach(es) to be employed;
- the types of problems that can be dealt with;
- the counselling environment – location, room type, furnishings, etc.

However, no matter the reasons why a therapist may have decided to enter into private practice, there are a number of professional and practical considerations that usually need to be addressed if the practice is to succeed (Pritchard, 2006). After all, at the end of the day, private practice in the talking therapies is just another business and the commercial demands of the real world have to be met. Potential private practitioners need to ask themselves the following questions and they need to have realistic answers ready.

- Are you ready to be your own boss?
- Are you a sufficiently competent practitioner to be able to work without colleagues providing a professional safety net?
- What sorts of clients will you see? What sorts of clients won't you see?
- Where are you going to see your clients?
- Are you going to specialise?
- How much will you charge?
- What arrangements need to be made to ensure your personal safety?
- Do you want to work as a single practitioner or in a small collective setting?
- How are you going to deal with the professional isolation that working as a lone private practitioner might entail?

Current issues

So, what sorts of tales about themselves do private practitioners need to put before their prospective customers? What are their 'unique selling points'? After all, clients who are thinking about going to a private therapist for the first time are usually facing a confusing array of practitioners vying for their custom. The counselling and psychotherapy marketplace is fiercely competitive and its practitioners can be vociferous in their sales patter. In any given therapeutic high street there is usually an abundance of therapists to buy from. Which one should the clients pick? How do they make their choices?

Professional standards

One immediate problem comes from a simple fact that the public are probably mostly unaware of and, if it came to their attention, it might well shock people. It is this. In the UK absolutely anyone can call themselves a counsellor or a psychotherapist and set up in business. There are currently no restrictions, although this may no longer be the case in a few years' time (see Chapter 10: Counselling & psychotherapy – the next story). This means that psychotherapy's prospective customers have no obvious official reference points or national standards by which they can evaluate the quality of the various practitioners offering them their services. Few, if any, therapists currently find themselves publicly graded by customers who might post the equivalent of an internet 'product review'. However, trends in online advertising that encourage publicly available customer feedback suggest that this apparent immunity might well be about to end. Nevertheless, right now, there is very little consumer protection for any of counselling and psychotherapy's clients.

In some cases, private practitioners claim to comply with one or other of the ethical rulebooks. However, it is also the case that a significant number of private practice therapists have decided not to belong, even on a voluntary basis, to any of the professional counselling bodies or organisations. Currently, this is a matter of professional choice and such memberships are certainly not a requirement for UK counsellors and psychotherapists (at least for now – again, see Chapter 10). Indeed, some practitioners might react with horror should they eventually be compelled to belong to one of the professional associations. This is because they view such organisations as likely to subject practitioners to restrictive professional covenants – ones that they claim could potentially weaken the therapeutic power of the client–therapist relationship. Whether or not this is a valid argument is still subject to considerable, and often passionate, debate. However, prospective clients need to be aware that, if they do consult unregulated practitioners, they are unlikely to have anywhere to take a complaint if they feel aggrieved in any way. This also means that underperforming practitioners are subject to no sanctions or penalties for failing to meet acceptable standards. Private practice therapists need not subject themselves to any form of professional policing.

Professional qualifications

It is likely that client confusion is likely to deepen further when they discover that, even among the supposedly more formally qualified and professionally disciplined private therapists, there is a bewilderingly wide range of training and qualification levels. For example, some counsellors are accredited by the British Association for Counselling and Psychotherapy (BACP). However, this does not mean that all such practitioners are equally qualified. This is because, while working towards achieving BACP accreditation, all these accredited counsellors will have undergone differing levels of counsellor training, ranging from FE college basic certificate courses to doctoral degrees from the major universities. To add to the client confusion, it is not even necessary for BACP members to be formally accredited before practising as counsellors. For example, in October 2008, of the then 30,379 BACP members, only 7,672 were fully accredited (personal communication, BACP Membership Department, 14 October 2008).

Choosing a therapist

However, even when therapists are suitably experienced or apparently qualified to practise privately, they seem to offer a baffling menu of specialities and techniques for their potential clients to select from. Anyone reading their adverts will find a therapeutic embarrassment of riches on offer. How are the prospective clients, with no particular knowledge of modern therapeutic techniques, supposed to distinguish between, say, gestalt, humanistic, CBT, solution-focused, Adlerian, person-centred, or any of the many, many other treatment types being urged upon them? Which approach should they choose? How can they choose? Which is the best treatment? How can these prospective clients make an informed choice? After all, many clients often do not really understand what it is that they need help with, let alone what sort of help it is they require. They only know that something is wrong and they have heard somewhere that counselling and psychotherapy might somehow help.

If all this is not sufficiently confusing, there is yet another question that clients have to ask themselves before deciding to enter into private therapy. This is a question that counsellors, too, must ask themselves before agreeing to accept a client for therapy. The question is this. Even if someone has the sort of problem that therapy might be able to help with, say for example mild depression or perhaps generalised anxiety, is emotional therapy necessarily the best way forward for that client? Would it be better (or quicker) to take some pills, get more exercise, tough it out, join an evening class, get a social life and so on? Can anyone be sure that counselling will not actually make things worse?

So, anyone interested in private practice counselling and psychotherapy, whether as providers or as recipients, might be well advised to take some time out to reflect on what they are trying to do and on what they might actually be able to achieve. What sorts of professional stories should the private practitioners be telling their clients? What sorts of stories do the clients want to hear? What sorts of stories will the clients feel themselves able to tell their therapists? It might be a good starting place, for clients and therapists alike, to reflect upon the following Reflection Point.

Clearly, there are many difficulties involved in setting up in private practice and many issues to consider. Nevertheless, private practice can be a rewarding job and one that can test properly trained therapists to their professional limits. Unfortunately, at best, private counselling and psychotherapy today is only likely to provide its practitioners with a part-time level of income. However, what it certainly will do is offer therapists a satisfying level of professional fulfilment.

Case study 7.1

Jean telephoned David, a private therapist, to ask for help with her problems. David asked her why she wanted to come along, as he needed to make sure that he was the right person to help her. Of course, had he decided that it would be better to refer her on, he could easily do so. This is because, although he worked as a lone practitioner, he also made sure that he kept in touch with people working in the associated professions and the social welfare agencies. In other words, he practised alone but he was not professionally isolated.

Jean described her problem. It became clear that she was emotionally depressed. Jean also mentioned that she had had an operation on her thyroid a couple of years ago and that she felt she had never got over it. David asked Jean if she had seen a doctor about any of her problems and he was concerned to learn that she had not been to see her GP for about 12 months. He urged Jean to see her GP for a check-up before she came along for her first therapy session.

When Jean did come along for the first session, she seemed to be very dispirited. She cried a lot and she seemed to find it hard to look at David. He asked Jean why she had come and she said that, actually, she nearly hadn't. When she had initially phoned, she had been feeling a little bit better that day and had hoped that someone might be able to make her 'better all the time'.

It was clear that Jean was very depressed. It also seemed that her mood might be too low for her to be able to connect with the counselling process. David asked Jean if she had seen her doctor. Jean said she had, but, when pressed, Jean mumbled about 'not having seen the doctor as such, just the practice nurse'.

David realised that it was likely that Jean would need some medication to help lift her mood enough for counselling to begin. There was also the thyroid issue. David knew that a dysfunctional thyroid could lower someone's mood. He encouraged Jean to book an early appointment with her doctor.

When she next came to see David, Jean was obviously feeling a bit better. She told David that the doctor had said that physically she was fine. However, as she was very depressed, the GP wanted her to take some medication. David explained that it was sometimes necessary for medication and counselling to work together. Jean agreed to start taking her pills and David suggested that they should meet again, but not for a fortnight, so as to give the medicine time to work. When they next met, it seemed to David that her mood had lifted so much that it was almost as if a stranger was walking through the door – now her therapy could start.

REFLECTION POINT

Do some internet research on local therapy agencies and find out their policies on:

- what sorts of people they think should be offering private counselling sessions;
- what sorts of professional activities they think private counsellors should undertake;
- what sorts of professional activities they think private counsellors shouldn't undertake.

THE STORY OF EMPLOYEE ASSISTANCE PROVIDERS

It was not until well into the 1980s that the employee assistance provider (EAP)-led provision of workplace counselling in the UK, much as we would recognise it today, began to be more widely available. This seems to have happened not so much as a planned development, but more as a result of a series of troubleshooting reactions to some specific workplace difficulties. For example, after two separate incidents in which employees committed suicide, a doubtlessly very worried Boots the Chemists responded by setting up an employee counselling service (Coles, 2003). In yet another example, a concerned Post Office began to offer counselling as an antidote to high levels of employee tension after too many stress-related incidents seemed to be occurring (Tehrani, 1997). Other incidents in other organisations resulted in similar employee counselling services becoming established elsewhere.

Today, EAPs offer much more than counselling for emotionally troubled workers (Grange, 2005). They also offer a wide range of psychological interventions (management consultancy, coaching, mentoring, training, awareness programmes, etc.), as part of an extensive package of overall human relations provisions (Carroll, 2002). The workplace counsellor's story seems to be ever-expanding and, nowadays, organisational counsellors are commonly found to be operating more or less everywhere, and at all levels, in the world of work. There are a number of possible explanations of why this might be so. Indeed, why is workplace counselling so often seen as being helpful to troubled employees? Of course, it might be that the explanation is a simple one. Perhaps it is just that both employers and their employees find workplace counselling to be generally useful. In other words, they do it because it appears to work (Oher, 1999). As McLeod (2001) argues, workplace counselling apparently provides personal benefits to many employees and it also seems to provide organisational benefits to their employers, too. However, such a simple explanation might not be enough. Other observers might take a more worldly view and wonder if employers sometimes use workplace counselling to try to reduce the ever-increasing levels of damages claims from employees who claim to have been psychologically injured at work (Hughes and Jenkins, 2003; Kinder, 2003, etc.).

Current issues

At a basic level, workplace counselling might be nothing more than routine, everyday counselling that just happens to be paid for by the employer. Like subsidised canteens and staff discounts, funding workplace counselling might just be a sort of employee perk not dissimilar to private health insurance. Perhaps this is why most workplace counselling services are required to assist both the employees and their immediate dependants, and to deal with all sorts of emotional or psychological difficulties. Could this mean that workplace counselling and general purpose counselling are actually the same as each other – it is only the funding source that differs? Alternatively, it might be argued that workplace counselling is genuinely different from mainstream counselling because it has its own distinguishing features. For example, the workplace counsellor might bring into play specific, workplace-sensitised knowledge and skills that are of particular benefit to the workplace-based client (Feltham, 1997; Summerfield and van Oudtshoorn, 2000).

It could also be argued that workplace counselling is different from traditional counselling because operationally it is known to be beneficial to employing organisations as well as to individual employees (Orlans, 2003). After all, the cost benefits to employers of having a psychologically healthy workplace are well established (Goldberg and Steury, 2001), and there is strong evidence to suggest that promoting good-quality interpersonal relationships between workers is vital for good organisational performance (Nuttall, 2004). It seems that workplace counselling might also be potentially helpful in managing the psychological stresses and dysfunctions that result from the ever-present drive for change that overshadows so many of today's employment situations (Wainwright and Calnan, 2002). Perhaps workplace counselling is indeed very different from everyday counselling.

REFLECTION POINT

Jot down your answers to the following questions.

- What are the differences between workplace counselling and everyday counselling?
- What are the similarities between workplace counselling and everyday counselling?
- Whose interests come first – employees' or employers'? Are you sure?

What is workplace counselling?

What workplace counselling actually is can be a difficult question to answer. To start with, we know that there are many ways in which it can be provided. These include in-house services, out-sourced EAPs, individual practitioners, face-to-face therapy, telephone-based therapy, internet-based therapy, conference calls and so on (Colon, 1996; Cutter, 1996; Grange, 2005; Wright, 2001). In the UK at least, the overwhelming majority of workplace counselling is probably provided on a face-to-face basis by the externally sourced EAPs and their affiliate counsellors. However, even knowing who provides it and what the arrangements are for its provision still does not really tell us very much about what workplace counselling actually is. It might even be that the answer really depends on who is asking the question and who is answering it. In other words, one definition is that workplace counselling is 'context dependent . . . if it is carried out at work then it is workplace counselling' (Orlans, 2003). Alternatively, Woolfe (2003) considers workplace counselling to be a form of psychological staff-support, whereas McLeod (2001) defines workplace counselling as 'the provision of brief psychological therapy for an employee . . . paid for by the employer'. It rather looks like the answer to the 'What is workplace counselling?' question is 'You pays your money and you takes your choice.'

Perhaps we can find out what workplace counselling is by looking at some of the things that workplace counsellors do. Among the tasks that Schwenk (2006) suggests workplace therapists might carry out are:

- employee therapeutic counselling;
- training and health education;
- advising the organisation; welfare and emotional/psychological health;
- facilitating organisational change;
- critical incident support; trauma management;
- managing conflict situations; using mediation and facilitation skills.

We could add in many other objectives, for example:

- providing services to employees' dependants;
- stress reduction training;
- staff support;
- work/life balance management;
- well-being strategy planning, and many more.

Another way of finding out what workplace counselling is, is to look at some of the reasons why organisations decide to offer their employees access to counsellors. Friery's (2006) reasons include those shown in Table 7.1.

Major reasons	Lesser reasons
Provide additional support to employees	Enhance the staff welfare provisions
Satisfy their duty of care to their employees	Support the Human Resources Department
Support employees through major changes	Protect the organisation from litigation
Help alleviate stress	Encourage staff retention and loyalty Address sickness and absence levels

Table 7.1: Friery's reasons for the provision of workplace counselling.

How workplace counsellors relate to their clients

Nevertheless, whatever it is that you believe workplace counsellors should do (who they should work with, who they should work for, what sorts of services should they offer), it is arguable that there is at least one major difference between workplace counselling and everyday, general counselling. It is this: in traditional counselling only two parties are involved; in workplace counselling multiple stakeholders have a genuine, direct interest. These include the employing organisation itself, its line managers, its

Human Resources and Occupational Health Departments and, of course, the employee-client's workmates, colleagues and family.

As we have noted, in most general practice counselling relationships, there is only a client and a counsellor. No one else intervenes unless a clinical supervisor is consulted. Professional ethics keep the counselling sessions confidential. Therefore, there are only two stakeholders in the standard counselling relationship, as can be seen in Figure 7.1.

Figure 7.1:
The everyday general counselling relationship.

However, in the case of workplace counselling, the professional relation-ships start to get more complicated because the organisation (and its constituent parts) is also an essential stakeholder. Therefore, there are a minimum of three partners in the workplace counselling relationship, and often more, as can be seen in Figure 7.2. This complexity also has an effect on the power balance between the various involved parties (see Figure 7.3).

Figure 7.2:
The basic workplace counselling relationship.

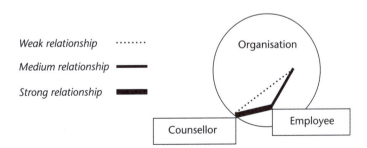

Figure 7.3: Workplace counselling power structure
(adapted from Coles, 2003, p98).

Not only are the relationships between the interested parties more complicated than they are in ordinary counselling, but these relationships are further complicated by the possibility that they might vary with the type of task or purpose that the workplace counselling session is focusing on. Possibly, the workplace counselling is really much more of a three-cornered relationship – one that has three partners (client, organisation, counsellor) and three points of focus (administrative, psychological, professional). Figure 7.4 is my interpretation of Towler's (1997) take on how this all works.

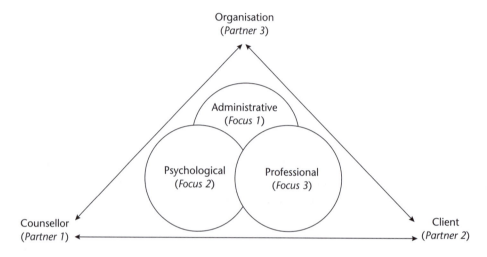

Figure 7.4: The three-cornered relationship (slightly amended by the author).

So, it seems arguable that EAP counsellors do have a different story to tell from that of the everyday, mainstream counsellor. This might be because workplace counsellors operate within some much more complicated relationships and power structures. Perhaps this difference can be better illustrated by means of the following Case study (which is, of course, only another story).

Case study 7.2

Paul is a freelance counselling affiliate with a major UK EAP agency that contracts with a number of companies. One of those companies often sent work teams abroad on extended work packages. Quite near the end of their return home flight, one such team was involved in an on-board emergency. A fire warning sounded and the pilot announced that they would be making an emergency landing. After a nerve-racking, but actually safe, landing the passengers were told that a computer glitch had generated a false alarm. Nevertheless, the incident was very frightening for the passengers.

These events first came to Paul's notice when Bill came to see him via the EAP agency. Bill had been one of the returning technicians. When he restarted work in the UK office, Bill found that he was becoming unreasonably angry with his colleagues. Bill wasn't being like Bill! His manager referred him to the firm's workplace counselling service.

Bill described his circumstances to Paul and it quickly became clear that he was probably suffering from a psychological condition known as acute stress disorder (ASD). When Paul explained to Bill that ASD was a common occurrence in people who had been subjected to the sort of scare that Bill had experienced on the aeroplane, Bill's relief was immediate. He had been frightened that he was going mad. He was so relieved to hear that his condition was recognisable and explainable. It even had a name and was also treatable. Learning these simple facts was a huge boost for Bill and this marked the turning point in his recovery. With Paul's support, Bill managed to cope with his mood swings during the four or five weeks that it took the ASD to fade away and for his life to get back to normal.

REFLECTION POINT

- Workplace counsellors can get involved in all sorts of multidisciplinary tasks – would you want to?
- Some companies require workplace counsellors to tell them if an employee is misusing alcohol or other drugs – how would you feel about 'snitching' on a client?

SUGGESTED FURTHER READING

Carroll, M and Walton, M (1997) *Handbook of Counselling in Organisations.* London: Sage.

Probably the most comprehensive study available – good, but dated.

Hemmings, A and Field, R (eds) (2007) *Counselling & Psychotherapy in Private Practice.* East Sussex: Routledge.

Hughes, R (ed.) (2004) *An Anthology of Counselling at Work II.* Lutterworth: ACW/BACP.

A wide range of topics and authors.

Hughes, R and Kinder, A (2007) *Guidelines for Counselling in the Workplace.* Lutterworth: BACP.

Routine information, but useful for newcomers to EAP work. Available as a free download from www.counsellingatwork.org.uk (accessed Summer 2009).

Palmer, S, McMahon, G and Wilding, C (2005) *The Essential Skills for Setting Up a Counselling and Psychotherapy Practice.* East Sussex: Routledge.

Lots of useful ideas for the newly established practitioner. There are some very useful chapters on business skills, law and the practicalities of providing a private practice service.

CHAPTER 8

Working in the educational sector

CORE KNOWLEDGE

- Counsellors and psychotherapists have worked in UK schools and colleges for over 100 years.

- Counsellors work with under-18s in primary and secondary education and with post-18s in tertiary and higher education.

- There are major legal and ethical issues involved when working with the under-18s that can vary across the age ranges. The principal concerns are:
  - client confidentiality;
  - duty of care to pupil/student clients;
  - information disclosure.

- There are numerous stakeholders in schools counselling; these include parents, teachers, the authorities and child protection workers.

- Confidentiality in schools counselling may sometimes have to be a team function rather than purely being the counsellor's responsibility.

- Therapists working in schools and colleges have two essential tasks:
  - attending to the emotional welfare and the mental health of the student/pupil client;
  - contributing to maximising the pupil/student learning experience.

INTRODUCTION

Education sector counselling is often thought of in terms of providing psychotherapy and guidance to troubled under-18-year-olds. Typically, these sorts of services are targeted at pupils in primary and secondary schools. These pupil-clients are nearly all under 18 and so legally they must be treated differently from adults. In addition, this is a client group that is still very much progressing through age-related emotional and psychological development, so it presents therapists with some very specific professional challenges.

A further area of interest to the educational sector practitioner is the provision of counselling and psychotherapeutic services for the mostly post-18-year-old students in further or higher education. Obviously, post-18-year-olds have the same rights (and no doubt many of the same troubles) as any other adult group in society. Therefore, at first glance it might be assumed that their needs would be no different from anyone else's. However, as we shall see later in this chapter, the provision of psychological services to young adults who are still in full-time education has it own specific concerns. For example, university or college therapists will often find themselves having to address the particular needs of young people who may be living away from home for the first time in their lives. Clearly, it would be a mistake to assume that all such young adults are 'street wise'.

This chapter will begin by exploring the various concerns and issues faced by counsellors working with school pupils. It will then go on to examine the difficulties that are faced by practitioners who are working with university and college students.

SCHOOLS COUNSELLING – A HISTORY

Counselling in schools is not actually such a modern innovation as might sometimes appear to be the case. Child guidance, including elementary forms of pupil counselling, has been a feature of educational services and children's health provisions since the beginning of the last century (Lines, 2006). For example, the London County Council appointed Cyril Burt as its first child psychologist in 1913 (Institute of Education Archives, 2007). In another example, one of the earliest instances of a child guidance service in the USA can be found in nineteenth-century Detroit, where a basic pupil counselling service was set up in 1898 (Bor et al., 2002).

However, in the UK, schools counselling in its more modern form began to emerge as a result of the Newsom Report (1963). This recommended that schools should employ counsellors who could particularly focus their efforts on students who were apparently underperforming across a range of educational and social measures. At that time, it was believed that the primary task of schools counsellors was to help pupils enhance their educational experiences. Therefore, it was proposed that only experienced and qualified teachers should be trained for this role.

Unfortunately, subsequent constraints in education budgets, and shifts in opinion about the proper responsibilities of workaday teachers, soon began to undermine the specialist teacher-counsellor role. Therefore, by the mid-1970s/early 1980s, counselling (at least in the pastoral sense) was mostly downgraded to being just one of the multitude of allegedly integrated activities that all teachers should routinely undertake. It was no longer seen as the exclusive province of specially trained experts (Hamblin, 1986).

However, as we have seen over the last 25 years, the workload imposed on school staff has greatly increased and indeed is still increasing. Teachers are more and more subject to performance monitoring. The professional demands on them from an ever-expanding National Curriculum are forever growing. All these developments, with their correspondingly huge time requirements, have resulted in an exponential increase in teachers' work-loads, together with a tendency to depersonalise many of their functions (Watkins, 2008). This has meant that an already overstretched teaching profession has found it extremely difficult, sometimes even impossible, to find the time or the personal resources necessary to maintain a combined educator/counsellor role. Something had to give and all too often that something was pupil counselling. However, this did not stop the youngsters bringing their emotional and social difficulties to school. Their educational and personal developments were still at risk. There was huge demand for counselling, but teachers were being denied the wherewithal to meet it. Something had to be done.

SCHOOLS COUNSELLING TODAY

Nowadays, ways of providing assistance for troubled pupils increasingly include the introduction of trained counsellors into schools to help pro-vide a specific, student-focused pupil support service. In such cases the counsellors often form part of a wide range of student support provision that includes mentors, young people's advice workers, educational social workers, health workers, educational psychologists, learning support assistants, peer counsellors and, of course, the school's teaching staff (Lines, 2006). This expanding use of counsellors has been made possible by the huge increase in recent years of available practitioners emerging from counsellor training programmes. However, few of these training pro-grammes appear to sufficiently address the needs of embryonic schools counsellors and their clients. This means that newly employed schools counsellors have to resolve a number of procedural and ethical issues, including the following.

Confidentiality

For most counsellors and psychotherapists, confidentiality is absolute and there have even been cases of practitioners risking prison rather than divulging a client's confidences (Jenkins, 2002). However, in a school set-ting, client confidentiality is not absolute and sometimes certain disclosures are demanded by UK law, by local child protection committee rules, and by a range of local authority best-practice guidelines. In addition, most schools that employ counsellors will have their own policies on such matters and, of course, many head teachers will vigorously guard their personal, in-house authority.

All these competing demands for information about pupil-clients combine to create ethical minefields for schools counsellors. After all, at base, counsellors too have a moral responsibility to protect the overall welfare of minors and this means that they may not always be able to offer children the same rights and privileges that are enjoyed by adults. Clearly, this very problematic issue is further compounded as the pupil-clients' ages vary and, obviously, different standards will apply to, say, 9- or 10-year-olds from those that will apply to 16- or 17-year-olds. For example, on the one hand, counsellors working with primary-age children will normally need to obtain parental consent before any therapy can commence. On the other hand, counsellors working with secondary-age children usually do not require parental consent. This is because the 'Fraser Guidelines' (formerly known as the 'Gillick Competence Test') apply to protect the older pupils' rights to privacy.

Good practice suggests that the consent rules applicable in UK medical treatment settings generally should also normally apply to schools counselling. These are comprehensively set out in the UK Department of Health (2001a) publication, *Reference Guide for Consent for Examination or Treatment*, and the very latest information can be found at the 'Every Child Matters' website (**www.ecm.gov.uk/informationsharing**). As a general rule, best practice permits the sharing of confidential information without client consent (with the relevant authorities only), if there is reason to believe that the child is, or may be, exposed to risk or significant harm. This includes harm to others.

School management responsibility

All head teachers are required to act *in loco parentis*. In other words, they have the rights, duties and responsibilities of a parent while a child is in their charge. It might be that, during a counselling session, the therapist becomes privy to important information that the head teacher is unaware of. This might also be the sort of information that the head teacher would normally, perhaps even urgently, want to act upon in the child's best interests. It might be vital for the head teacher to consult colleagues, the child's parents or social services.

Can head teachers rely on the schools counsellor to reveal such information? Indeed, in such cases should the counsellor break counselling-room confidentiality? In fact, this problem is actually much more complex than it might seem at first sight because, apart from self-referral, there are numerous ways in which a young person might be referred to the schools counsellor. These include referrals from special needs coordinators, class teachers, year heads, pastoral tutors, parents, carers and so on. All these people have a stake in the counselling process and all may feel that they are entitled to appropriate direct feedback. In fact, it might even be in the child's best interests that referrers quickly become aware of a child's difficulties or personally adverse circumstances. Again, the question is, must the counsellor divulge such information and indeed should the counsellor do so?

Taken all round, the issue of client confidentiality in schools counselling is nothing less than a moral maze. There appears to be no simple answer.

REFLECTION POINT

- If you were a schools counsellor, who would you feel primarily responsible to: the child; the school; the parents; society?
- What would you do if your pupil-client says, 'Don't tell anybody but . . .'?

Case study 8.1

Maddy lived next door to Caroline who had a 13-year-old daughter, Tracy. Tracy was normally a cheerful child, but just lately seemed to be very quiet and withdrawn. Maddy asked Tracy if anything was wrong. Tracy said that there was something, but she could only talk about it if Maddy promised never to tell anyone. Maddy replied that she was good at keeping secrets but that, if she ever found out that Maddy was in real trouble, she would do whatever she felt was right in trying to help her.

Tracy then told Maddy enough to make her suspect that Caroline's long-term boyfriend was being abusive. This was really a matter for the police or the social services. Tracy was possibly in serious danger and needed help. What should Maddy do? What could she do?

Maddy decided to have a word with Tracy's head teacher. She did not ask Tracy's permission, though, and at first she only talked to the head about 'one of her pupils'. The head asked Maddy where she lived and, after finding this out, asked if it was a nearby neighbour's child that she was concerned about. When Maddy confirmed this was so, the head was able to tell Maddy that she was pretty sure that she knew who the child was and that steps were already in hand to try to help her. Maddy felt sufficiently reassured to be willing to confirm Tracy's identity.

Unknown to Maddy, Tracy was already considered to be at possible risk and the child protection team was already aware of her situation. As it happened, Tracy was already seeing the schools counsellor who, now forewarned, was able to encourage Tracy to tell her just what was going on. Tracy had been made aware from the start that the counsellor might have to tell the head what was happening. She made a bit of a half-hearted complaint about that, although it seemed to the counsellor that, underneath all the bluster, Tracy appeared to be secretly relieved that somebody cared enough about her to want to actually do something.

ACTIVITY 8.1

- Sketch out an action plan that sets out how you would have handled Tracy's problems.
- How would you have decided what was in Tracy's 'best interests'? What might have helped? What might have hindered?

WHY DO WE NEED SCHOOLS COUNSELLORS?

Schools counsellors will almost certainly find that the problems brought to them by their student-clients are as diverse, as comprehensive, and sometimes just as intractable, as the problems that might be brought by any client, anywhere, to any therapist. Bor et al. (2002) argue that ordinary everyday life itself can be stressful and problematic for any child, irrespective of individual personal strengths. They include in their list of potential stress areas worries about issues such as competitiveness, bullying, social exclusion, racism, family crises, sibling rivalry, underachievement, abuse, homophobia, peer pressure and substance abuse. Clearly, this list is far from exhaustive. Geldard and Geldard (2004) even imply that pressures from the expected and routine experiences of adolescence might, just by themselves, appear to generate psychological conditions that could even require treatment. Sometimes it seems that adolescence is almost akin to a psychological 'illness'. So, are all adolescents emotionally 'diseased'? No doubt, a good many of their parents, especially when feeling sufficiently harassed, would probably agree.

So, the task of the schools counsellor, from the moment that a referred pupil first knocks on the counselling-room door, is complex, demanding and pressured. The counsellor's immediate concern is obviously the child but, behind the child, rather like ghosts slipping surreptitiously into the room, is a whole army of 'others' (teachers, family, friends, social services, etc.), all of whom have a direct interest in the therapy session and who have a vital stake in the counselling process. The counsellor also has to take into account some other, equally ghostly, although perhaps more indirect, forces from the wider world (professional/ethical concerns, child protection law, society's demands, etc.). Keeping all these influences in balance and doing right by the child is almost a superhuman task. The 'ideal' schools counsellor needs the wisdom of Solomon, the patience of Job and the tenacity of Robert the Bruce, together with highly developed sensitivity and finely honed interpersonal skills. The rest of us, those of us who don't reach such lofty perfections, and who are not such counselling paragons, must rely on the essential quality that Napoleon looked for in his generals; we need good luck!

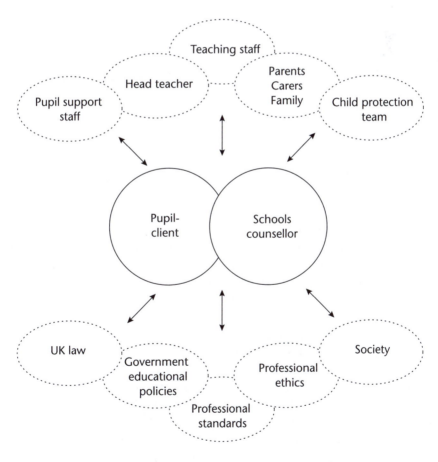

Figure 8.1: The schools counsellor's world.

COUNSELLING IN COLLEGES AND UNIVERSITIES

So far this chapter has concentrated on the issues faced by counsellors working in primary and secondary education. Another important area of counselling for therapists working in education is that targeted at meeting the needs of students in FE or HE. Counsellors working with these usually post-18-year-olds, who are mainly full-time students, are very often operating from within a university or college in-house counselling service. The differences between working with this older student client group and the younger school pupils group will be more clearly illustrated by the following tale from a practising university counsellor.

PRACTITIONER REFLECTIONS – PAULA BILES-GARVEY

A university counsellor's story

It is my experience, and that of my colleagues, that our work in a well-known university's counselling service is expanding. We are seeing significant increases in the numbers of our student-clients who present with mental health problems. These include anxiety states, panic attacks, self-harm, risk-taking behaviour, excessive drinking, substance misuse, eating disorders, obsessive-compulsive disorder and depression. All of these conditions seem to be on the increase within the student population.

Nowadays, our counselling service, like many university counselling schemes, is linked with the NHS general practice (GP) surgeries that serve our resident student population. This very convenient connection has resulted in these GPs becoming much more willing to refer suitable student patients to our counselling service. Sometimes, this is because the NHS treatment waiting lists are too long and sometimes this is because they believe the free, friendly, local service provided by the university's own counsellors will be better tailored to the needs of the university's own students. It is very encouraging to note that local GP practices will often set up joint meetings between the counselling service practitioners and medical staff to discuss matters of mutual concern and perhaps even to consider the specific needs of some of the student-patients.

Over the course of the last three years I have found more GPs sending their student-patients to me as clients (not their terminology). Often the client arrives with only a 'post-it note' (usually on a pharmaceutical company's 'freebie'), with the GP's diagnosis on it together with a recommended level of counselling. Typically, such a 'prescription' might say 'Alcohol problems – 12 Steps' or 'Low self-esteem – 6 weeks of CBT'. These sorts of referrals (although obviously welcome in themselves) raise a number of ethical and procedural issues for me and my university counselling colleagues. For example, it is a rather casual system that does not feel very confidential in the way that information is so informally transmitted between the GPs and the university counselling service. It is also a system in which I as the counsellor feel that I have been instructed by the GP, even though I work for the university's counselling service and not for the NHS. Furthermore, it somehow goes against the grain to be told what therapeutic interventions to use with my clients. After all, I am a professional practitioner and wish to apply my own skills and knowledge. I, too, may well have an opinion about the correct assessment of a client's problems and my own plan of how to address them. Finally, this referral method somehow seems to suggest that we university counsellors are seen by the GPs as adjunct 'assistant therapists' to the NHS and not as independent professionals in our own right.

It is now often the case that many universities are starting to advertise the various computer programs or online services that are available to people suffering from mild emotional disorders (e.g. **www.depressionalliance.org**). These have been extensively evaluated and it seems that these online services are often helpful. It appears from student-client feedback that they can offer significant short-term help in such cases as mild depression or anxiety, for example. However, it seems to me that online services are unlikely to provide the benefits that longer-term, face-to-face, therapeutic relationships can bring about. This is particularly so in cases where the current symptoms may be related back to early-years developmental traumas. From my point of view, working with a client in a long-term therapeutic setting is extremely rewarding, especially, for example, when I see the damaged attachment issues presented by some of my young clients being repaired as we work through their problems together.

A particular area of professional difficulty arises when student-clients ask me to contact their therapists back home. They want me to find out what those therapists think and what they have been doing. Clearly my clients do not want their original therapy disrupted. They want rapid and effective help, but I know that building a new, quality, counsellor–client relationship with me will take as long as it takes. There are no shortcuts. It is not possible for one therapist to suddenly replicate another. Apart from causing problems around confidentiality, these sorts of requests place pressure on me as a university counsellor if I decline to contact the original therapist.

A very new form of psychological pressure, and one that is particularly applicable to student populations, can come from the extensive, negative, use of modern information technology. In effect, this can often be very powerful 'cyber-bullying'. This sort of bullying usually takes place on social networking sites. For example, by using mobile phones, videos of date rapes are shared, intimate pictures from relationships are made public, or very adverse comments about people are published. These 'cyber assaults' very often occur after a relationship ends. Hearing or seeing the outpourings of clearly depressed young people being shared with total strangers can be damaging to the victims. They might feel betrayed by their friends; they might not even be aware that their friends are commenting on their supposed behaviour and opinions. The internet makes it far easier today for someone to be betrayed, humiliated or socially destroyed. For example, some students have reported that they have had to take down their profiles from social networking websites after future employers discovered web postings showing them in inebriated states.

Counselling in university settings can bring a whole new set of professional and ethical concerns for the students' therapists. For me, a typical example might arise if I were to become aware of a pre-existing mental health problem for, say, a student teacher – one who is engaged in teaching practice at a local school. It might well be the case that the student does not wish to tell a future employer or even the faculty board about such concerns – they do not want to be stigmatised. For instance, it is possible that the student might be suffering from an obsessive-compulsive disorder. Perhaps the student feels compelled frequently to leave the nursery, classroom or playground to wash hands, check doors and so on. This might mean that the counsellor has every reason to believe that pupils, perhaps sometimes including very young children, might sometimes be left unsupervised or otherwise at risk. By coming to the counselling service, the client is also effectively acknowledging that these behaviours are getting out of control. However, the standard counselling ethical position on confidentiality precludes the counsellor from informing the school's management or the university authorities.

I know of one real-life case that led to such an ethical dilemma. That particular case involved a disturbed student who looked after nursery-age children during his teaching practice. The counsellor concerned rather cleverly resolved the resulting ethical dilemma by asking permission from the university's academic board to make a presentation to the academic staff generally about the possible impacts of mental health problems on any of the students engaged on any of the university's professional work experience programmes. The counsellor sought guidance from academic staff about what students were indeed required to declare as medical problems in such cases. The counsellor also wanted to hear their views on what might be considered to be minor or major mental health issues or acceptable levels of medication that might be considered safe when students were in engaged in safety sensitive work. This counsellor's rather enterprising initiative resulted in letters being written to several government departments and to several counselling professional bodies to try to clarify both the legal reporting requirements and the confidentiality/ethical issues.

With child protection issues, the rules about reporting reported or disclosed child sexual abuse are clear, but there is often a gap in practice for young people aged between 16 and 18. At 17, young people are considered no longer to be minors and are not treated by the child mental health services. However, it is not until they are 18 that they are entitled to treatment from the adult mental health services. Many college or university counsellors are very well aware that the 17–18 group of young people do not get the help that they need or are entitled to as they fall between the two provisions. This is an area of special concern to the university counsellor who might meet such clients.

Like so many students, my university's young people, too, are away from home, often for the first time. They might be vulnerable to all sorts of emotional and psychological difficulties, ranging from homesickness to major depression. Sometimes, these youngsters find that psychological reactions to previous traumatic incidents are triggered during their time at university. These incidents include bereavement, violent attacks, neglect by parents, phobias and so on. Excessive freedom for the first time in their lives combined with the misuse of drugs and alcohol can also be problematic for young people. With the greater movement of international students, cultural misunderstandings and problems, often relating to drugs, alcohol and sex, can also arise. All these issues, too, are of particular concern to the university counsellor.

The recent setting up of NHS early psychosis intervention services for the crisis management of young people is very welcome, particularly as it seems that these sorts of incidents are most likely to occur during teenage years or early twenties and, if treated appropriately, can be ameliorated, preventing serious mental health problems later in adult life. Early intervention is an approach favoured in the NHS now to prevent longer-term high mental health costs arising. The local early psychosis intervention teams have given presentations to my university's counselling service in a bid to publicise the support that they can provide. This is especially important given the apparent increase in psychosis resulting from recreational drug use.

University counselling and psychotherapy is interesting and challenging work. We are often the unseen glue behind the scenes helping to keep the young people on-programme. University managers need to properly understand the vital role counselling services play in student retention. Personal one-to-one support and contact can often be the essential holding element that is missing when students are away from home.

Paula's story is interesting from two very specific viewpoints. First, she sets out the special practice issues that counsellors working in educational settings have to deal with. She is clearly responding beyond the basic psychotherapeutic needs of her clients and trying to help them cope with some major personal developmental issues in their lives. Second, it is clear from Paula's tale that she and her colleagues have to work well beyond the traditional counselling boundaries. They are bravely responding to an obvious need for them to assume a measure of pro-active responsibility for guiding and assisting their young clients in all aspects of their lives. It would appear that these educational counsellors have long bypassed the purist/realist therapist debate.

SUGGESTED FURTHER READING

Axline, V (1964, reprinted 1990) *Dibs: In search of self.* London: Penguin.

A warm and charming story of a real-life case – read this book.

Geldard, K and Geldard, D (2008) *Counselling Children: A practical introduction*, 3rd edition. London: Sage.

A useful book for those intending to specialise in working with children. Part 3, 'Skills', is excellent.

Lines, D (2006) *Brief Counselling in Schools.* London: Sage.

A helpful, 'workaday' book. Chapter 1 gives an excellent overview of this topic.

CHAPTER 9

Working in the
National Health Service

CORE KNOWLEDGE

- Counselling and psychotherapy services in the National Health Service (NHS) have grown largely in parallel with the growth of the NHS.

- Counselling in the NHS has two main functions:
  - providing an EAP service for staff;
  - providing treatments for patients.

- Counselling has had difficulty in finding a suitable niche for itself within the NHS hierarchy – this issue remains unresolved.

- Counsellors working in the NHS face issues over:
  - sharing information about patients;
  - working within imposed time limits;
  - working in a cost-effective manner;
  - working with imposed directives about how to treat clients.

- The Government's policies on *Improving Access to Psychological Therapies* are likely to bring about significant changes in counselling and psychotherapy service delivery within the NHS.

- Accounts of real-life NHS counselling (as told by real-life NHS therapists) suggest that counselling within the NHS has a number of significant differences from counselling as practised elsewhere.

INTRODUCTION

In one sense, it is obvious that the story of counselling and psychotherapy in the National Health Service (NHS) could not have possibly begun before 1948. How could it? Before 1948, there was no NHS. However, in another sense, it might be argued that the tale of the psychological therapies and public healthcare provision might actually have begun as far back as 1896. This was when Lightner Witmer (who had trained under the pioneering psychologist, Wilhelm Wundt, in Vienna) opened what was probably the world's first public-access psychological clinic at the University of

Pennsylvania. However, to begin with, those early-days psychologist-practitioners were not particularly interested in therapy as such. They were much more interested in investigating the technical applications of psychology to human behaviour and in promoting the academic study of psychology; they were not particularly bothered about being clinicians (Reisman, 1991). However, eventually, these psychological pioneers did make some tentative attempts at patient treatment when they experimented with what today we would probably call 'psycho-educational therapy'. In Witmer's clinic, the clinicians' usual treatment methods were mainly centred on trying to promote 'good mental health' by teaching 'correct' behaviours to patients whose lifestyles were supposedly deviant.

During the early days of mental health treatments, those advocating the use of clinical applications of psychology in patient care (especially in its later guises in the counselling and psychological therapies) faced many problems in becoming established within what then was a medical hierarchy that jealously guarded its status. In part, this was because the psychotherapies emphasised talking to, and respecting, the patient and this very much contradicted professional attitudes that were prevalent during the late nineteenth- and early twentieth-century practice of scientific medicine. Traditionally, there used to be a tendency among doctors to subjugate their patients (Moynihan, 1993). Patients were merely the carriers of the disease; they could play no part in helping their scientific 'saviours' to combat illness. Patients were there to be cured; they were not there to chat with their doctors.

Nevertheless, even in those early days, the importance of responding to the psychological health needs of patients was slowly beginning to be accepted. Some doctors were starting to listen to their patients. Slowly, things improved. For example, in 1920, the Tavistock Clinic, with its emphasis on doctor–patient dialogue and patient mental welfare, was established. In 1926, the Pioneer Health Centre in Peckham was set up to promote 'positive health consciousness' in partnership with its patients (Moynihan, 1993). Gradually, what was initially seen to be a form of 'mental hygiene', in which the patient played a constructive role, was viewed by more and more doctors as being an essential part of promoting patient well-being.

THE NATIONAL HEALTH SERVICE IS BORN

The year 1948 was momentous for patient care in the UK. This was the year in which the National Health Service (NHS) was launched into what was expected to be a brave, new, socially conscious, egalitarian, post-war world. From its very beginning, the NHS recognised that the universal provision of physiological/medical treatments for physical ailments was not enough to meet the needs of all its patients. Their levels of psychological 'fitness' also needed addressing. Therefore, plans were drawn up to ensure that mental health services became an essential part of the embryonic NHS.

To begin with, mental health provision within the NHS was what we would call today a second-tier function. It was rarely available at the local surgery. Patients accessed the then mental health services via their GPs, who referred them to specialist regional units. It was not until 1971 that the Isis Centre in Oxford opened the UK's first walk-in, locally accessible psychological health clinic, which included the provision of psychotherapy and coun-selling as part of its routine treatment menu. However, the reality is that the take-up of counselling throughout the NHS, and its recognition (at least in some quarters) as being a valid treatment option, took at least another 20 years. Indeed, some might argue that counselling has still not been fully accepted throughout the NHS culture.

Counselling has not found it easy to claim a respected place within the NHS healthcare professions. The medical world has been described by East (1995) as 'a tribal village society' that is often hostile to newcomers. It could be argued that the pioneer NHS counsellors were viewed with great suspicion by many in the NHS establishment who have zealously guarded their own professional empires. For example, in an article typical of its era, Harris (1994) claimed that, by including counselling as part of overall healthcare, the government 'may be turning its back on two centuries of careful and dedicated work by doctors' and 'we may be deserting medicine for magic'. Gradually, however, more positive views of counselling began to prevail among GPs. For example, Cocksedge (1997) strongly supported the inclusion of counselling, psychotherapy and psychological services as an everyday part of most GP practices. Counselling was gradually coming to find its place as one of a number of acceptable treatment choices on the public healthcare 'bill of fare' (Hemmings, 2000).

Initially, counselling appeared within the NHS in two main forms. In its first form, counsellors provided employee assistance programmes for NHS staff. However, there is no immediately obvious reason to assume that NHS workplace counselling is any different from any of the other forms of employee counselling that have already been discussed in Chapter 7. Therefore, in this chapter we can ignore that side of counselling's NHS story.

A different approach to treatment

Treating patients (the second main form of NHS counselling) began to develop as the counselling therapies started to become more and more available at many local GP surgeries. During the late 1990s, there was a huge expansion in counselling provision in primary care. This was fuelled in part by the GPs' growing frustration with the long waiting lists for the then

NHS specialist psychological services (Davies, 1997). Over time, these GP surgery-based counsellors gradually came to be seen not as merely being a second-class substitute for the supposedly specialist psychological services, but as a viable, alternative, professional healthcare provision. One great attraction of this new treatment approach was that it could be tailored to the immediate needs of individual patients. Another advantage was that it provided an on-demand and localised, patient-friendly service (Hemmings, 2000).

The newly emerging, primary care-based counselling treatments were mainly delivered by freelance counselling practitioners who were individually contracted to (or associated with) local GP practices. The local surgeries could use their then status as NHS fundholders to finance this counselling provision (Brennan and Hollanders, 2006). This particular method of providing counselling for their patients gave the GPs the marked advantages of local control and a direct ownership of the in-house counselling services that were working with their patients (Davidson, 2000). However, between 1997 and 2000, yet another of the NHS's policy changes reduced the GPs' fundholding powers, so much of the local funding for primary care counselling services began to disappear (Foster, 2000).

Counsellors versus psychologists

It is unfortunate that, over the years, the ups and downs of NHS funding for patient mental welfare services have sometimes served to exacerbate the rivalry that a vocal minority within the psychological services already felt towards the incoming counselling 'upstarts'. Clearly, a scarcity of funds will often tend to generate operational rivalries. Regrettably, it is also the case that, for some observers, the image of professional counsellors, especially those working from the voluntary sector, used to be that they were merely part-time, pin-money earning, middle-class 'do-gooders', who were only amusing themselves with an undemanding 'hobby' (Hudson-Allez, 1999). It is even arguable that, 20 or 30 years ago, such an evaluation might not always have been entirely groundless. This is certainly not the case today.

The negative assessments that some of the healthcare professions held about counsellors were worsened by the then scarcity of sound, practice-based evidence in support of the shorter-term mental health treatments, such as counselling or brief psychotherapy (Roth and Fonagy, 1996, etc.). It is also unfortunately arguable that the early disdain felt by some counselling therapists towards any sort of scientific enquiry into their work did not help counselling's case for demanding professional respect.

The debates and disputes between the psychologists and the counsellors have rumbled on. On the one hand, the psychologists seem to have at least conceded that there might be a case for using counsellors to help them with their excessive caseloads by taking on some of their apparently less demanding patients (Burton et al., 1995; Kemp and Thwaites, 1998). On the other hand, many counsellors still seem to be uncomfortable with many of the methodological and theoretical viewpoints advanced by their allegedly more 'scientific' therapeutic cousins. Green (1994) summarised the earlier territorial conflicts between the counsellors and the psychologists as being one in which the psychologists might grudgingly be prepared to allow counsellors to assist them with their work, if they were willing to offer low-grade support to selected patients, whereas the counsellors wanted to be recognised as independently skilled practitioners who were the psychologists' professional equals.

RECENT HISTORY

Over the last five years or so, the position of counselling within the NHS seems to have altered yet again. Reviews of funding and management policies have resulted in changes in the ways in which counsellors are employed in primary care. The tendency now is for health authorities to purchase and manage counselling services through the primary care groups or community trusts (Davidson, 2000). This has changed the status of counsellors based in GP surgeries from being independent operators to being established as part of the overall NHS structure. Indeed, nowadays, many of the originally independent counsellors have actually become NHS employees.

The result of these changes in their employment conditions has been to create professional demands on primary-care counsellors that some of their still independent colleagues (especially those practising outside the NHS) might find unacceptable. Is it possible that the NHS counselling culture inevitably clashes with some of the traditionally held beliefs about what constitutes ethically sound therapeutic practice? For example, conflicts might arise if externally imposed time constraints or instructions from GPs about how to treat patients clash with the high value that many counsellors place on their professional independence and their ability to offer their clients creative and unhurried help. Other conflicts might arise for counsellors who strictly guard patient confidentiality, when they are confronted by the NHS need for patient information to be held in common within any of the care teams.

Paying close attention to some of the admirable (but regrettably idealistic) traditional counselling scruples may not always be possible in the context of a professionally managed, frantically busy NHS, with its waiting lists, its demands for rapid responses and, above all, its insistence on cost-effective results. Traditionally trained counsellors who find themselves undertaking primary care work might find that they are exposed to 'culture shock'. This can hit them as soon as they encounter the full force of NHS organisational bureaucracy and the pressure to work within certain national policy guidelines, for which they may feel no particular sense of ownership. NHS counsellors are also required to be responsible for their professional practices, and to be publicly accountable for these practices, within the overall NHS structure – 'It is crucial that the professional standards developed nationally continue to be responsive to changing service needs and to legitimate public expectations' (Department of Health, 1997). The NHS is a robust, demanding, organisationally driven, performance-demanding world for which few, if any, counsellor training courses prepare their graduates.

PRACTITIONER REFLECTIONS – TINA GRAHAM

A GP surgery counsellor's story

Parking up, I'm immediately thinking about who I'm seeing first today. My nine o'clock is an intelligent woman with high motivation. A pleasure to work with and indeed I know that the session will very likely flow with ease. She has good insight regarding her life and particularly her personal development.

Reviewing my caseload is so important for us here within the NHS, to manage not just the business of it but also the diversity and demands of each individual who accesses the service. This can be a challenge in itself. That's why my next client, on this particular day, is more demanding. She needs more from me than my first client does in terms of her own ability to see herself in her situation. I have to work hard at keeping her focused. She needs lots of reassurance and time to go over her issues and problems at length. Her pace is very different from that of my first client.

Entering the building I greet my colleagues – nurses, receptionists, doctors, secretaries – as I climb the stairs to my room. First things first: answer phone messages – a couple of queries and a cancellation. Next stop: visit my in-tray and look at the new referrals that have come from the GPs, health visitor and the practice nurses. This counselling service usually has at least ten referrals a week with a client uptake of about 60 per cent.

I enter my room and flick the 'engaged' sign over; I shut the door and hope for a little bit of quiet time before work proper begins. If I have made good time on my journey to work, I make a few phone calls; otherwise I adjust the chairs, reach for the clock and the tissues, place them accordingly and open my filing cabinet. Reading my client notes and having time to reflect upon previous work before sessions is enormously important and useful – I make sure I'm back in the picture and story of each client before their arrival. I review the work to date, think about what the clients might benefit from, intervention-wise, or indeed cast my mind back to clinical supervision discussions.

I fire up my PC and log into my sessions for the day. It saves a wasted trip downstairs as the patients here check in with reception before I collect them. The work is very varied; a typical morning like the one outlined above is the norm. Sometimes I only see two clients before lunchtime, but mostly I will see three clients. I prefer to do the bulk of my clinical work before lunch as I often notice my energy levels depleting in the afternoon. Again, it depends upon my client cases, but I generally try to scatter them so that my more needy, less motivated, clients are interspaced with my more motivated ones. It's a juggling act at times and it is not always possible to do this as we do try our best here to accommodate people who are late and slot them in at the times they are best able to attend. Demands upon us have certainly increased with the implementation of the *Improving Access to Psychological Therapies* paperwork. We have had, as colleagues, to negotiate the best ways forward as far as the data collection. There have been battles with the local health trust not only for our jobs, but also as far as how and what data is needed from our clients.

I try to go out for a walk at lunchtime and just revitalise myself and freshen myself up for the afternoon's work. After my lunch, I usually come back to more messages or an urgent referral that has come hot off the press from the secretaries. Often I might need to have a chat with or visit from a concerned GP about a patient. Working together as a team is so very important; it's a vital part of working in an integrated NHS service. There is a team confidentiality that can at times be very useful, especially when we are holding some very fragile patients. Contact with the GP helps to bring in appropriate higher-intensity interventions should they become necessary. Discussion about the effectiveness of medication can be conveyed between counsellor and GP – with the GP possibly reconsidering a medication if things haven't improved for a patient.

My colleague knocks on my door with a concerned look – 'Can you spare a minute?' Nodding, I usher her in and close the door. She is reviewing a referral and has concerns as the patient is 30 weeks pregnant, and has been placed on an antidepressant. We both query this decision and wonder how best to approach the GP concerned as we are wondering about the thinking behind this decision. She leaves and, by chance, another of our GPs appears and he's in a buoyant mood. We exchange small talk and I gently broach the subject and ask for his technical knowledge reference the referral. He clarifies the position for me and tells me about the drug companies and the research into medication, the stage of development of the baby and how the potential for developmental harm is minimal now the gestation period is coming to an end. He explains how the foetus is fully formed at 26 weeks and we have a discussion over balancing the patient's emotional needs with minimising harm to the baby. It's a very informative conversation and settles my mind as to the decisions and reminds me of the responsibilities GPs have to undertake every day. I thank him for his time and input as it's helped me to develop my own knowledge a little bit further. I convey the conversation to my colleague and return to my afternoon's work.

> I see another two clients and I make sure my notes are all up to scratch. I shut my filing cabinet. I think over my day and the interventions and the people I have encountered. This is a typical day and other days might appear much the same on the surface, at least the structure might, aside from days when I supervise the two volunteers we have here. What's never the same is the diversity and the challenges that each new client brings to me; the developments and difficulties I face as I try to help people move forward never stop being unique. The reality is that each day in the life of a GP surgery counsellor is actually a one-off.

DO NHS COUNSELLORS WORK DIFFERENTLY?

There are those who would argue that NHS counselling, particularly counselling in primary care settings, might be heading towards becoming a distinct psychotherapeutic profession in its own right (Hudson-Allez, 2000). This argument is further supported by the observation that many counsellors, including those working in GP surgeries, often appear to end up practising in similar ways to each other despite their probably having originally come from different training backgrounds or initially claiming allegiance to differing counselling schools (Mearns, 1999, etc.).

Workload

At first sight, the overt differences between working in a GP surgery and, say, working in private practice or perhaps in some parts of the voluntary sector are obvious. The private practitioner can elect to offer clients an unhurried, time-generous service that is delivered in a calm and discreet environment. Private clients can choose to have as many counselling sessions as seems appropriate. Private practice counsellors can decide for themselves when they should engage in reflection and personal or professional development (as indeed ideally should all counsellors). In addition, such private practitioners can opt to include sufficient time for administrative matters as a routine part of their normal working day. However, the counsellor working in the maelstrom of a busy GP surgery has a very different set of working experiences. There is often a hurried, even harried, working environment, lots of people around, hustle and bustle, and a never-ending demand for the counsellor's time. The amount of time available to treat each patient is limited and there is rarely, if any, time available between sessions for reflection or personal development. NHS counselling is usually time-limited and clients do not usually get more than six sessions with their counsellors.

Outside the NHS, a seven-hour working day probably involves about four hours of actual face-to-face client time, with a recommended weekly limit of some 18–20 client hours (BACP, 2008). This leaves ample time available for administrative tasks, reading and research. However, in primary care, a seven-hour working day will often involve at least six, and sometimes even seven, face-to-face counselling sessions and very often includes a need to fit in an urgent or emergency additional referral as well (in some way or another). Somehow the relevant paperwork also has to be squeezed into this overly crowded working day, usually by the counsellor working 'voluntary' overtime. NHS counsellors in full-time posts could be providing upwards of 30 client sessions every working week. This is a formidable, even daunting, workload. There is very little 'surplus' time for anything else, unless the counsellor is prepared to allocate some private time to such professional demands as reading, reflection and clinical casework discussions with colleagues. It seems that, in NHS counselling as actually practised, there can often be a huge gap between the real and the ideal.

Confidentiality

Client confidentiality is another area of potential divergence between NHS counselling and counselling in other settings. The general counselling ethical maxim that nothing goes outside the counselling room without the client's express consent simply does not apply in NHS settings, where team confidentiality is the order of the day. The referring doctors often require feedback and counsellors may well wish to discuss the overall care of some patients with the relevant GPs. After all, it is always possible that the counsellor might obtain some vital information from the patient that the doctor needs to know. It is also possible that the counsellor might be able to offer some useful advice about the patient's general treatment package to the surgery medical team. (These sorts of complications were compellingly set out earlier in this chapter in Tina's Practitioner Reflections.)

Such clear limitations to counsellor–client confidentiality are further compromised by the ever-increasing legal requirements on all counsellors to disclose certain information about their clients to the authorities. So far, this list includes drugs trafficking, child abuse, terrorism and money laundering, and doubtlessly it will be expanded over time. Taking all these factors into account strongly suggests that NHS counsellors need to develop a new, possibly independent, ethical code – one that takes context and law into account while at the same time protecting both the counsellors and the clients. Some attempts to resolve this issue have been made, although proposals for a comprehensive solution are likely to be debated for some time to come.

No doubt, counsellors who are already practising in the NHS would be able to highlight yet more areas of difference, or even conflict, between their mode of counselling and that as practised by other counsellors in other contexts. It is also very likely that there are more differences yet to be identified. Therefore, it seems arguable that NHS counselling approaches might eventually come to diverge permanently from other forms of counselling in a number of significant ways. Whether these professional differences need only to be procedural within certain contexts, or whether they indicate fundamental changes in professional approaches to client care, will no doubt cause yet another intense, ongoing debate between counselling's pragmatists and counselling's purists.

PRACTITIONER REFLECTIONS – BARBARA ALLEN

Counselling and psychotherapy in an NHS primary care mental health team

In my particular NHS area, there is no primary care counselling service. We have a primary care mental health team, which is a multidisciplinary team made up of nurses, occupational therapists and counsellors and, although I trained as an integrative counsellor, I am employed as a mental health practitioner. This team was developed in 2002 as a direct response to the recommendations of the National Service Framework for Mental Health. Despite our different professional orientations we have identical roles, assessing patients within GP surgeries, signposting them to other services or, if appropriate, providing a flexible number of brief therapeutic interventions. There is no exact limit to the number of sessions provided. 'Brief counselling' in this instance means as few, or as many, sessions as are needed as long as the patient problems or issues are manageable and meet the criteria of the primary care remit. Patients are never 'discharged' from our service in the same way as patients are never 'discharged' by their GPs.

Like my colleagues, all my experience has been within the primary and secondary care mental health service. There are some similarities, and also some fundamental differences, in the way we work. In other words, rather like the various schools of psychotherapy, we do the same job but differently. These differences sometimes become apparent during our weekly peer supervision sessions. We may use different language for core concepts, which, when discussed, reveal a shared understanding. With this weekly supervision we have cultivated a transdisciplinary approach, exchanging views and expertise, thereby enhancing individual core skills.

The workload leans heavily towards assessments at which a decision must be made as to the mental state/health of the patients and whether our service is able to meet their needs. This means that assessment skills are of paramount importance. Rapport and relationship building, and the use of perception and intuition during information gathering are essential parts of our work. Referral to secondary care services is a possibility. However, it is necessary for certain criteria to be met in order to warrant such a referral and it is often the case that the primary care patients are not considered to be 'ill enough' to warrant referral. Despite this, they have presented to our service suffering some form of mental 'dis-ease' and often in need of professional services in order to ease their distress.

This means that, although I am a counsellor, I often find myself working in ways that may be at odds with some of the more orthodox approaches to counselling. This causes some tension and challenges to my own core beliefs. For instance, although I usually note information during assessment and subsequent sessions, brief factual details and significant information is logged straight on to the computer system within the GP surgery and handwritten information is destroyed. Patients are alerted to this fact from the outset and are also informed of the limits to confidentiality in respect of harm to self or others. The breaking of confidentiality in order to protect others has sometimes felt very uncomfortable dynamically, but if a patient does disclose information (for example, regarding abuse they have suffered) and indicates that others may also be a risk, I have a duty of care to report such risks.

At the end of each session it is necessary for the patient to contact my office in order to book a further appointment. This means I do not have control of my own diary and, if the patient decides not to book a further appointment, I have no recourse for follow-up. The GP would, of course, be aware (via the computer system) that the patient has chosen not to engage and would either re-refer or contact secondary services if deemed appropriate at that time.

Due to the waiting list and volume of patients seen, it is often four weeks (at least) between appointments. In order to meet the needs of a large number of patients, we organise and make good use of other interventions such as workshops and groups, as well as providing self-help material in the form of booklets (bibliotherapy).

At assessment I may identify that a patient would benefit from attending one of our psycho-educational workshops on anxiety, mood management or assertion before seeing me for a follow-up appointment. Each workshop is a one-off educational session lasting three hours, run by an occupational therapist and a counsellor. It may be that the patient could benefit from reading a publication specific to their particular difficulty. We have an arrangement with the local library service whereby they administer the loans and renewals of books available on a 'book prescription', which we are able to provide. Following attendance at the workshop or reading a selection of publications, I find the patient often returns for further appointments having gained some insight, learned helpful coping strategies or recognised issues they feel might be beneficial to explore.

I think these interventions can sometimes provide worthwhile time-saving shortcuts for the motivated patient. I am aware that use of such materials may cause some to feel this is a complete abandonment of a counselling approach. However, the building of the therapeutic relationship and developing a client–counsellor working alliance is, I feel, of greater importance. This is especially so when such emphasis is placed on the patient's ability to engage in such activity and can be helpful in allowing the patient to own their recovery and realise their own power to implement change.

For some patients with less capacity for insight, or for some appropriately motivated patients, it might be beneficial to employ a more CBT approach and I make good use of homework sheets and session formats when working with some anxious or depressed patients. Sometimes, when embarking on such a programme, it is beneficial to see patients weekly for the first few sessions. I have discovered that, when the patient has an understanding of the principle of using homework sheets to challenge their negative auto-matic thoughts or to modify behaviour, it is possible to squeeze half-hour sessions in at the end of my surgery to monitor progress and set new goals. They may then make use of workshops following this in order to make further gains.

I have found it helpful to adopt a flexible approach to try to accom-modate the vast variety of presenting problems and provide whatever the patients need to help them on their road to recovery. The approach is driven by the patient, not by theory. Time is a commodity in short supply and I (like all counsellors) always hold in mind the importance of every therapeutic hour spent with each patient and so we maximise opportunities.

PRACTITIONER REFLECTIONS – ALEXANDRA BOSSMAN

Counselling and psychotherapy in an NHS secondary care mental health team

I am a specialist counsellor and I work in NHS secondary services, which can be also defined as the acute or emergency part of treatment offered to patients who need mental healthcare. It is distinct from primary services, as patients will be referred in and discharged out once treatment is completed. Referrals come from all the other sectors of the health services, although GPs refer the greatest proportion. It is also a more specialist end of the care spectrum and those needing interventions will have complex needs and often will have more than one diagnosis. They may be in crisis and require admis-sion. They may be in crisis and not require admission, but can potentially be managed at home by crisis intervention teams. Patients may be frequent service users or presenting for the first time and they may have more than one clinician offering support to them.

Our team is called Community Mental Health and we are a multi-disciplinary group comprising psychiatrists, clinical psychologists, community psychiatric nurses, social workers, psychological therapists, counsellors, support workers and psychotherapists. We have a team meeting once a week where patients will be discussed and treatment options defined, because it is not unusual for patients to need the support of each specialism. Essentially, psychiatry will be responsible for medication and diagnosis, although not exclusively; social care matters such as housing or benefits will be managed by either the nurses or social workers, and therapy will be undertaken by potentially all of us in some form.

So what therapy is on offer? Patients once referred into secondary care must be seen within 18 weeks (Department of Health, 2004 – 'No one will have to wait longer than 18 weeks from GP referral to hospital treatment'). Given the downward pressure to see patients as soon as we can, interventions are governed by time too. Generally, patients are offered 20 sessions of one-to-one therapy or one year of the same. The therapies on offer are cognitive-analytic therapy, cognitive-behavioural therapy, psychodynamic counselling, gestalt therapy, psychoanalytical approaches and systemic psychotherapy with couples/families. Currently, we are developing group work approaches and these will be either educationally oriented, where symptoms are discussed and thought about (obsessive and compulsive disorders, for example), or more therapeutically oriented, where group processes drive the recovery of individuals. There is also a dialectical therapy group, which offers a mixture of skills and therapy for those with personality disorders (borderline disorder in particular). Just to add to the complexity of this team, very often nurses and social workers undertake additional training and are able to offer therapy as well as their other skills. In addition, some of the psychiatrists also practise as therapists.

Assessment and treatment – who decides?

When patients are referred there will be a referral letter, which will outline the symptoms, current medications, risks of self-harm and general life situations. These case narratives will be discussed by a group consisting of managers and clinicians and together they evaluate how best a patient can be helped. If the therapy route is chosen, patients will be allocated to a therapist for assessment for psychological mindedness, and this process will be carried out in depth and sometimes over a number of meetings. This represents two main aspects. First, a good, thorough assessment enables both parties to really think about what therapy will be about and how prepared patients are to think about change. Second, for some people this might be the first time they have had the opportunity to tell the whole story and feel that the facts and the emotions attached to these events have been truly understood. Doing this may be therapeutic in itself and sometimes a choice is made at this point not to continue with further work.

Counselling at this point is very specific and usually focused on one or two key areas that will have been identified at assessment. Although I will not specifically be asked to diagnose, I will be looking for symptoms or features that may suggest where the main area of difficulty may lie.

My work pattern is to offer therapy as a contract on which both therapist and patient collaborate. It is not something that I just do to them. We will talk about timings of appointments, and how we might expect to see the impact of them. For instance, we would acknowledge the possibility that there might be an increase in distress symptoms initially and we discuss what that could mean. This is a form of rehearsal for the therapy itself and it is helpful for patients to be able to imagine what the reality of this type of work is. For instance, if someone is attending therapy and becomes upset, they might want to think about how they handle that on an ongoing basis. Furthermore, we will discuss how they might manage a crisis. Who would they ring and what other resources might they have at their disposal? Confidentiality is an issue that will be discussed. The NHS is a bureaucracy and has paperwork that is an essential requirement legally, and also there are psychological tools for measuring change in the patients' perceptions and thus gaining an indication of how therapy may have helped them. Paperwork of this type is usually done at the first session, at a midway point, and at the end. Therefore, the level of confidentiality that a patient can expect is not what it might be if one was a sole practitioner in private practice.

In the NHS, we have legal obligations and responsibilities as well as the usual ethical and clinical dilemmas. However, notwithstanding this, I will ensure patients understand how confidentiality works for them. If I need to speak to another clinician, the psychiatrist say, about medication, I will ask permission first. Alternatively, I will encourage the patient to speak for themselves if there is an issue. There is also an electronic data recording system and I will record meeting times and, if there is a clinical need, extra information regarding the patient's mental health. This is necessary if patients are actively suicidal and needing extra help from crisis services. I may be asked to attend discharge planning meetings for patients if they have had an admission locally or perhaps have been referred to a specialist eating disorder unit. Here, again, confidentiality is negotiated and therapy is seen as a piece of work that dovetails with others, and is more like an integrative model at this point.

As well as working as an individual therapist, I am also one half of a team that offers systemic couple/family therapy. We see couples or families who again may be referred by GPs or perhaps from within secondary services. A typical day for me (if there is such a thing) will involve four or five therapy sessions and then the necessary paperwork, liaison with other health professionals and attending meetings if required to do so. Living and working in a rural area, there is also a component of travelling to and from various bases, where we see those who prefer to be seen in their communities.

WHERE NHS COUNSELLING IS TODAY

Despite all the historical wrangling about the rightful place of counselling in the NHS, it seems that, by 2000, at least 50 per cent of all GP practices had some sort of access to a counsellor (Mellor-Clark et al., 2001). A major reason why this was necessary was that GPs were (and probably still are) spending up to 30 per cent of their working week dealing with patients' mental and emotional health problems. Much of this workload was (and probably still is) centred on anxiety, depression and apparently psycho-somatic conditions (Davidson, 2000). As it is very likely that this wide range of mental health problems originated from an equally wide range of causes, it seems reasonable to assume that no one method (or school) of counselling therapy would be universally applicable. One size would almost certainly not fit all. Therefore, primary care counsellors are developing a wide range of therapeutic skills and techniques in order to meet these very varying demands. We can see clear evidence of the essential need for an innovative multi-school approach in all three Practitioner Reflections.

NHS counsellors and psychotherapists are continually required to demon-strate that their skills and techniques are likely to be successful in the treatment of their patients. Fortunately, modern research (Elliot et al., 2008; Stiles et al., 2006; Ward et al., 2008, and many others) indicates that counselling and psychotherapy is indeed cost-effective and of provable efficacy for the care of the psychologically disturbed. Not only that, but mega-studies such as that of Brettle et al. (2008) specifically support the notion that counselling is an economically justified, valid treatment choice for primary care patients who suffer with non-specific, generic psycho-logical problems. This study indicates that counselling is as equally effective as are all other treatment modalities and, probably most importantly of all, is likely to be equally cost-effective. On the surface this might be an argument for claiming that counselling's place within a modern NHS has been established. However, modern developments (such as the Govern-ment's *Improving Access to Psychological Therapies* policy) seem to favour the possible, even probable, dominance of CBT within the NHS's counselling and psychotherapy services.

As CBT and similar 'rapid-fire' therapies are likely to be delivered by speedily trained psychological 'technicians', the whole question of counselling's professional status has been put back on the table. These issues are further discussed in the next section of this book – Part 4: Where is counselling & psychotherapy going?

ACTIVITY 9.1

Set out your own ideas and make some notes about these questions:

- What can counsellors and psychotherapists offer the NHS that other healthcare practitioners cannot?
- How could counselling and psychotherapy evolve to 'fit' the evolving NHS?
- How could the NHS develop such that it could make better use of the specific skills that counsellors and psychotherapists can bring to patient care?

SUGGESTED FURTHER READING

Bryant Jeffries, R (2005) *Workplace Counselling in the NHS*. Abingdon: Oxford University Press.

This is a specialist text for those with a particular interest in this topic.

Department of Health (2008) *Improving Access to Psychological Therapies Implementation Plan: National guidelines for regional delivery*. Crown copyright. Available online at www.dh.gov.uk (accessed Summer 2009).

Again, this is for those with a specialist interest.

Tempest, M (2006) *The Future of the NHS*. St Albans: XPL Publishing.

An informative text, but one that needs to be read in conjunction with all the rapidly emerging online NHS publications.

PART 4

WHERE IS COUNSELLING & PSYCHOTHERAPY GOING?

CHAPTER 10

Counselling & psychotherapy – the next story

CORE KNOWLEDGE

- The statutory regulation of the psychological therapies is imminent.

- Regulation will be controlled by the Health Professions Council (HPC).

- Regulation might separate counselling and psychotherapy into two different professions.

- Regulation will probably result in a new set of *Standards of Proficiency* for both counsellors and psychotherapists.

- Regulation might result in counsellors and psychotherapists having different levels of professional qualifications.

- The talking therapies might well evolve as a degree-based profession.

- The Government's current policies within the NHS are emphasising the alleged superiority of cognitive-behavioural therapy.

- The counsellors of the future might evolve as 'supershrinks', who are able to work in whatever ways are necessary, or they might become sector specialists, each with a unique service to offer.

- Every therapist, from trainee to the leadership, can and should have something to say about how their profession should, or could, develop.

REGULATING THE PROFESSIONAL THERAPIST – THE DEBATE

In many ways it could be argued that the co-disciplines of counselling and psychotherapy are already established as professional occupations. After all, together they already have their own discrete body of knowledge (professional discourse) – one that is well established at all levels of higher education and academic scholarship and supported by peer-reviewed research. However, the talking therapies do currently lack what some would claim to be two of the other essential attributes of a high-level calling. First, therapists in the UK have no official status; they have no established professional recognition. Second, they do not have a centrally authorised, nationally approved, minimum standard of practitioner training and certi-fication. There are no officially established UK performance thresholds that clients could (or should) expect from their therapists.

Precisely what it is that turns a 'job' into a 'profession' is open to argument. For some, this process necessarily involves regulation and enforceable discipline, whereas for others it is an attitude of mind. The imminent statutory regulation of counselling and psychotherapy is bringing these sorts of disputes to the fore throughout the talking therapies. Of course, as with most contested issues in psychotherapy, the concept of professional-isation attracts passionate argument. It is a wide-ranging debate that includes disputes over the basic purposes of counselling and psychotherapy, together with disagreement about desirable qualification levels, perform-ance standards, quality controls, ethics and many other equally contentious issues.

The 'against' argument

On the anti-regulation side are the many practitioners who would argue that professionalisation and regulation would effectively 'kill' the talking therapies (Shannon, 2009, for example). This is because they see such processes as effectively being 'anti-therapy'. Many of these anti-regulationists claim that, if therapy is confined within defined limits, it cannot encompass the whole of the human psyche and experience. For example, the newly established (April 2009) Alliance for Counselling and Psychotherapy Against State Regulation (**www.allianceforcandp.org**) argues that official regulation would fatally reduce client choice and inappropriately medicalise the therapist's calling. The Alliance also argues that there is no evidence to support claims that regulation might bring desirable operational or practical benefits (public respect, interdisciplinary recognition, accountability, etc.) to the therapy trade. Many of regulation's dissenters particularly object to the plan to use the Health Professions Council (HPC) as the regulatory body. They believe that the HPC does not have the appropriate expertise. Such objectors would claim that only therapists can understand the needs of therapists. Gladstone (2008) sums up many of their arguments by calling therapy regulation 'illusory, unethical and hazardous'.

For many of the anti-regulationists, counselling and psychotherapy are art forms that cannot be given any official restrictions and so cannot be constrained. Many of the anti-regulationists claim that therapy is beyond discipline. It is a 'way of being' rather than a 'way of knowing'. They say that psychological counselling is a freestyle approach to people and their needs. It cannot be a proficiency-based activity based on a measurable set of aptitudes, abilities and techniques. This, they say, means that therapy is a personal approach to psychological well-being; it is an attitude that is gradually acquired rather than a definable skill that can be systematically taught.

Another major concern for many of those opposing counselling's professionalisation is their belief that regulation would improperly award power and expertise to the therapist. These dissenting theorists argue that therapists and their clients should be equally authoritative, equally knowledgeable and equally responsible co-explorers in their therapeutic worlds. Therefore, they claim that the potential personal authority and status that professionalisation could possibly confer on therapy's practitioners would destroy such an equality-based, interpersonal power balance. For example, Proctor (2008) argues that 'professionalisation and regulation will lead to therapy as an increasingly elite profession, bolstering claims to expert knowledge through university accredited courses and gatekeeping entry'.

The 'for' argument

The supporters of professionalisation and regulation argue that the public would be better served by an officially recognised therapeutic profession. Many such pro-regulationists would argue that, were the perceived status of the counselling professions to increase, so too would the quality and dependability of the therapy provisions and services available to the public. This, they argue, would come about because high-status professions have an imperative to disconnect from inadequate 'fellow travellers'. Therefore, the supposedly negative outcomes that Proctor (2008) suggests might result from regulation are seen by the pro-regulationists as actually being very positive and very desirable. They want official recognition, respect and status for their calling. They want control. The pro-regulationists argue that the currently unfettered and unmonitored proliferation of therapies and therapists only serves to confuse the public and to expose clients to exploitation. Many pro-regulationists might also argue that the lack of an authoritative regulatory body weakens consumer protection and means that there is no provision for the disciplining of underperforming practitioners. In addition, many pro-regulationists also claim that the public has a right to demand that all therapists will have undertaken some form of nationally accepted standards of education and training. It is certainly true that no such standards currently exist.

Some modern practitioners support therapy's probable imminent regulation on the grounds that they expect it to promote what they see as being some very desirable higher levels of professional services and responsibilities. In a typical example, Kierski (2009) interviewed four very eminent psychotherapeutic practitioner-theorists (Emmy van Deurzen, Holly Connolly, Alan Frankland and Elizabeth Campbell). Collectively, they supported regulation of the talking therapies. All four argued that regulation will lead to enhanced public confidence in counselling and promote better and more rigorous standards of practice. Aldridge (2009) argues that there is no evidence that regulation will (as some claim) destroy creativity or therapist autonomy. She also rejects the argument that regulation will enforce unnecessary or unethical professional limitations or practice boundaries. Aldridge refers to the seemingly beneficial effects that regulation has had on art therapy as a practical example of the positive side of controlled professionalisation.

Freedom or repression?

It is possible that much of the 'for and against' war currently being fought over the statutory regulation and professionalisation of counselling and psychotherapy is simply a reprise of similar battles that took place at earlier times in other professions prior to their eventual or imminent statutory regulation (nursing, teaching, social work, etc.). In one sense, these debates could be seen as just being particular versions of the 'nanny state' versus 'personal licence' arguments that have long existed and that still create widespread dispute within society generally. The main thrust of society's pro-regulators (in earlier times and now) seems to target an alleged need to protect the public, to set out service/performance benchmarks, to drive up professional standards and to enhance practitioner status. The main thrust of the anti-regulators (then and now) seems to be concerned with worries about the potential diminished levels of innovation/creativity and practitioner autonomy that might arise if the freedom of professional practitioners is in anyway curtailed. So, both in the world as a whole and in psychotherapy in particular, when does freedom become anarchy? Alternatively, when does regulation become repression? Can anyone be sure?

REGULATING THE PROFESSIONAL THERAPIST – THE REALITY

The 'pro and con' therapy regulation argument rages. It will probably do so for the foreseeable future. However, in recent years, the inevitability of state intervention in the direction of the talking therapies has come to be more and more accepted as a likely political reality. As a result, the main UK bodies concerned with psychotherapy and psychological therapies (including, principally, the British Association for Counselling and Psychotherapy (BACP), the United Kingdom Council for Psychotherapy (UKCP) and the British Psychological Society (BPS)) moved to a position whereby they have accepted (in some quarters very reluctantly) that regulation is going to happen. Indeed, for the psychologists, statutory regulation is already happening.

Nevertheless, the organisations claiming to speak for the UK's talking therapies have continued to quarrel with the government about the methods to be employed (see accounts by Aldridge, 2006; Aldridge and Pollard, 2005). In particular, they objected to the proposal that the HPC should be the national regulatory body for the psychotherapeutic professions. As a result, a Representative Group of nine of the main organisations involved with the provision of psychological therapies in the UK was set up (BPS, 2006). The Representative Group collectively accepted the need for regulation, although they rejected the Government's proposal that the HPC should be the regulator. They wanted therapist regulation to be undertaken by an independent 'Psychological Professions Council', which would, in some ways, have mimicked the UK's General Medical Council. As Miller (2006) put it, 'our proposal for a new Independent Regulator . . . developed because we regard the HPC route as unworkable . . . regulation via the HPC would be disastrous'. The Representative Group's underlying premise, that therapists are best regulated if they are *self*-regulated, was not accepted by the Government. Equally importantly, the Group's argument that, if regulation must come about, the HPC should not be the regulator, has also been firmly rejected.

To all intents and purposes, the apparently irresolvable debate about professionalising the therapy trade is increasingly irrelevant. Unless there is a radical change in Government policy, the pro-regulationists have won. The fact is that, although many within the therapy profession will continue to dissent, the Government is actively arranging for the statutory regulation of the psychological therapies to be carried out under the remit of the HPC. Furthermore, the Government has announced its intention to expedite the statutory regulation of the counselling and psychotherapy professions. Ministers have also stated that they are firmly against the proliferation of regulatory bodies and have ruled out the possibility of creating a separate Psychological Professions Council.

The Government's current intentions are that counselling will become an HPC-regulated profession during 2011 (Pointon, 2008). The HPC has set up an advisory Professional Liaison Group (PLG), chaired by Professor Diane Waller. The PLG has now made its recommendations to the HPC. In turn, the HPC will now advise the Government. The PLG has recommended (subject to public consultation) that:

- counsellors and psychotherapists should be on different registers from each other;
- certain professional titles (counsellor, psychotherapist, etc.) should be legally protected;
- practitioners currently registered with certain existing voluntary bodies (BACP, UKCP, etc.) should be automatically transferred to the new statutory register;
- certain currently unregistered practitioners should be eligible for HPC registration through a 'grandparenting' scheme;

- registered counsellors should have attained an academic award at National Qualifications Framework (NQF) Level 5 (HE diploma, Year 2 honours degree; foundation degree);
- registered psychotherapists will need an NQF Level 7 (master's degree) qualification.

It is expected that following the HPC report to the Government the appropriate statutory orders will swiftly follow. It seems likely, therefore, that regulation will come about some time before 2012. Clearly, the eventual nature and style of the statutory orders will be of vital concern to everybody in the talking therapies. They will profoundly affect the personal therapy trade for years to come. Whatever the outcomes of the next few months, the HPC's recommendations and the Government's conclusions will shape the prospects for most of personal therapy's practitioners for the foreseeable future. At the time of writing, no one can say with any certainty what sorts of people, with what sorts of backgrounds, education or training tomorrow's therapy practitioners will be. We do not know how they will be officially recognised. We do not know where they will be working. We can only guess at what sorts of services they will be offering to what sorts of clients. Today's therapists do indeed seem to be living in 'interesting times'.

REFLECTION POINT

- Would any of therapy's great thinkers and innovators have been able to develop their ideas had they been subject to statutory regulation?
- Statutory regulation of counselling and psychotherapy – the 'nanny state' at its worst or a safeguard for an often vulnerable group of clients?

TRAINING THE PROFESSIONAL THERAPIST – IDENTIFYING THE GAPS

As we know, there are no officially recognised training schemes or qualification standards for counsellors and psychotherapists (except in the particular case of certain chartered psychologists). The situation is that, at present, anybody, apparently qualified or not, can call themselves a counsellor or a psychotherapist. As a result, people claiming to have the necessary expertise to offer some sort of talking therapy can, and do, have all sorts of backgrounds and training (spurious or curious), or even none at all. Just look in any of the local directories under 'Counselling and Advice' or 'Psychotherapy'. You will find all sorts of people claiming to be therapists, ranging from the weird and wonderful to those who, at least on the surface, appear to be adequately or appropriately qualified. Even those who seem to be among the better qualified (according to their adverts at least) have huge variations in their actual training levels that range from basic six-week introductory courses to postgraduate degrees. The simple truth is that, at present, anyone looking for a therapist is very much in danger of 'buying a pig in a poke'.

There are, of course, a number of voluntary organisations in the UK that claim to represent, and in some ways qualify, various groupings of counsellors and psychotherapists (chartered psychologists excepted). Probably the most widely known of these more or less nationally accepted bodies are the British Assocation for Counselling and Psychotherapy (BACP) and the United Kingdom Council for Psychotherapy (UKCP). However, only a minority of those offering personal therapy in the UK are actually BACP accredited or UKCP registered or have equivalent endorsements (COSCA – Scotland, etc.). This is an unfortunate state of affairs because it helps to maintain the currently woeful lack of consumer protection. However, even the professional policing of practitioners who do choose to be BACP/UKCP or similarly accredited remains limited. Neither the BACP nor the UKCP, nor any of the other voluntary therapy organisations, has any statutory teeth. They can only refuse to endorse defective practitioners, they cannot stop them practising.

It is also the case that neither the BACP nor the UKCP takes on the task of directly training those of their members who they might eventually recognise as being 'proper' therapists. In all cases they apparently leave this job to the various training organisations that each of these two professional associations has deemed to have achieved Approved Training Establishment status. It is, of course, true that the content and circumstances of the training offered by any of the BACP/UKCP-approved training organisations have to meet some very specific, openly published criteria. In the case of the BACP, these criteria are set out in its *Accreditation of Training Courses* (2009), informally known as the 'Gold Book'. In the case of the UKCP, its minimum training criteria are set out in the *UKCP Standards of Education and Training* (2008). Broadly speaking, both sets of criteria tend to be somewhat in line with each other.

It is clearly arguable that learning to conform to the BACP/UKCP criteria might be an admirable ambition for aspiring talking therapists, but is such an attainment actually sufficient to qualify them to practise? One potential educational weakness in both these training schemes is typified by the UKCP's 2009 website statement that 'Psychotherapy is both an art and a science and as such it is not possible to identify purely objective methods to assess an individual's readiness to practice' (**www.psychotherapy.org.uk**). In other words, it seems that both of these professional bodies set out some extremely desirable (although arguably limited) aims for training therapists, but neither sets out specific directions on how to achieve these targets. Furthermore, neither body apparently defines any nationally agreed benchmarks against which the students' accomplishments might be measured. As a result, the levels of training received by those currently practising under the BACP and UKCP banners vary from something that is probably little more than a FE certificate/diploma to doctoral-level qualifications.

TRAINING THE PROFESSIONAL THERAPIST – PLUGGING THE GAPS

In the UK, some of the confusion about what are the proper ways of training professional psychological therapists is probably about to be untangled. There are two sets of national training and practice protocols currently under development. The first is the *National Occupational Standards for Psychological Therapies* (NOS) and the second is the *National Standards of Proficiency for Counselling and Psychotherapy* (NSP). Details of these are as follows.

National Occupational Standards for Psychological Therapies

A set of national occupational standards that applied to counselling only was originally developed by the Employment National Training Organisation (ENTO). These were largely an extension of the UK's National Vocational Qualification (NVQ) system and do not seem to have been very influential with the counselling training agencies. ENTO began a systematic review of these standards in 2005. However, in 2006, Skills for Health (the Healthcare Skills Development Council) began a development project to provide a set of *National Occupational Standards for Psychological Therapies* (NOS). This is a separate and much more wide-ranging process than that being undertaken in the ENTO review. The ENTO review is apparently an updating of an existing set of counselling protocols; the Skills for Health initiative is intended to provide a set of performance standards for all the psychological therapists working in healthcare situations. The Skills for Health report was due at the time of writing. It seems likely that the Healthcare Skills Project will incorporate, or combine with, some of the ENTO proposals when it finally reports. You can keep abreast of all these developments at **www.skillsforhealth.org.uk** and at **www.ento.co.uk**.

At present, Skills for Health have developed, or are developing, Draft NOS for four of the common therapeutic approaches or, as they call them, therapeutic modalities. These are:

- cognitive-behavioural therapy;
- psychodynamic psychotherapy;

- systemic family therapy;
- humanistic therapy and counselling.

The NOS are concerned with providing performance standards for therapists irrespective of the working title that any individual practitioner uses. So, as far as the NOS are concerned, it does not matter what sort of therapist you call yourself or what sort of training you have had. It is only when you are working in one of the above modes that your clients can expect you to be performing at the levels proposed by Skills for Health.

It should be noted that the NOS are standards of therapist practice and not standards of therapist education. They are intended as working tools to help individuals and organisations evaluate their therapeutic services as they are delivered. The NOS are not a set of rules or academic curricula nor are they professional qualification benchmarks. In other words, the NOS will, at best, only inform the HPC as it finalises its proposals for the standards of proficiency that therapists will be required to achieve in order to gain HPC registration.

National Standards for Proficiency in Counselling and Psychotherapy

The Draft Report to the HPC from the Psychotherapists and Counsellors Professional Liaison Group includes some proposals for a set of *National Standards for Proficiency in Counselling and Psychotherapy* (NSP). This report is likely to form an important part of the HPC's final recommendations to the Government. The main purpose of the NSP will be to define the minimum standards of expertise required by all HPC registered practitioners. Unlike the Skills for Health proposals, the NSP is generic and applies across all branches of counselling and psychotherapy – it is *not* mode specific. The NSP qualify the worker, not the work.

The NSP do not by themselves provide the education and training organisations with a set of syllabi. However, in order to gain HPC approval, such organisations will need to prove that their programmes produce graduates who are capable of meeting the minimum practitioner thresholds set out in the NSP. This is because the HPC will eventually be defining the acceptable practitioner education and training levels. In the Draft NSP there are some 50 suggested *Standards of Proficiency* that could be shared by all registered counsellors and psychotherapists. There is one proposed additional standard that supposedly will only apply to registered psychotherapists and one other proposed additional standard that will allegedly only apply to registered counsellors. The first additional standard assumes that psychotherapists have a particularly advanced understanding of severe mental health issues. The second assumes that counsellors have a special understanding of their clients' concerns about well-being, life issues and personal transitions. Updates on these developments can be found at **www.hpc-uk.org**.

The HPC's proposed *National Standards* generate some potential disputes. Are the apparently different educational needs of counsellors and psychotherapists borne out by reality? The claimed differences in training levels might fade away in times to come. The psychotherapist's alleged superior understanding of severe mental health issues might be equalled by that of counsellors, should counselling eventually emerge as an honours degree-entry profession. Is it really the case that counsellors diverge from their psychotherapist colleagues because they have a genuinely superior understanding of well-being, life issues and personal transitions? It is quite likely that many, if not most, psychotherapists would claim a similar level of understanding of human need.

TRAINING THE PROFESSIONAL THERAPIST – ISSUES AND DEBATE

As far as psychotherapists are concerned, therapy is supposedly already a mainly postgraduate-entry profession. This is the minimum educational standard that psychotherapists have decided their registered practitioners need to attain. However, a survey of the UKCP's list of approved training bodies, and the programmes that they offer, gives us reason to wonder if the true standards of every one of these approved training programmes are truly at such an admirably high level. It also seems that the study content of some of these programmes might vary widely. Of course, it is always open to debate whether such educational variety is, or is not, a 'good thing'.

The educational situation, as far as current trainee counsellors are concerned, is not dissimilar, except that their claimed minimum training standards are lower. These standards are possibly (but not universally) usually at about HE diploma level. Although psychotherapists claim to have undergone a more in-depth training than counsellors routinely undertake, this is generally only a defendable assertion as far as the differences between the BACP and the UKCP minimum qualification standards are concerned. For the newly emerging breed of graduate counsellors, these alleged training differences are sometimes more than made up in the third year of the increasingly available honours degree-level counselling training programmes.

It is clearly arguable that, currently, there is a somewhat confused mix of apparently uncoordinated approaches to UK therapist professional training. This is unlike the situation in most of the other major professions, where there are nationally accepted base syllabi that are offered by approved training establishments via courses that have been independently validated by the Quality Assurance Agency for Higher Education. In the other major professions the training routes first require the student to undergo generic training at bachelor's level. This is followed by a period spent in gaining professional experience under an experienced and fully qualified mentor. Finally, specialised or advanced training is undertaken by postgraduate study and research. This is rarely the case in UK therapist tuition, except in cases where the student has first enrolled on one of the growing numbers of integrated, degree-based therapist training programmes. Will statutory regulation change this state of affairs? Might it become the case that an emerging combined counselling and psychotherapy profession will eventually demand an honours degree as a minimum entry-level qualification?

At present, the HPC's draft proposals for therapist education only appear to generally endorse (or 'officialise') the current situation for therapy trainees. It appears that the existing programmes approved by therapy professions' main representative bodies (BACP, UKCP, BPS, etc.) will satisfy the proposed HPC registration thresholds. So far there has been no move to set up a fully thought-out career training path for therapists. Interestingly, other sectors of the socially active professions have been through similar reviews/ regradings of their practice and training standards over the years. In many cases (social work, for example), they have gradually evolved as HE-based callings with structured career paths. This rather suggests that the pro-regulationists' apparent victory in therapy's 'regulation wars' is, as yet, far from absolute. It might be that they have only been successful in the opening skirmishes. It might also be that there are many battles yet to be fought over the appropriate educational and training standards that will come to be expected from the therapists of the future.

REFLECTION POINT

- Should there be any differences in the training or professional practices of counsellors and psychotherapists?
- What would you include in an educational programme for talking therapists? What would you leave out?
- The talking therapies – are they Art or Science?

TRAINING THE PROFESSIONAL THERAPIST – A WAY FORWARD

Let us suppose that, eventually, all therapists will be required to have obtained a minimum, entry-level educational standard equivalent to an honours degree. Therefore, if gaining such a degree were to become an essential first professional step, it would seem likely that eventual entry into one of therapy's specialisms or advanced practice areas would probably require postgraduate education. In other words, advanced professional therapeutic practitioners are likely to evolve as master's-level specialists. Bearing in mind the personal and professional advantages that having a rewarding career path might bring to therapists, does Figure 10.1 suggest a suitable way forward for tomorrow's professional counsellors and psychotherapists?

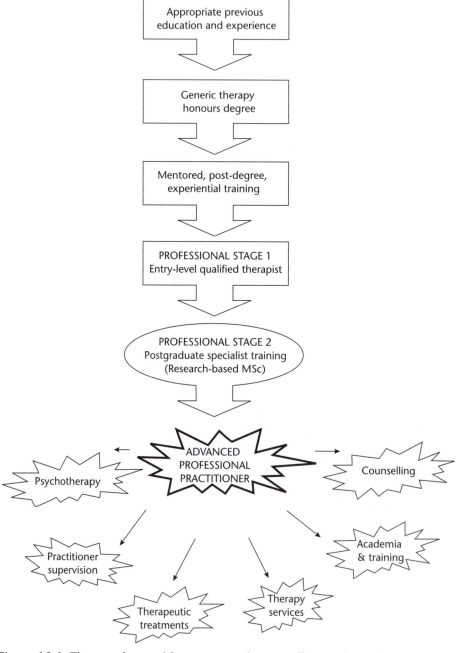

Figure 10.1: The way forward for tomorrow's counsellors and psychotherapists?

THE TALKING THERAPIES AND THE NHS – THE COMING YEARS

In today's NHS, the talking therapies are very often made available to appropriately diagnosed patients. This is especially so in primary care settings. It seems that patients' experiences have caused them to come to highly value counselling as a treatment choice (Brettle et al, 2008). It also seems that GPs, too, value counselling, particularly when delivered through their local surgeries. Apparently, they feel that it helps them to retain direct control of their patient's welfare (Brettle et al, 2008).

Importantly for today's NHS counsellors and psychotherapists, the general trend of the research (Antonuccio et al., 1995; Roth and Fonagy, 2005, and many others) seems to show that the drug-based treatments and the talking therapies are, when taken in the round, about equally helpful in cases of psychological and emotional disturbance. These sorts of studies also suggest that most of the talking therapies (including CBT) are roughly speaking about as effective as each other (see the reviews by Cooper, 2008). The important point here is to note that none of the psychological therapies used in the NHS is likely to be any less (or any more) useful than CBT. Therefore, it is no doubt surprising to many therapists and non-therapists alike to find that CBT has become the psychotherapeutic 'flavour of the month' throughout the NHS (see NICE *Guideline 23*, 2004, for example).

The CBT debate

CBT's pre-eminence is not likely to diminish in the near future. It appears that current NHS planning is largely based on the policy makers' assumption that CBT will continue to enjoy its enhanced and allegedly superior status. This optimistic view stems in part from the Layard Report (2006). Further support for the extensive use of CBT comes from the undeniable fact that it has been very well defended by its supporters as being a properly researched, legitimate, flexible and effective form of psychotherapy (Veale, 2008, and many others). Nevertheless, a significant number of counsellors and psychotherapists remain doubtful about the true place of CBT within the overall psychotherapeutic remit. For some of these doubters, CBT is simply not 'proper therapy' and probably never will be. Of course, for those therapists who believe that the talking therapies should be combined to form an 'inclusive church', with no significant distinctions between its practices or its practitioners, such doubts are irrelevant. This is because they consider that the overwhelming trend of the evidence still tells us that, as far as the competing psychological therapies are concerned, indeed 'everybody has won and all shall have prizes'. Nevertheless, the question remains: 'Why should CBT be so popular?' However, perhaps a much more important question to ask is: 'Will CBT really fulfil the NHS policy makers' expectations?'

Although it might be argued that the 'who supports CBT' debate is increasingly irrelevant for modern talking therapists, it is still the case that the high value that the NHS places on CBT is of vital concern to all NHS-based counsellors and psychotherapists. One of the attractions that CBT has for today's NHS largely comes from the fact that CBT has been robustly evaluated by numerous outcome studies as being an effective and rapid treatment method (see Roth and Fonagy, 2005, and many others). Another attraction is that it is apparently cheap to deliver. Brief intervention CBT has also received significant support from extensive outcomes-based research and this is clearly of telling importance for the cost-effectiveness-driven NHS policy makers. This happy state of affairs (for CBT anyway!) is not yet the case for the other counselling-based therapies, although the research deficiencies, at least, are being rapidly corrected (see Cooper, 2008; Lambert, 2004; Stiles et al., 2006, and many, many others).

The practical reality is that CBT's apparently provable efficacy, its assumed superiority, and its hoped-for low cost, have all combined to cause the NHS management to decide that CBT should become the future treatment of choice for most of the mental health problems that patients bring to their doctors (Department of Health, 2001b, 2001c). Today, the popular 'cure all' prescription for the psychologically troubled seems to be to provide them with about six sessions of CBT. This seems to be the favoured treatment in almost all cases. One reason why this might be so could be because this is precisely what the national NHS directives recommend. Among the problems that CBT is claimed to be effective in treating are:

- anxiety disorders, including phobias, panic attacks and panic disorder;
- depression and other mood disorders;
- eating disorders;
- psychosomatic disorders;
- obsessive-compulsive disorders;
- anger;
- post-traumatic stress disorders;
- sexual and relationship problems;
- adverse habits, such as facial tics;
- drug or alcohol abuse;
- sleep problems;
- chronic fatigue syndrome (ME);
- chronic (persistent) pain.

This CBT-based treatment policy was endorsed by the National Institute for Health and Clinical Excellence (NICE) in 2004. The NICE *Clinical Guidelines 9, 22* and *23* recommend CBT as the most suitable treatment for anxiety, depression and eating disorders. It is indeed a one-size-fits-all policy and, what is more, this type of treatment is cheap. This is because the recommended 'dose' of six or so sessions can allegedly be delivered by apparently very quickly trained workers. This means that CBT is easy to manage, easy to plan for and easy to budget for. It is also claimed that it will be easy to find the practitioners to provide it and inexpensive to educate them. All in all, CBT is an NHS manager's dream.

As a result of these developments and the impact of Layard's very influential report, the Government is making a pump-priming investment of £170 million in the NHS initiative, *Improving Access to Psychological Therapies* (IAPT) from 2008 onwards (NHS, 2007). More investment is planned. The Government's objectives are set out in the *IAPT Implementation Plan* (Department of Health, 2008a). Their intentions are quite clear. There is going to be a huge expansion in the availability of CBT throughout the NHS and a similarly huge expansion in the number of CBT therapists who will have been trained to carry out this work. Whether this new group of therapists will be drawn from a practitioner pool that will necessarily include many of today's other talking therapists yet remains to be seen. None of this appears to augur well for non-CBT psychological therapists in tomorrow's NHS, unless they are prepared to radically reconsider their styles of practising.

TRAINING TOMORROW'S CBT DELIVERERS FOR THE NHS

It seems that there will be two standards of CBT training made available for what will be two classes of CBT practitioners.

1. *Curriculum for high-intensity therapy workers* (Department of Health, 2008b)

> *Courses for high-intensity workers will aim to provide a post-qualification training in evidence-based CBT for adults with depression and/or any of the anxiety disorders.* ***The courses will be at postgraduate diploma level or equivalent.*** Recruitment for the courses will be aimed at postgraduates, with trainees drawn from clinical psychologists and psychotherapists, as well as people with experience of delivering mental health in other professional capacities such as nursing and counselling (and including graduate mental health workers who can demonstrate professional and academic equivalence).*

(* Author's emphasis)

2. *Curriculum for low-intensity therapy workers* (Department of Health, 2008c)

> *The curriculum is based on a modular structure of four modules delivered over 45 days in total. Although each module has a specific set of foci and learning outcomes, the clinical competencies build module upon module*

*and courses will be expected to focus the majority of their classroom activity on clinical competency development through clinical simulation/ role play. All modules will be assessed on participants' practical demonstration of competencies, according to pass/fail criteria. **Participants will not necessarily possess previous clinical or professional expertise in mental health*,** and will be able to undertake academic assessments at either undergraduate or postgraduate level, depending on their prior academic attainment. Skills-based competency assessments will be independent of academic level and must be achieved according to a pass/fail criterion.*

(* Author's emphasis)

It would not take a genius (or a confirmed cynic) to work out that, almost certainly, more resources will be allocated to training the cheaper low-intensity workers than will be allocated to training the more expensive high-intensity workers. The key issue here is that the person specification for the low-intensity trainees states that they need not 'possess previous clinical or professional expertise in mental health'. So this question arises – low-intensity CBT workers might well be cheap to train and cheap to employ, but is the NHS's rapidly emerging heavy reliance on CBT (effectively making it the preferred therapy) really in the best interests of the patients or in the best interests of the NHS bean counters?

DOES COUNSELLING AND PSYCHOTHERAPY HAVE A FUTURE IN THE NHS?

One result of the growing primacy of CBT treatments is that, in an increasingly expanding number of NHS areas, the non-CBT counselling services are in danger of being either discontinued or greatly reduced. If uncorrected, this potential trend is likely to accelerate as more and more of the new CBT technicians complete their training and come into post. In addition, it is inevitable that ongoing NHS budget restraints and operating stresses will continue to demand ever-higher levels of patient throughput. This all means that, if the existing NHS generalist counsellors and psychotherapists want to survive, they might well find themselves having to fundamentally adapt their treatment methods. Counselling practice could well find itself having to evolve in order to meet the demands of the highly pressured, cost-based contexts within which counsellors will find themselves working. Of course, not all therapists will be willing to do this. Totton (1997), for example, argues that working within such externally imposed limits diminishes the potential benefits of therapy.

However, it can also be argued that the NHS counselling services are only required to deliver optimum levels of benefits to each patient. A 'four-star' service is not always necessary – sometimes 'adequate' will do. Therefore, NHS counsellors will rarely be able to indulge in the luxury of the endless personal or client self-explorations that constitute the therapeutic ideal of psychotherapy's purists. In other words, NHS counsellors and psychotherapists will probably find themselves having to choose between one of two options. Neither appears very attractive, at least from the traditional therapist's point of view. They might have to either elect to deliver some form of time-restricted, 'that-will-do', therapy that suits the then prevailing circumstances – or be sacked. The choice might be between providing 'good enough' therapy and providing no therapy at all. In the real world, complying with NHS budget constraints and priority choices is a routine operational fact of life and is likely always to be so (Tinsley, 1999). Perhaps the harsh message for tomorrow's NHS counsellors and psychotherapists will be 'adapt or die!'

REFLECTION POINT

- Is CBT a 'proper' counselling therapy?
- Do NHS counsellors 'see clients' or do they 'treat patients'?
- What sorts of people should the NHS's new CBT workers be?

NEW THERAPISTS FOR A NEW CENTURY

The talking therapies are rapidly evolving – no question of that! But what of the therapists themselves; are they evolving too? What might be happening to them? Some theorists believe that the therapists of tomorrow will evolve into being very different types of practitioners, working in different branches of the therapy trade, each division requiring different areas of professional expertise. Could this mean that counselling and psychotherapy will really end up as disparate vocations? After all, McLeod (2009) has already suggested that there are some essential differences between the ways in which counsellors and psychotherapists each view their clients. For example, it may be that perhaps counselling reflects society's needs, whereas psychotherapy supposedly reflects the individual patient's needs.

Other theorists see the therapists of the future as developing into much better, much more effective practitioners; superior practitioners even. Irrespective of their original training, outside the confines of their therapeutic 'schools', the measure of these new 'improved-quality' therapists might come from their outcome-evaluated, advanced professional competencies rather than from assessing their ability to conform to schoolistic theory. These new practitioners might evolve into what, in much earlier times, Ricks (1974) was already describing as a new breed of tackle-any-thing, wonder-therapists – the 'supershrinks'.

The supershrink

The notion of a supershrink is fundamental to the future of the talking therapies. This is because a 'supershrink profession' might be much more powerful and with a much higher status than is generally the case with today's talking therapies. It seems that the concept of a supershrink does have some research-based support. Wampold and Brown (2005) found evidence that, for whatever reasons, some therapists were consistently better than others when measured by the quality of the treatment outcomes. Other studies, for example Project MATCH (1997), seem to support such a finding. Is there a secret ingredient that makes the super-shrinks stand out? One possible explanation of the supershrink phenom-enon is that it is simply happenstance. Perhaps some people are just naturally much better therapists than others. Is there such a being as a 'great' therapist?

Fortunately, all is not lost for the rest of us who were not born with a natural 'greatness'. Performance studies, both within therapy and in the outside world (see Colvin, 2006), usually find that, generally speaking, hard work usually makes up for any apparent lack of giftedness or innate superior talent. Further studies suggest that there are strategies that all therapists could adopt that might help them to improve their effectiveness with their clients. For example, Miller et al. (2006) found that formally engaging with client feedback has a marked effect on therapist performance. Miller et al. have summed up these strategies into three components.

- *Think*: First, decide upon the therapeutic objectives and then plan how to achieve them.
- *Act*: Second, start work with the client and monitor your performance by obtaining ongoing client feedback – find out if your treatment strategy is working.
- *Reflect*: Third, reflect on your performance and, if necessary, adopt alternative strategies.

According to Miller et al. (2006), it seems that hard work and effort are the true keys to success in any calling, including the talking therapies (see the review by Ericsson et al., 2006). As the old joke goes, 'Can you tell me how to get to the Albert Hall please? Yes; practise, practise, practise!' An interesting point here is that, if Miller et al. (2008) are right, tomorrow's supershrink is likely to be a highly skilled technician working within laid-down operating procedures and obedient to measurable outcomes. That is a far cry from the unrestrained, creative practitioners that some see as the rightful heirs to the true future of 'proper' counselling and psychotherapy.

Counsellors and psychotherapists – a parting of the ways?

There seems to be a possibility that, in a few years' time, statutory regulation will initially divide counselling and psychotherapy into two different callings with two different levels of training requirement. This could mean that these two trades might effectively become two different professions. Some theorists have already anticipated (even welcomed) this possibility. For example, McLeod (2009) argues that now is the time to undertake a radical review of the nature of counselling. This is because he suggests that counselling is really what he calls a 'front-line' community-based activity within the helping professions. He suggests that counselling should be a collaborative activity between the therapist and the client – one that is targeted at helping the client to deal with life and life's difficulties. This would indicate that counsellors should concentrate on understanding people and their interrelationships in terms of their social, cultural and organisational contexts. This is different, he argues, from psychotherapy, which is more exclusively targeted on the individual patient and on providing specific remedies for individual problems. In other words, psychotherapy tends to be a narrow, focused approach to the individual, whereas counselling tends to be a wider, society-based activity. Put crudely, this argument seems to suggest that psychotherapy is about finding cures, whereas counselling is about acceptance, learning and change.

If these suggested differences actually do underpin a true divergence between counselling and psychotherapy, it seems reasonable to suggest that these co-professions will devolve into being providers of two different types of service, delivered by two different types of therapeutic practitioner. Each of these two disciplines might then evolve by striving to satisfy different professional demands. For example, the psychotherapists might advance their profession by developing new therapies (cures?). After all, in the UK today there is a huge, often unmet, ever-growing demand from patients needing immediate mental healthcare 'fixes' (McCrone et al., 2008). Could the psychotherapists find productive ways of filling those gaps? Alternatively, perhaps the counsellors might promote their own professional discipline by becoming more embedded within their communities. Perhaps if counsellors came out from their consulting rooms, they might find themselves becoming much more socially pro-active. For example, it might be that schools counsellors could offer advice on child welfare, or perhaps workplace counsellors could help employers to devise more productive (and financially more advantageous?) interactions between their employees.

It is always possible that separating out counsellors from psychotherapists might actually strengthen the two callings. A parting of the ways might be beneficial to both professions. Yet again we can see that it is 'an interesting time' to be any sort of a talking therapist.

FINAL THOUGHTS

In this book, I have been setting out how I believe my version of the story about how counselling and psychotherapy has developed over the years. It is the story of the need that people often have to seek out someone to listen to them; someone to support them through their difficult times. Sometimes it really is as simple as that – people do not always want 'cleverology'; sometimes they just want 'tea and sympathy'. It can be a sobering lesson for any therapist to learn that, no matter what sort of a practitioner it is that you choose to be, for some of your clients all your carefully acquired skills and learning are not actually of very much interest. For some of our customers, just being heard is enough; just being really attended to is sufficient. Somehow, in some way, helping our clients to bring their stories out into the open, and helping them to give themselves a voice and to tell their tales to someone who is genuinely interested, seems to do the job. It appears that, in some cases, all that is needed, when we are trying to find a way to make someone feel whole again, is to help that someone to feel validated as a person. Clients talk; we listen – after all, that is how the talking therapies got their name.

A central theme throughout this book has been my belief that counselling and psychotherapy, indeed the talking therapies generally, are all just different sides of the same coin. Of course, my ideas may have to be revised, at least temporarily, if regulation does separate these two callings in legal terms. Whether such a separation would be anything other than artificial, and whether it will stand the test of time, currently remains a very open question. Obviously, for many other theorists and investigators it is actually an irrelevant question, because they are firm in their belief that all the therapy types are inherently different.

It seems to me that the really interesting puzzle comes not from wondering where therapy came from, but in trying to work out where it might be going. Some theorists believe that it will go down a science-based route, achieve practical and theoretical integration and emerge as a 'super-therapy'. Other theorists argue that the individual therapy modalities cannot be combined and so a meta-theory that could underpin a mega-therapy cannot emerge. For yet other thinkers, the existing therapy types should be envisaged as art forms to be worked at by unrestricted, creative practitioners. They would claim that each therapy modality, and each interpretation of it, is unique. As ever, some therapists want regulation; some want freedom. Some prefer professional controls; others are more comfortable with therapeutic anarchy.

Of course, as well as wondering where therapy is going, we also need to think about where the therapists themselves are going. Will they continue to be loyal adherents of their various 'schoolisms'? Will they become practitioners of a united form of therapy or will counsellors and psychotherapists remain independent of each other? Will tomorrow's therapists need advanced education? A very important question concerns the growing power of the cognitive-behavioural therapists. Are we moving towards a psychotherapeutic world in which 'CBT is King!'? Sometimes we define therapists by the services that they provide (family therapist, drugs adviser, workplace counsellor, etc.). What if, in the future, we were to develop some new overarching service areas for counsellors and psychotherapists (social systems designers, conflict resolvers, change managers, etc., etc.)? Would such developments simply require us to find additional ways to define therapists? Alternatively, would such evolutions require us to develop some new-style 'super-therapists' or perhaps today's practitioners simply have to cope and get on with things if they happened to find themselves working in these new sorts of service areas?

So, I am leaving you with many questions needing many answers! Do you have any? Can you work something out? As for me, this is it. My tale is told; my story is done. Now you tell yours!

SUGGESTED FURTHER READING

Cooper, M (2008) *Essential Research Findings in Counselling and Psychotherapy: The facts are friendly.* London: Sage.

READ THIS BOOK! This is an excellent account of all the core issues in therapy research. Chapter 7 is the key to the future.

Yalom, I (1991) *Love's Executioner and Other Tales of Psychotherapy.* London: Penguin.

Current literature: *Therapy Today, Counselling & Psychotherapy Research, Counselling Psychology Quarterly, British Journal of Guidance & Counselling and The Psychotherapist.*

References

Aldridge, S (2006) Update on regulation. *Therapy Today*, 17(1): 34–5.

Aldridge, S (2009) Making your mind up. *Therapy Today*, 20(4): 18–20.

Aldridge, S and Pollard, P (2005) *Interim Report to Department of Health on Initial Mapping Project for Psychotherapy & Counselling*. Available online at www.bacp.co.uk (accessed Summer 2009).

Allport, G and Odbert, H (1936) Trait-names: a psycho-lexical study. *Psychological Monographs*, 47(211).

Antonuccio, D, Ganton, W and DeNeslky, G (1995) Psychotherapy versus medication for depression: challenging the conventional wisdom with data. *Professional Psychology: Research and Practice*, 26(6), December 1995: 574–85.

Appignanesi, R and Zarate, O (2007) *Introducing Freud: A graphic guide to the father of psychoanalysis*. Cambridge: Icon Books.

Australian Bureau of Statistics (2003) *ABS Labour Survey, Trend Data to May 2003*. Canberra: ABS Publications. Available online at www.abs.gov.au (accessed Summer 2009).

Axline, V (1964, reprinted 1990) *Dibs: In search of self*. London: Penguin.

Bandura, A (1977) *Social Learning Theory*. Englewood Cliffs, NJ: Prentice Hall.

Barkham, M (2007) Remarks to the November 2007 NHS Psychological Therapies Conference. *Therapy Today,* December 2007: 8–9.

Beck, A (1963) Thinking and depression 1: idiosyncratic content and negative distortions. *Archives of General Psychiatry*, 9: 324–33.

Beck, A (1964) Thinking and depression 2: theory and therapy. *Archives of General Psychiatry*, 10: 561–71.

Beck, A (1975) *Cognitive Therapy and the Emotional Disorders*. Madison, CT: International Universities.

Beck, A (1991) *Cognitive Therapy and the Emotional Disorders*. London: Penguin.

Beck, A (1999) *Prisoners of Hate: The cognitive basis of anger, hostility and violence*. New York: HarperCollins.

Beck, A, Rush, A, Shaw, B and Emery, G (1979) *Cognitive Therapy for Depression*. New York: Guilford Press.

Beck, JS (1995) *Cognitive Therapy: Basics and beyond*. New York: Guilford Press.

Beck, U (1992) *Risk Society: Towards a new modernity*. London: Sage.

Beer, S (2003) *Demystifying EAPs*, paper presented at the 2003 Association for Counselling at Work Conference, Geneva, 13–17 April.

Bennett, M (2005) *The Purpose of Counselling and Psychotherapy*. Basingstoke: Palgrave Macmillan.

Bennett-Levy, J, Butler, G, Fennell, M, Hackmann, A, Mueller, M and Westbrook, D (eds) (2004) *The Oxford Guide to Behavioural Experiments in Cognitive Therapy*. Oxford: Oxford University Press.

Bettleheim, B (1983) *Freud and Man's Soul*. New York: Alfred A. Knopf.

Blow, A, Sprenkle, D and Davis, S (2007) Is who delivers the treatment more important than the treatment itself? The role of the therapist in common factors. *Journal of Marital & Family Therapy*, 33(3): 298–317.

Bor, R, Ebner-Landy, J, Gill, S and Brace, C (2002) *Counselling in Schools*. London: Sage.

Bordin, E (1979) The generalisability of the psychoanalytic concept and the working alliance. *Psychotherapy: Theory, Research and Practice*, 16: 252–60.

Bowlby, J (1969) *Attachment and Loss, Volume 1*. London: Hogarth Press.

Bowlby, J (1973) *Attachment and Loss, Volume 2*. London: Hogarth Press.

Bowlby, J (1980) *Attachment and Loss, Volume 3*. London: Hogarth Press.

Boyes, C (2008) *Cognitive Behavioural Therapy* (Collins 'Need to know?'). Glasgow: Collins.

Brennan, J and Hollanders, H (2006) Trouble in the village? Counselling and clinical psychology in the NHS. *Psychotherapy and Politics International*, 2(2): 123–34.

Brettle, A, Hill, A and Jenkins, P (2008) Counselling in primary care: a systematic review of the evidence. *Counselling and Psychotherapy Research*, 8(4): 2007–214.

British Association for Counselling & Psychotherapy (BACP) (2008) *Counselling and Psychotherapy Workloads: Information Sheet G4.* Available online at www.bacp.co.uk (accessed Summer 2009).

British Psychological Society (BPS) (2006) *Proposals for a Psychological Professions Council (PPC).* Leicester: BPS.

Browne, S (2008) The therapy maze. *Therapy Today,* 19(5), June: 9–18.

Bryant-Jefferies, R (2005) *Workplace Counselling in the NHS.* Abingdon: Radcliffe.

Buber, M (1970) *I and Thou* (trans. W. Kaufmann). New York: Touchstone Scribner (original publication 1923).

Burton, M, Sadgrove, J and Selwyn, E (1995) Do counsellors in general practice surgeries and clinical psychologists in the NHS see the same patients? *Journal of the Royal Society of Medicine,* 88: 97–102.

Cain, D and Seeman, J (eds) (2002) *Humanistic Therapies: Handbook of research and practice.* Washington, DC: American Psychological Association.

Carroll, M (1996) *Workplace Counselling.* London: Sage.

Carroll, M (2002) Memories of the future: scenarios for counselling at work. *ACW Journal,* 38: 10–12.

Carroll, M and Walton, M (1997) *The Handbook of Counselling in Organisations.* London: Sage.

Carver, C and Scheier, M (2000) *Perspectives on Personality* (4th edition). Boston, MA: Allyn & Bacon.

Castonguay, L, Constantino, M and Holtforth, M (2006) The working alliance: where are we and where should we go? *Psychotherapy,* 43: 271–9.

Cattell, RB (1965) *The Scientific Analysis of Personality.* Baltimore, MD: Penguin Books.

Claringbull, N (2003) An informal workshop, in Claringbull, N (2004) *A Fourth Wave in Workplace Counselling – Its professional specialisation?* Available online at www.bacp.co.uk/research/conference2004/index.html (accessed Summer 2009).

Claringbull, N (2004a) *A Fourth Wave in Workplace Counselling – Its professional specialisation?* Available online at www.bacp.co.uk/research/conference2004/index.html (accessed Summer 2009).

Claringbull, N (2004b) Specialist practitioners – the next wave in workplace counselling. *ACW Journal – Counselling at Work,* 44, Spring.

Claringbull, N (2006) The fourth wave in workplace counselling – towards the understanding and the development of the professional specialisation of workplace counselling, unpublished doctoral thesis, University of Middlesex.

Clarke, L (Chief Executive, BACP) (2008) *Personal communication,* BACP Research Conference, Cardiff, 9–10 May.

Clarkson, P (1995) *The Therapeutic Relationship.* London: Whurr.

Clarkson, P (2003) *The Therapeutic Relationship* (2nd edition). London: Whurr.

Cocksedge, S (1997) A GP perspective. *Clinical Psychology Forum,* 101: 22–5.

Coles, A (2003) *Counselling in the Workplace.* Maidenhead: Open University Press.

Colon, Y (1996) Chatter(er)ing through the fingertips: doing therapy online, in Murphy, L and Mitchell, D (eds) When writing helps to heal: e-mail as therapy. *British Journal of Guidance & Counselling,* 26(1) (1998).

Colvin, G (2006) Secrets of greatness: what it takes to be great. *Fortune Magazine.* Available online at www.CNNMoney.com (accessed Summer 2009).

Constantino, M, Castonguay, L and Schut, A (2002) The working alliance: a flagship for the 'scientist-practitioner' model in psychotherapy, in Tryon, G (ed.) *Counselling Based on Process Research: Applying what we know.* Boston, MA: Allyn & Bacon.

Cooper, M (2003) *Existential Therapies.* London: Sage.

Cooper, M (2008) *Essential Research Findings in Counselling and Psychotherapy.* London: Sage/Leicester: BACP.

Cooper, M, O'Hara, M, Schmid, P and Wyatt, G (eds) (2007) *The Handbook of Person-centred Psychotherapy and Counselling.* Basingstoke: Palgrave.

Crocker, SF (1999) *A Well-lived Life: Essays in gestalt therapy.* Cleveland, OH: Gestalt Institute of Cleveland Press.

Cullup, S (2005) From CEPC to ACW. *ACW Journal – Counselling at Work,* 49: 28–9.

Cushman, P (1990) Why the self is empty: towards a historically situated psychology. *American Psychologist,* 45: 599–611.

Cutter, F (1996) Virtual psychotherapy? *PsychNews International.* Available online at www.cmhc.com (accessed Summer 2009).

Davidson, L (2000) Meeting the challenges of the new NHS for counselling in primary care: a service manager perspective. *British Journal of Guidance and Counselling,* 28(2): 191–201.

Davies, D (1997) *Counselling in Psychological Services*, Buckingham: Open University Press.

Department of Health (1997) *The New NHS – Modern, Dependable*. Crown Copyright. Available online at www.dh.gov.uk (accessed Summer 2009).

Department of Health (2001a) *Reference Guide for Consent for Examination or Treatment*. Crown Copyright. Available online at www.doh.gov.uk/consent (accessed Summer 2009).

Department of Health (2001b) *Treatment Choice in Psychological Therapies and Counselling*. Crown Copyright. Available online at www.dh.gov.uk (accessed Summer 2009).

Department of Health (December 2001c) *Choosing Talking Therapies*. Crown Copyright. Available online at www.dh.gov.uk (accessed Summer 2009).

Department of Health (2004) *The NHS Improvement Plan*. Crown Copyright. Available online at www.dh.gov.uk (accessed Summer 2009).

Department of Health (2008a) *Improving Access to Psychological Therapies Implementation Plan: National guidelines for regional delivery*. Crown Copyright. Available online at www.dh.gov.uk (accessed Summer 2009).

Department of Health (2008b) *Improving Access to Psychological Therapies Implementation Plan: Curriculum for high-intensity therapy workers*. Crown Copyright. Available online at www.dh.gov.uk (accessed Summer 2009).

Department of Health (2008c) *Improving Access to Psychological Therapies Implementation Plan: Curriculum for low-intensity therapy workers*. Crown Copyright. Available online at www.dh.gov.uk (accessed Summer 2009).

Dollard, J and Miller, N (1950) *Personality and Psychotherapy: An analysis in terms of learning, thinking and culture*. New York: McGraw-Hill.

Draper, M, Jennings, J, Baron, A, Erdur, O and Shankar, L (2002) Time-limited outcome in a nationwide college counselling centre. *Journal of College Counselling*, 5(1): 26–38.

Dryden, W (2005) *Rational Emotive Behaviour Therapy in a Nutshell (Counselling in a Nutshell)*. London: Sage.

Dryden, W (2007) *Dryden's Handbook of Individual Therapy* (5th edition). London: Sage.

Duncan, B, Solovey, A and Rusk, G (1992) *Changing the Rules: A client-directed approach to therapy*. New York: Guilford Press.

East, P (1995) *Counselling in Medical Settings*. Buckingham: Open University Press.

Egan, G (1975) *The Skilled Helper*. Pacific Grove, CA: Brookes/Cole.

Ehrenwald, J (1976) *The History of Psychotherapy: From healing magic to encounter*. New York: J Aronson.

Ellenburger, H (1970) *The Discovery of the Unconscious: The history and evolution of dynamic psychiatry*. London: Allen Lane.

Elliot, R, Cooper, M and Friere, B (2008) *Empirical Support for Person-centred Experiential Psychotherapies: Meta-analysis update 2008*, paper presented at the BACP Research Conference, Cardiff, 9–10 May.

Ellis, A (1962) *Reason & Emotion in Psychotherapy*. Secaucus, NJ: Lyle Stuart.

Ellis, A (2001) *Overcoming Destructive Beliefs, Feelings and Behaviors: New directions for rational emotive behavior therapy*. New York: Prometheus Books.

Employee Assistance Professionals Association (EAPA) – USA (2004) *EAP Chapters List*. Available online at www.ieaspassn,org (accessed Summer 2009).

Employee Assistance Professionals Association (EAPA) – USA (2008) *Employee Utilisation Data*. Available online at www.ieaspassn,org (accessed Summer 2009).

Ericsson, A, Charness, N, Feltovitch, P and Hoffman, R (2006) *The Cambridge Handbook of Expertise and Expert Performance*. Cambridge: Cambridge University Press.

Erikson, E (1965) *Childhood and Society*. London: Penguin Books.

Evans, K and Gilbert, M (2005) *Introduction to Integrative Psychotherapy*. Basingstoke: Palgrave Macmillan.

Eysenck, H (1952) The effects of psychotherapy: an evaluation. *Journal of Consulting Psychology*, 16: 319–24.

Eysenck, H (1967) *The Biological Basis of Personality*. Springfield, IL: Charles C Thomas.

Eysenck, H (1990) *Decline and Fall of the Freudian Empire*. Washington, DC: Scott-Townsend.

Eysenck, H (1990) Biological dimensions of personality, in Pervin, LA (ed.) *Handbook of Personality: Theory and research*. New York: Guilford Press.

Eysenck, H (1991) Dimensions of personality: the biosocial approach to personality, in Strelau, J and Angleitner, A (eds) *Explorations in Temperament: International perspectives on theory and measurement*. London: Plenum.

Eysenck, H (1992a) Four ways five factors are not basic. *Personality and Individual Differences*, 13: 667–73.

Eysenk, H (1992b) The outcome problem in psychotherapy, in Dryden, W and Feltham, C (eds) *Psychotherapy and its Discontents*. Buckingham: Open University Press.

Fairbairn, W (1952) *Psychoanalytic Studies of the Personality*. London: Tavistock/Routledge.

Feltham, C (1997) *The Gains of Listening: Perspectives on counselling at work*. Buckingham: Open University Press.

Fiedler, F (1950) Comparison of therapeutic relationships in psychoanalytic, non-directive and Adlerian therapy. *Journal of Counselling Psychology*, 14: 436–45.

Foster, J (2000) Counselling in primary care and the new NHS. *British Journal of Guidance and Counselling*, 28(2): 176–90.

Freedheim, D (1992) *A History of Psychotherapy: A century of change*. Washington, DC: American Psychological Association.

Freeman, A and Simon, K (1989) Cognitive therapy of anxiety, in Freeman, A, Simon, K, Beutler, L and Arkowitz, H (eds) *Comprehensive Handbook of Cognitive Therapy*, New York: Plenum Press.

French, T (1933) Interrelations between psychoanalysis and the experimental work of Pavlov. *American Journal of Psychiatry*, 89: 1165–203.

Freud, A (ed.) (1986) *Sigmund Freud: The essentials of psychoanalysis*. London: Penguin.

Freud, S (2002) Jung and Freud: false prophets, in Evans, K and Gilbert, M (2005, p9) *Introduction to Integrative Psychotherapy*. Basingstoke: Palgrave Macmillan.

Friery, K (2006) Workplace counselling – who is the consumer? *Counselling at Work*, 54, Autumn: 24–6.

Funder, D (1997) *The Personality Puzzle*. New York: Norton.

Gay, P (1998) *Freud: A life for our times*. London: Dent.

Geldard, K and Geldard, D (2004) *Counselling Adolescents*, 2nd edition. London: Sage.

Geldard, K and Geldard, D (2008) *Counselling Children: A practical introduction*, 3rd edition. London: Sage.

Gendlin, E (1981) *Focussing*. New York: Bantam Books.

Gilbert, P (2005) *Compassion: Conceptualisation, research and use in psychotherapy*. Hove: Brunner-Routledge.

Ginger, S (2007) *Gestalt Therapy: The art of contact*. London: Karnac Books.

Gladstone, G (2008) Eleven good reasons to oppose SR. *Ipnosis*, June 2008. Available online at ipnosis.postle.net/ (accessed Summer 2009).

Goldberg, R and Steury, S (2001) Depression in the workplace: costs and barriers to treatment. *Psychiatric Services*, 52: 1639–43.

Grange, C (2005) The development of employee assistance programmes in the UK: a personal view. *Counselling at Work*, 49, Summer. Available online at www.bacpwork place.org.uk/journal_pdf/act_summer05_a.pdf (accessed Summer 2009).

Green, B (1994) Developing a primary care and community psychology service. *Clinical Psychology Forum*, 101: 18–21.

Gurman, A and Messer, S (2005) *Essential Psychotherapies*. New York: Guilford Press.

Hall, C, Lindzey, G and Campbell, J (1997) *Theories of Personality*, 4th edition. Hoboken, NJ: Wiley.

Hamblin, D (1986) The failure of pastoral care? *School Organization*, 6(1): 141–8.

Harris, M (1994) *Magic in the Surgery: Counselling in the NHS – A licensed state friendship service*. Bury St Edmunds: Social Affairs Unit.

Heidegger, M (1962) *Being and Time*. Oxford: Blackwell.

Hemmings, A (2000) Counselling in primary care: a review of the practice evidence. *British Journal of Guidance and Counselling*, 28(2): 232–52.

Hemmings, A and Field, R (eds) (2007) *Counselling & Psychotherapy in Private Practice*. Hove: Routledge.

Hollanders, H (2000a) Historical developments, in Palmer, S and Wolfe, R (eds) *Integrative and Eclectic Counselling and Psychotherapy*. London: Sage.

Hollanders, H (2000b) Integrative and eclectic approaches, in Palmer, S and Wolfe, R (eds) *Integrative and Eclectic Counselling and Psychotherapy*. London: Sage.

Hopkins, R (2005) From little oaks mighty acorns grow. *Counselling at Work*, 49, Summer. Available online at www.bacpworkplace.org.uk/journal_pdf/acw_summer05_d.pdf (accessed Summer 2009).

Horvath, A Greenberg, L (eds) (1994) *The Working Alliance: Theory, research and practice*. Chichester: Wiley.

Hubble, M, Duncan, B and Scott, D (2000) *The Heart and Soul Of Change*. Washington, DC: American Psychological Association.

Hudson-Allez, G (1999) Brief versus open-ended counselling in primary care: should the service be extended to include both models? *European Journal of Psychotherapy, Counselling & Health*, 2(1): 7–18.

Hudson-Allez, G (2000) What makes counsellors working in primary care distinct from counsellors working in other settings? *British Journal of Guidance and Counselling*, 28(2): 203–13.

Hughes, R (ed.) (2004) *An Anthology of Counselling at Work II*. Lutterworth: ACW/BACP.

Hughes, R and Kinder, A (2007) *Guidelines for Counselling in the Workplace*. Lutterworth: BACP.

Hughes, R and Jenkins, P (2003) Legal perspectives, *ACW Journal*, 46. Available online at www.counsellingatwork.org.uk (accessed Summer 2009).

Husserl, E (1977) *Phenomenological Psychology*. The Hague: Nyhoff.

Inglis, F (1989) Managerialism and morality, in Carr, W (ed.) *Quality in Teaching: Arguments for a reflective profession*. Lewes: Falmer Press.

Institute of Education Archives (2007) *Subject Guide 5: Child Psychology*. London: Institute of Education, London University.

Jacobs, M (1992) *Sigmund Freud*. London: Sage.

Jacobs, M (1998) *The Presenting Past*, 2nd edition. Buckingham: Open University Press.

Jacobs, M (2003) *Sigmund Freud*, 2nd edition. London: Sage.

Jacobs, M (2004) *Psychodynamic Counselling in Action*, 3rd edition. London: Sage.

Jacobs, M (2005) *The Presenting Past*, 3rd edition. Buckingham: Open University Press.

Jamieson, A (2004) ACW Conference 2004 – keynote speech. *Counselling at Work*, 45: 2–5.

Jenkins, P (2002) *Legal Issues in Counselling & Psychotherapy*. London: Sage.

Jones, E (1959, republished 1990) *Free Associations: Memories of a psycho-analyst*. New Brunswick, NJ: Transaction Publishers.

Jung, C (1965) *Man and His Symbols*. New York: Doubleday.

Jung, C (1970) *Collected Works, Volume 10*. London: Routledge and Kegan Paul.

Karasu, T (1986) The specificity against nonspecificity dilemma: towards identifying therapeutic change agents. *American Journal of Psychiatry*, 143: 687–95.

Kelly, G (1955) *The Psychology of Personal Constructs, Volumes 1 and 2*. New York: Norton.

Kemp, E and Thwaites, R (1998) A comparison of adult mental health patients allocated to counselling and clinical psychology. *Clinical Psychology Forum*, 121: 13–16.

Kierski, W (2009) The future of psychotherapy. *Contemporary Psychotherapy*, 1(1), April. Available online at contemporarypsychotherapy.org/journals/ (accessed Summer 2009).

Kinder, A (2003) Stress in court, *Counselling at Work*, Winter: 16–19.

Kinder, A (2005) Workplace counselling – a poor relation? *Counselling at Work*, Spring. Available online at www.bacpworkplace.org.uk/journal_pdf/acw_spring05_f.pdf (accessed Summer 2009).

King, P and Steiner, R (1991) *The Freud–Klein Controversies 1941–45*. London: Routledge.

Klein, M (1997) *Envy and Gratitude and Other Works: 1946–1963*, New edition. London: Hogarth Press.

Lambert, M (2004) *Bergin and Garfield's Handbook of Psychotherapy and Behaviour Change*, 5th edition. New York: Wiley.

Lane, D and Corrie, S (2006) *The Modern Scientist-Practitioner: A guide to practice in psychology*. Hove: Routledge.

Latner, J (1986) *The Gestalt Therapy Book*. New York: The Gestalt Journal Press.

Layard, R (2005) *Therapy for All on the NHS*, Sainsbury Centre for Mental Health Lecture, 12 September. Available online at www.cpc-online.co.uk/documents/ (accessed Summer 2009).

Layard, R (2006) *The Depression Report: A new deal for depression and anxiety*. London: The Centre for Economic Performance's Mental Health Group, London School of Economics. Available online at www.lse.ac.uk (accessed Summer 2009).

Leahy, R (2003) *Cognitive Therapy Techniques: A practitioner's guide*. New York: Guilford Press.

Lemma, A (2007) Psychodynamic therapy: the Freudian approach, in Dryden, W (ed.) *Dryden's Handbook of Individual Therapy*. London: Sage.

Lietaer, G (1990) The client-centered approach after the Wisconsin Project, in Liataer, G, Rombauts, J and Van Balen, R (eds) *Client-centered and Experiential Therapy in the Nineties*. Leuven: Leuven University Press.

Lines, D (2006) *Brief Counselling in Schools*. London: Sage.

Lishman, W (1996) *Organic Psychiatry: The psychological consequences of cerebral disorder*. Oxford: Blackwell.

Luborsky, L, Singer, B and Luborsky, L (1975) Comparative studies of psychotherapy: is it true that everyone has won and all will have prizes? *Archives of General Psychiatry*, 32: 995–1008.

Maddi, S (1996) *Personality Theories: A comparative analysis*, 6th edition. Toronto: Brooks/Cole.

Mahoney, M and Arnkoff, D (1978) Cognitive and self-control therapies, in Bergin, AE and Garfield, SS (eds) *Handbook of Psychotherapy and Behaviour Change*, 2nd edition. New York: Wiley.

Mander, G (2000) *A Psychodynamic Approach to Brief Therapy*. London: Sage.

Martell, C, Addis, M and Jacobson, N (2001) *Depression in Context: Strategies for guided action*. New York: Norton.

Maslow, A (1943) A theory of human motivation. *Psychological Review*, 50: 370–96.

Maslow, A (1962) *Towards a Psychology of Being*. New York: Van Nostrand.

Maslow, A (1973) *The Further Reaches of Human Nature*. New York: Viking.

Masson, J (1992) *Against Therapy*. London: HarperCollins.

McCrae, R and Costa, P (1997) Personality trait structure as a human universal. *American Psychologist*, 52: 509–16.

McCrone, P, Dhanasini, S, Patel, A, Knapp, M and Lawton-Smith, S (2008) *Paying the Price: The cost of mental health care in England to 2026*. London: King's Fund.

McLeod, J (2001) *Counselling in the Workplace: The facts*. Rugby: BACP.

McLeod, J (2003) *An Introduction to Counselling*, 3rd edition. Maidenhead: Open University Press.

McLeod, J (2008) *Counselling in the Workplace: The facts*, 2nd edition. Lutterworth: BACP.

McLeod, J (2009) Counselling: a radical vision for the future. *Therapy Today*, 20(6), July. Available online at www.therapytoday.net/article/show/532/ (accessed Summer 2009).

McLeod, J, Johnson, J and Griffin, J (2000) A naturalistic study of the effectiveness of time-limited counselling with low-income clients. *European Journal of Psychotherapy, Counselling & Health*, 3(2): 263–77.

Mearns, D (1999) *Present and Future Challenges for Counselling*, Conference presentation to the Aberdeen Association for Counselling, 12 June.

Mearns, D and Thorne, B (2000) *Person-Centred Therapy Today: New frontiers in theory and practice*. London: Sage.

Mearns, D and Thorne, B (2007) *Person-Centred Counselling in Action*, 3rd edition. London: Sage.

Mellor-Clark, J, Simms-Ellis, R and Burton, M (2001) *National Survey of Counsellors Working in Primary Care: Evidence of growing professionalisation?* London: Royal College of General Practitioners.

Miller, R (2006) President's Column. *The Psychologist*, 19(12): 707.

Miller, S, Duncan, B, Brown, G, Sorrel, R and Chalk, M (2006) Using formal client feedback to improve retention and outcome. *Journal of Brief Therapy*, 5: 5–22.

Miller, S, Hubble, M and Duncan, B (2008) Supershrinks. *Therapy Today*, 19(3), April: 4–9.

Mitchell, S and Black, M (1995) *Freud and Beyond: A history of modern psychoanalytic thought*. New York: Basic Books.

Moore, S (2006) Voluntary sector counselling: has inadequate research resulted in a misunderstood and underutilised resource? *Counselling and Psychotherapy Research*, 6(4): 221–6.

Moynihan, J (1993) *A Guide for the Healthcare Professional*. Cambridge: Probus.

Mulhauser, G (2008) *History of Counselling & Psychotherapy*. Available online at counsellingresource.com (accessed Summer 2009).

Musgrave, A (2007) Competencies consultation response: letter to BACP, *Ipnosis*, April 3. Available online at ipnosis.postle.net/ (accessed Summer 2009).

National Health Service (NHS) (2007) *Improving Access to Psychological Therapies*. Available online at www.iapt.nhs.uk/ (accessed Summer 2009).

National Institute for Health and Clinical Excellence (NICE) (2004) *Clinical Guidelines 9, 22 and 23*. Available online at www.nice.org.uk (accessed Summer 2009).

Nelson-Jones, R (2008) *Basic Counselling Skills: A helper's manual*. London: Sage.

Nettle, D (2007) *Personality: What makes you the way you are*. Oxford: Oxford University Press.

Newsom, J (1963) *Half our Future* (*Newsom Report*). London: Central Advisory Council for Education/HM Stationery Office.

Norcross, J (1986) *Handbook of Eclectic Therapy*. New York: Brunner/Mazel.

Norcross, J (2002) *Psychotherapy Relationships that Work: Therapist contributions and responsiveness to patients*. New York: Oxford University Press.

Norcross, J and Goldfried, M (1992) *Handbook of Psychotherapy Integration*. New York: Brunner/Mazel.

Norcross, J and Goldfried, M (eds) (2005) *Handbook of Psychotherapy Integration*, 2nd edition. New York: Oxford University Press.

Nuttall, J (2004) Modes of interpersonal relationship in management organisations. *Journal of Change Management,* 4(1): 15–29.

Oher, J (1999) *The Employee Assistance Handbook*. New York: Wiley.

Orlans, V (2003) Counselling psychology in the workplace, in Woolfe, R, Dryden, W and Strawbridge, S (eds) *Handbook of Counselling Psychology*, 2nd edition. London: Sage.

Padesky, C (1996) *Guide Discovery using Socratic Dialogue*. Oakland, CA: New Harbinger.

Palmer, S and Bor, R (2008) *The Practitioner's Handbook: A guide for counsellors, psychotherapists and counselling psychologists*. London: Sage.

Palmer, S and Woolfe, R (eds) (2000*) Integrative and Eclectic Counselling and Psychotherapy*. London: Sage.

Palmer, S, McMahon, G and Wilding, C (2005) *The Essential Skills for Setting Up a Counselling and Psychotherapy Practice*. Hove: Routledge.

Patterson, T (2007) Person-centered personality theory: support from self-determination theory and positive psychology. *Journal of Humanistic Psychology*, 47(1): 117–39.

Paul, G (1967) Strategy in outcome research in psychotherapy. *Journal of Consulting Psychology*, 31: 109–18.

Pavlov, I (1927) *Conditional Reflexes*. London: Oxford University Press.

Perelberg, R (ed.) (1999) *Psychoanalytic Understanding of Violence and Suicide*. London: Routledge.

Perls, F (1948) Theory and technique of personality integration. *American Journal of Psychotherapy*, 2: 565–86.

Perls, F, Hefferline, R and Goodman, P (1951) *Gestalt Therapy: Excitement and growth in the human personality*. New York: The Gestalt Journal Press.

Persons, J (1993) Case conceptualisation in cognitive-behaviour therapy, in Kuehlwein, KT and Rosen, H (eds) *Cognitive Therapies in Action: Evolving innovative practice*. San Francisco, CA: Jossey-Bass.

Pervin, L, Cervone, D and Oliver, J (2004) *Personality: Theory and research*, 9th edition. New York: Wiley.

Pointon, C (2008) An open process, *Therapy Today*, 19(8), October: 12–13.

Postle, D (1999–2008) All editions, *Ipnosis*. Available online at ipnosis.postle.net/ (accessed Summer 2009).

Pritchard, D (2006) Setting up in private practice, *Counselling at Work*, 51, Winter: 26–9.

Proctor, G (2008) Professionalisation: a strategy for power and glory, *Therapy Today*, October.

Project MATCH Research Group (1997) Matching alcoholism treatments to client heterogeneity. *Journal of Alcohol Studies*, 58(1): 7–29.

Rayner, E (1990) *The Independent Mind in British Psychoanalysis*. London: Free Association Books.

Reddy, M (1993) The counselling firmament: a short trip around the galaxy. *Counselling*, 4(1): 47–50.

Reddy, M (1997) External counselling provision for organisations, in Carroll, M and Walton, M (eds) *The Handbook of Counselling in Organisations*. London: Sage.

Reisman, J (1991) *A History of Clinical Psychology*, 2nd edition. London: Taylor & Francis.

Ricks, D (1974) Supershrink: methods of a therapist judged successful on the basis of adult outcomes of adolescent patients, in Ricks, D, Thomas, A and Roff, M (eds) *Life History Research in Psychopathology, Volume 3*. Minneapolis, MN: University of Minnesota Press.

Rogers, C (1942) *Counselling and Psychotherapy*. Boston, MA: Houghton Mifflin.

Rogers, C (1957) The necessary and sufficient conditions of therapeutic personality change. *Journal of Consulting Psychology*, 21: 95–103.

Rogers, C (1959) A theory of therapy, personality and interpersonal relationships, as developed in the client-centred framework, in Koch, S (ed.) *Psychology: A study of science*. New York: McGraw Hill.

Rogers, C (1961) *On Becoming a Person*. Boston, MA: Houghton Mifflin.

Rogers, C (1977) *Carl Rogers on Personal Power: Inner strength and its revolutionary impact*. New York: Delacorte Press.

Rogers, C (1980) *A Way of Being*. Boston, MA: Houghton Mifflin.

Romero, A and Kemp, S (2007) *Psychology Demystified: A self-teaching guide*. New York: McGraw-Hill.

Rosenzweig, S (1936) Some implicit common factors in diverse methods in psychotherapy. *American Journal of Orthopsychiatry*, 6: 412–15.

Roth, A and Fonagy, P (1996) *What Works for Whom? A critical review of psychotherapy research*. New York: Guilford Press.

Roth, A and Fonagy, P (2005) *What Works for Whom? A critical review of psychotherapy research*, 2nd edition. New York: Guilford Press.

Rotter, J (1981) The psychological situation in social learning theory, in Magnusson, D (ed.) *Toward a Psychology of Situations: An interactional perspective*. Mahwah, NJ: Lawrence Erlbaum.

Rotter, J (1982) *The Development and Applications of Social Learning Theory*. New York: Praeger.

Ryan, R (1998) Management role for counselling skills. *Counselling at Work*, 20, Spring.

Ryckman, R (1993) *Theories of Personality*, 5th edition. Belmont, CA: Brooks/Cole.

Ryle, A (1990) *Cognitive-Analytic Therapy: Active participation in change – A new integration of brief psychotherapy*. Chichester: Wiley.

Safran, J, Muran, J, Samstag, L and Stevens, C (2002) Repairing alliance ruptures, in Norcross, J (ed.) *Psychotherapy Relationships that Work: Therapists' contributions and responsiveness to patients*. New York: Oxford University Press.

Sanders, P (2002) *First Steps in Counselling: A student's companion for basic introductory courses*, 3rd edition. Ross-on-Wye: PCCS Books.

Schneider, K, Bugental, J and Pierson, J (eds) (2002) *The Handbook of Humanistic Psychology: Leading edges in theory, research and practice*. Thousand Oaks, CA: Sage.

Schustack, M and Friedman, H (2007) *The Personality Reader: Classic theories and modern research*. New York: Allyn & Bacon.

Schwenk, E (2006) The workplace counsellor's toolbox, *Counselling at Work*, 51, Winter: 20–3.

Scott, M and Dryden, W (1996) The cognitive-behavioural paradigm, in Woolfe, R and Dryden, W (eds) *Handbook of Counselling Psychology*. London: Sage.

Scott, M, Stradling, S and Dryden, W (1996) *Developing Cognitive-Behavioural Counselling*. London: Sage.

Segal, S, Williams, J and Teasdale, J (2002) *Mindfulness-based Cognitive Therapy for Depression: A new approach to prevent relapse*. New York: Guilford Press.

Shannon, B (2009) The end of an era. *Therapy Today*, 20(8), October: 20–2.

Shlien, J (1987) A countertheory of transference, in Levant, R and Shlien, J (eds) *Client-centred Therapy and the Person-centred Approach: New directions in theory, research and practice*. Westport, CT: Praeger.

Skinner, B (1953) *Science and Human Behaviour*. New York: Macmillan.

Skinner, B (1971) *Beyond Freedom & Dignity*. Indianapolis, IN: Hackett.

Spinelli, E (1994) *Demystifying Therapy*. London: Constable.

Spinelli, E (1996) The existential-phenomenological paradigm, in Woolfe, R and Dryden, W (eds) *Handbook of Counselling Psychology*. London: Sage.

Stampfl, T (1973) *Implosive Therapy: Theory and technique*. New York: General Learning Press.

Steele, D (1989) A history of job-based alcoholism programmes: 1955–1972. *Journal of Drug Issues*, 19(4): 511–32 .

Stevens, R (2008) *Erik H. Erikson: Explorer of identity and the life cycle*. Basingstoke: Palgrave Macmillan.

Stiles, W, Barkham, M, Twigg, E, Mellor-Clark, J and Cooper, M (2006) Effectiveness of cognitive-behavioural, person-centred and psychodynamic therapies in UK primary-care routine practice: replication in a larger sample. *Psychological Medicine*, 36(4): 555–66.

Stiles, W, Barkham, M, Mellor-Clark, J and Connell, J (2007) Effectiveness of cognitive-behavioural, person-centred, and psychodynamic therapies in UK primary-care routine practice: replication in a larger sample. *Psychological Medicine*, 37.

Stiles, W, Barkham, M, Mellor-Clark, J and Connell, J (2008) Letter to editor: Routine psychological treatment and the Dodo verdict: a rejoinder to Clark et al. (2007). *Psychological Medicine*, 38.

Stimpson, Q (ed.) (2003) *Clinical Counselling in Community and Voluntary Settings*. Hove: Brunner-Routledge.

Sullivan, H (1953) *The Interpersonal Theory of Psychiatry*. New York: Norton.

Summerfield, J and van Oudtshoorn, L (2000) *Counselling in the Workplace*. London: CIPD.

Tasker, B (2008) *Assessment in Counselling and Psychotherapy: Information sheet P13*. Available online at www.bacp.co.uk (accessed Summer 2009).

Tehrani, N (1997) Internal counselling provision for organisations, in Carroll, M and Walton, M (eds) *The Handbook of Counselling in Organizations*. London: Sage.

Tempest, M (2006) *The Future of the NHS*. St Albans: XPL Publishing.

Thorndyke, E (1932) *The Fundamentals of Learning*. New York: Teachers College.

Thorne, B (2002) Person-centred therapy, in Dryden, W (ed.) *Handbook of Individual Therapy*, 4th edition. London: Sage.

Thorne, B (2007) Person-centred therapy, in Dryden, W (ed.) *Handbook of Individual Therapy*, 5th edition. London: Sage.

Tinsley, M (1999) Letter to the editor. *Counselling in Medical Settings Journal*, 59(7).

Totton, N (1997) Inputs and outcomes: the medical model and professionalism. *Self & Society*, 25(4): 3–8.

Towler, J (1997) Managing the counselling process in organisations, in Carroll, M and Walton, M (eds) *The Handbook of Counselling in Organisations*. London: Sage.

Truax, C and Carkhuff, R (1967) *Toward Effective Counselling and Psychotherapy*. Chicago, IL: Aldine.

Tudor, K and Merry, T (2007) *Dictionary of Person-Centred Psychology*. Ross-on-Wye: PCCS Books.

Tyndall, N (1993) *Counselling in the Voluntary Sector*. Milton Keynes: Open University Press.

van Deurzen-Smith, E (1988) *Existential Counselling in Practice*. London: Sage.

van Deurzen-Smith, E (2002) *Existential Counselling & Psychotherapy in Practice*, 2nd edition. London: Sage.

Veale, D (2008) Psychotherapy in dissent. *Therapy Today*, February: 4–7.

Wachtel, P (1977) *Psychoanalysis and Behaviour Therapy: Towards an integration*. New York: Basic Books.

Wainwright, D and Calnan, M (2002) *Work Stress: The making of a modern epidemic*. Buckingham: Open University Press.

Wampold, B (2001) *The Great Psychotherapy Debate*. Mahwah, NJ: Lawrence Erlbaum.

Wampold, B and Brown, G (2005) Estimating variability in outcomes attributable to therapists: a naturalistic study of outcomes in managed care. *Journal of Consulting and Clinical Psychology*, 73(5): 914–23.

Ward, D (2001) World heritage honour for revolutionary mills. *The Guardian*, 15 December.

Ward, E, King, M, Lloyd, M, Bower, P, Sibbald, B, Farrelly, S, Gabbay, M, Tarrier, N and Addington-Hall, J (2008) Randomised controlled trial of non-directive counselling, cognitive-behaviour therapy and usual general practitioner care for patients with depression. *British Medical Journal*, 321: 1383–8.

Watkins, C (2008) Depoliticisation, demoralisation and depersonalisation – and how to better them. *Journal of Pastoral Care in Education*, 26(1), March: 5–11.

Watson, J (1925) *Behaviourism*. New York: Norton.

Welchman, K (2000) *Erik Erikson: His life, work and significance*. Buckingham: Open University Press.

Westbrook, D, Kennerly, H and Kirk, J (2007) *An Introduction to Cognitive Behaviour Therapy*. London: Sage.

Whitfield, G and Davidson, A (2007) *Cognitive Behavioural Therapy Explained*. Oxford: Radcliffe Publishing.

Wills, F (2008) *Skills in Cognitive Behaviour Counselling & Psychotherapy*. London: Sage.

Wilson, R and Branch, R (2006) *Cognitive Behavioural Therapy for Dummies*. Chichester: Wiley.

Winnicott, D (1965) *The Maturation Process and the Facilitating Environment*. London: Hogarth Press.

Wolfe, B and Goldfried, M (1988) Research on psychotherapy integration: recommendations and conclusions from an NIMH workshop. *Journal of Consulting & Clinical Psychology*, 22: 448–51.

Wolpe, J (1958) *Psychotherapy by Reciprocal Inhibition*, Stanford, CA: Stanford University Press.

Wolpe, J (1976) Behaviour therapy and its malcontents. *Journal of Behaviour Therapy and Experimental Psychology*, 3: 1–14.

Wolpe, J (1990) *Practice of Behaviour Therapy*. New York: Allyn & Bacon.

Woolfe, R (2003) The nature of counselling psychology, in Woolfe, R, Dryden, W and Strawbridge, S (eds) *Handbook of Counselling Psychology*. London: Sage.

Woolfe, R, Dryden, W and Strawbridge, S (2003) *Handbook of Counselling Psychology*, 2nd edition. London: Sage.

Wosket, V (1999) *The Therapeutic Use of Self*. London: Routledge.

Wright, J (2001) Developing on-line counselling in the workplace. *Counselling at Work*, 34: 4–6.

Yager, J (1999) The functioning physiology of personality: a start. *American Journal of Psychiatry*, 156: 252–7.

Yalom, I (1991) *Loves Executioner and Other Tales of Psychotherapy*. London: Penguin.

Index

Pages given in italic type contain relevant tables and figures.